Ernest Knight

Biddy Shillito

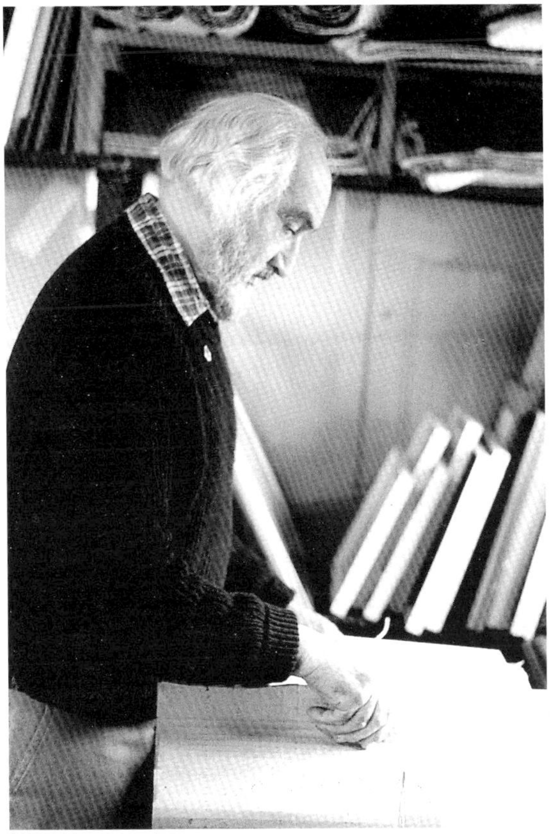

With 67 colour plates

Chapel Publications, Zelah

First Published 1997
Chapel Publications
Zelah Lane,
Zelah,
Cornwall, TR4 9HR

British Library Catalogue in Publication Data.

A CIP Catalogue Record for this book is available from the British Library.

ISBN No. 0 953 03090 3

Shillito, Biddy
ERNEST KNIGHT

Printed in Great Britain by
Rowe The Printers, Hayle, Cornwall.

Cover painting & Photograph.
The cover painting by Ernest Knight is of King's Tor, Vixen Tor & Pew Tor, Central Dartmoor.
Inset is a photograph of the artist.

Contents

Ernest Knight - A Collection of Paintings and Drawings.
Colour Plates

Black & White

The Ernest Knight African Collection
Colour Plates

60. Kululu - Isaac Banda
61. Tonga Village
62. Creation - Peter Kansenya
63. How Missionaries came - Peter Kansenya
64. The Crucifixion - Peter Kansenya
65. Simuchemba's Village - M. Simuchemba
66. Luapala River - D. Mukoshi
67. Smelter

Black and White

10. The Nativity - Samuel Katilungu
11. Rainmaking - Peter Kansenya
12. Witchdoctor at Work - Peter Kansenya
13. The Hunters - Samuel Katilungu
14. Man Chased by Lion - H.M. Chiyana
15. Witch Doctor - Peter Kansenya
16. Elephant Raiding - Isaac Banda
17. Swarm of Red Locusts - Martin Seconda
18. Man Attacked by Lion - H.M. Chiyana
19. The Village - Samuel Katilungu

Ernest Griset - Illustrations
Black and White

20. Nubian Lion
21. The Artist and Onlooker
22. The Theatre of Nature
23. Page of Improbables
24. The Lord Mayor's Dinner
25. The Academy
26. The Bears
27. The Animals' Ball
28. The Hatchet Throwers
29. A Comical Picnic
30. Punch

This book is dedicated to my sister Kit Knight, in memory of her years of happiness with Ernest. I thank her for the invaluable help she gave me in preparing this book.

Acknowledgements

My thanks to Grace Horseman and Pamela Topley for their help and encouragement, John Watton FRPS for his photographic advice and Lionel Lambourne for access to his book 'Ernest Griset, Fantasies of a Victorian Illustrator'

Dimensions are given in centimetres,
width before height.

Place names are as they were in the 1950's
Northern Rhodesia is now Zambia
Southern Rhodesia is now Zimbabwe
Tanganyika is now Tanzania
Nyasaland is now Malawi
Belgian Congo is now Zaire

Ernest Knight

Ernest Griset Knight was born on 24 March 1915 and named after his grandfather, a renowned Victorian artist and illustrator. His mother was Florence Annabella Griset.

Ernest grew up during the First World War. There were many hardships but he and his sister Bella had a happy childhood in spite of the problems of wartime. He went to a preparatory school in Winchester and then to Sutton Valence, a Boarding school in Maidstone, Kent. There were no art classes there and Ernest was glad as he felt he might have been influenced by the teaching before he went to the Chelsea College of Art, London.

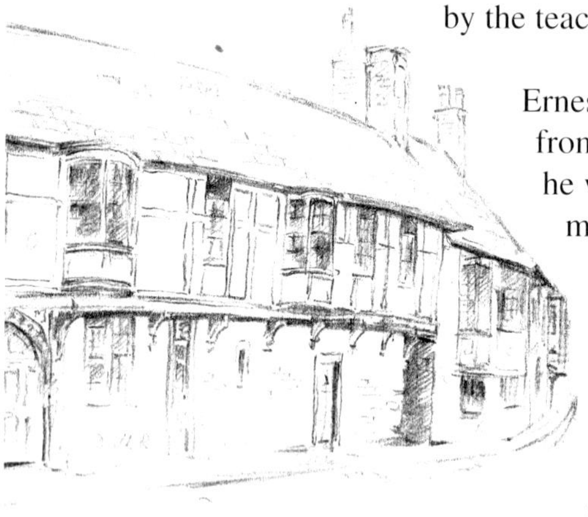

Ernest had a deep love of the countryside and he would escape from the life classes to paint the sky and landscapes whenever he was able. Studying in London gave him access to the major art galleries and it was Turner who influenced him greatly.

After completing his training at Chelsea, Ernest cycled throughout the West of England, painting as he went. Then in 1938 he went to South Africa with a friend and they settled in Johannesburg. The outbreak of war in September 1939 left him stranded there, so he did war work in a gold mine, being in charge of ventilation and working only with Zulus, whom he came to respect. He enjoyed their companionship and sketched them whenever he had a break from his arduous work. This led later to his deep interest in painting African portraits.

Ernest enjoyed the people and life in South Africa. He captured the atmosphere and light in the paintings that he did at that time.

In 1949 he took leave to go to England for six months and on the outward voyage he met Kit Solkhon. Kit also was on leave from her Northern Rhodesia Government post as Physiotherapist-in-charge. They were drawn together by their shared interest in books, finding that they had each brought copies of Aldous Huxley's Perennial Philosophy and Victor Gollancz' Anthology, and they both enjoyed music, art and working for peace. Ernest spent two weeks cycling around the coast of the West Country, painting and drawing as he went, and Kit was able to join him for a few days. Their friendship grew.

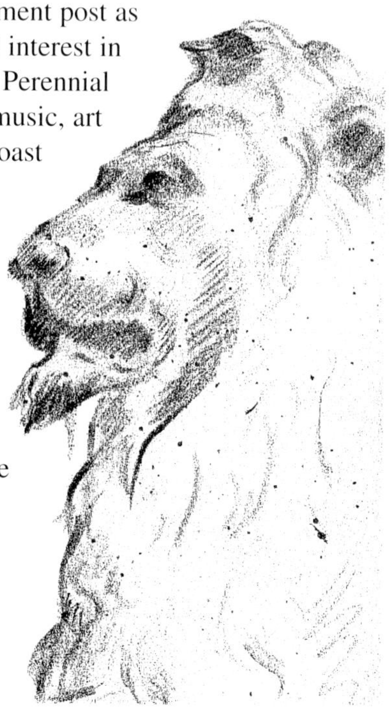

Kit returned to Lusaka in Northern Rhodesia and Ernest was offered a post as Principal of the Art School, Munali, a prestigious school for Africans in Lusaka. This enabled him to reside in the country and they were married in May 1952. On their honeymoon in the Vumba Mountains, Southern Rhodesia, Ernest could not resist painting and, as with all their subsequent holidays, the sale of the paintings paid all their travel expenses.

Kit went every few weeks to the Livingstone Hospital to check up on the African physiotherapist orderlies and Ernest used to drive her there so they stayed near the Victoria Falls at many different times of the year. Ernest painted all the moods of the Falls and there

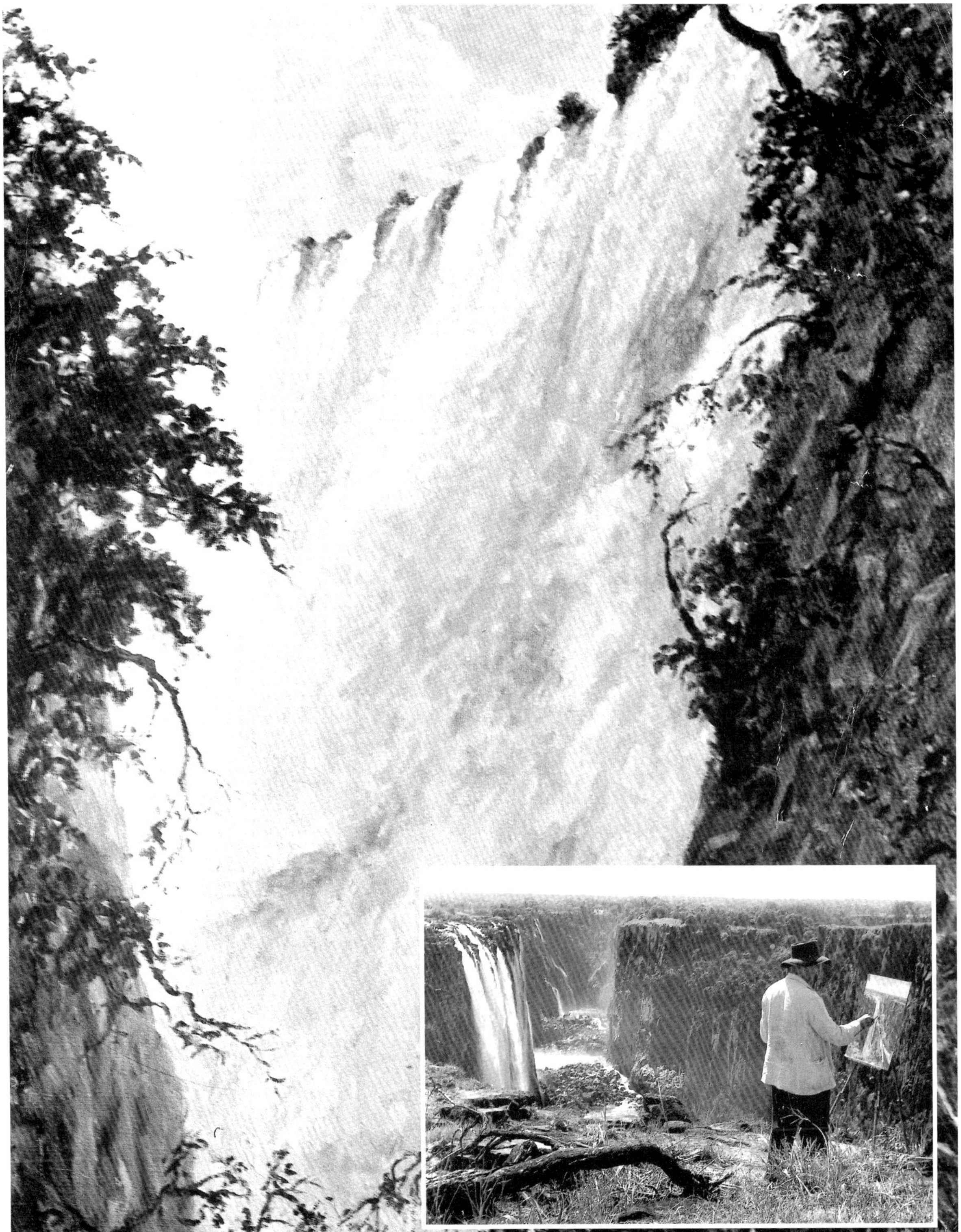

were constant changes. In the rainy season when the Zambezi River was at its fullest Ernest would convey the tremendous power of the water as it tumbled over the gorges and Devil's Cataract, the spray and sunshine creating mist and rainbows. As always, the light played the important part of his painting. Members of the Royal Commonwealth Society purchased one magnificent painting of the Eastern Cataract for their Headquarters in London. It was to commemorate the centenary of the discovery of the Falls by David Livingstone.

PAINTING OF VICTORIA FALLS UNVEILED

A PAINTING of Victoria Falls, presented to Headquarters by members living in Northern Rhodesia to commemorate the centenary of their discovery by David Livingstone, was unveiled on April 24th by Sir Gilbert Rennie, the High Commissioner of Rhodesia and Nyasaland.

The painting, which gives an excellent impression of the tremendous might of the Falls, is the work of Mr. Ernest J. Knight, for some time Principal of the Government African Art School in Lusaka ; he, with his wife, was present at the ceremony. It was much admired when it was exhibited locally and its acquisition was the praiseworthy conception of Mrs. D M. Talmage, at that time the Society's Honorary Corresponding Secretary in Ndola.

The painting has been hung at the end of the Rhodes Room, near to the marble bust of Cecil Rhodes, and has been set in a frame, designed by the Society's Architects (Sir Herbert Baker and Scott), let into the English oak panelling which was the gift of William Mallinson and Co. Ltd. when the building was constructed. In the room there is also a bust of Lord Milner.

SIR CHARLES PONSONBY, Chairman of Council, expressed gratitude to Mrs. Talmage and, in her absence in Rhodesia, warmly welcomed her parents and sister, Wing-Commander and Mrs. Grant Dalton and Miss Grant Dalton. He explained that when the picture was shown last year in the Copperbelt, Mrs. Talmage admired it very much and decided that it must be added to the Society's possessions at Headquarters. Following her lead, 83 members resident in Northern Rhodesia subscribed to make the gift possible. The Council and members generally were most grateful to Mrs. Talmage for her thought and for the energy with which she had carried it out, and also to the subscribers.

Before unveiling the painting, SIR GILBERT RENNIE paid a tribute to the initiative and generosity of the Society's members in Northern Rhodesia and, in particular, to Mrs. Talmage, who conceived the idea of the presentation. It was unfortunate that the ceremony could not be arranged to take place in the centenary year, 1955, but there was this gain—that the picture could now be unveiled in the presence of the artist and his wife, who were now in Britain.

Mr. Knight had done a great deal for art in Northern Rhodesia. By his teaching he had enabled Africans to express with much fluency and vigour their idea of colour and drawing, and his own paintings of many scenes in Northern Rhodesia had become deservedly popular.

It was particularly appropriate that the painting should be hung in the Rhodes Room of the Royal Empire Society. Rhodes and Livingstone, those two great men, were really the founders of Rhodesia and Nyasaland, and here they could be placed symbolically in close association.

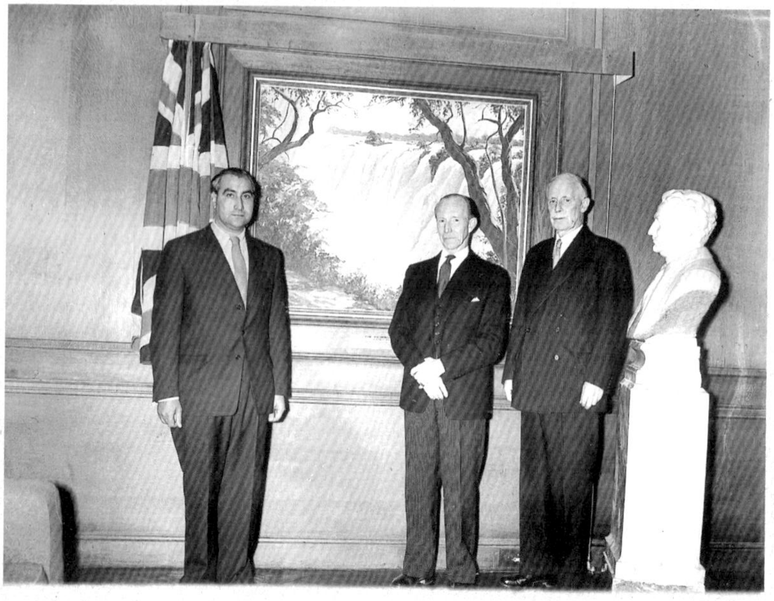

After the unveiling ceremony, Mr. E. J. Knight, the artist, was photographed standing beside his painting, with Sir Gilbert Rennie, the High Commissioner for Rhodesia and Nyasaland, and Col. Sir Charles Ponsonby, Chairman of Council. On the right is the bust of Cecil Rhodes.

Ernest constantly looked for changes in light and atmosphere. He travelled north, hitchhiking with his bare canvases, paints, palette and brushes in a haversack on his back, whilst Kit went by air to Zanzibar and met him there as she only had short leave from her work. At Kasama Ernest painted one old man in his village, and whilst waiting amongst the jostling crowds to board the steamer at Mwanza on the edge of Lake Tanganyika he saw an African woman in a red printed dress, with her baby strapped to her back. He asked if he could paint her portrait if he got her on to the boat - which he did.

They stayed in Dar-es-Salaam and Ernest painted the vivid market scenes and the crowded, narrow streets. They then crossed the stretch of ocean that divides West from East and reached Zanzibar, with its oriental atmosphere teeming with life and contrasting strikingly with the peace of the long, solitary sandy beaches. The painted canvases and drawings were taken back to Lusaka to hold an exhibition there.

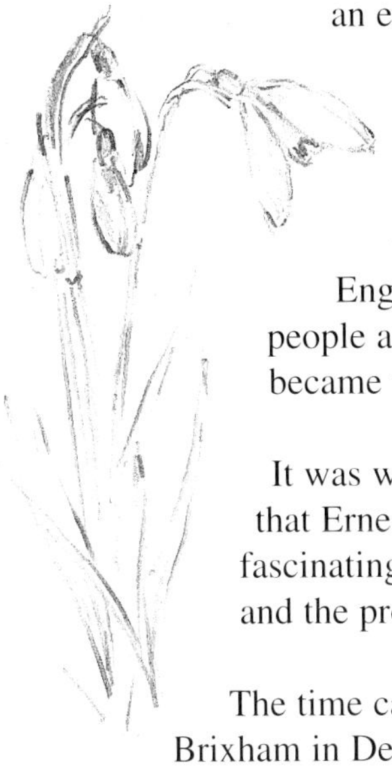

Always needing a change of atmosphere and light, Ernest travelled to Madagascar. This island seemed continental due to the strong French influence. In Tananarive Ernest looked down onto the colourful umbrellas of the market below. He loved to paint markets in Africa, England and Europe, for they were always full of colour, crowds of different people and alive with interest. The tropical palms and the deep blue of the sea became the backdrop for his Madagascar paintings.

It was while Kit was working at the Lusaka Government Hospital as physiotherapist that Ernest began art therapy for the long-term African patients. This led to a fascinating collection of paintings, which were exhibited in London, Vienna, Canada, and the provinces of the United Kingdom.

The time came for Ernest and Kit to return to England in 1956. They had decided that Brixham in Devon would make an ideal centre and were fortunate in securing a house overlooking Torbay, where they could add a studio. Ernest's paintings were prolific. The atmosphere of sea and sky, and the constant change and activity in the fishing harbour were his subjects. It was at this time that the replica of the Mayflower was being built at Brixham and Ernest looked down from his studio and recorded this.

During this period Ernest drove to London in his camper van and parked on the Thames' Embankment. He was ready to begin painting as dawn broke - his favourite time of day. Between 1972 and 1973 he completed a commission for thirty-five paintings of London.

However, it was Dartmoor, with all its changing moods through the seasons, the hills and mists, the heather and the gorse that drew him and in 1978 they left Brixham to live on Dartmoor. Their home stood in two and a half acres of woodland on a hill above Widecombe in the Moor. From his studio window there were magnificent views across the moor. Often they would set out before dawn so that Ernest could paint or draw and capture the mood of a landscape he had discovered on his endless drives across the moors. When asked how long it took to paint a scene he would explain that it began with exploring the moors and then catching the right light as he believed (as Turner had believed) that a painting is the light on a subject. The dawn produced the conditions he enjoyed most of all.

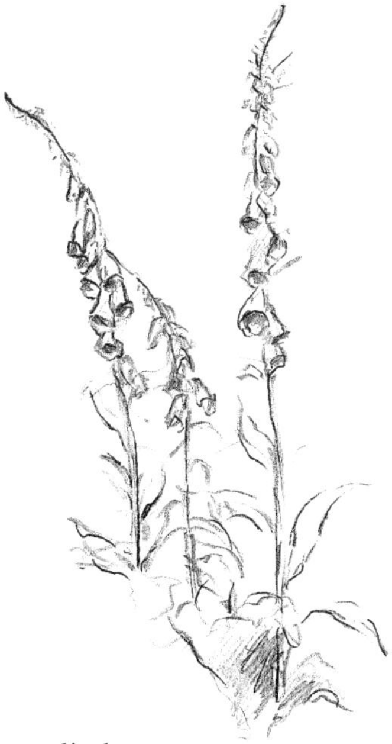

An atmosphere of peace surrounded their house, Torcroft. It was an idyllic sanctuary for birds and wild animals. Snowdrops, daffodils, bluebells and foxgloves covered the woodland through the seasons. Ernest's paintings of Dartmoor are among his greatest. The weather over the moors is so transient and as a landscape artist who loved his subject it was a great challenge.

In sun, rain and snow he was out with his canvas and paints. If the weather conditions were quite impossible he made drawings with annotations so that a painting could be completed in his studio; then he relied on his vivid visual memory.

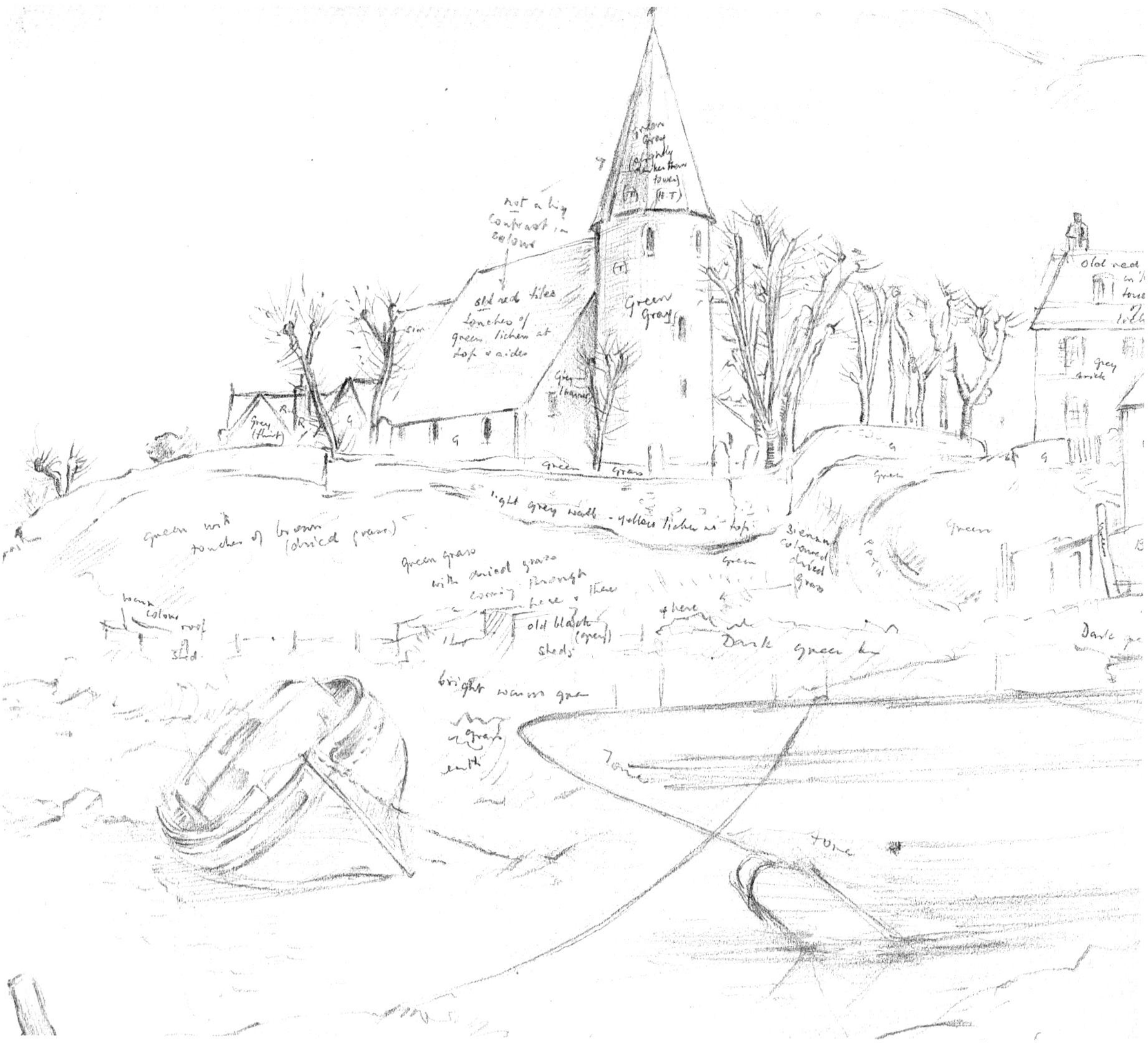

Ernest in his later years exhibited his paintings only in the gallery at Torcroft, Widecombe. Kit and Ernest both enjoyed meeting the countless visitors who came to view and perhaps buy a painting. Ernest just wanted people to enjoy the work that he had done.

Kit and Ernest spent their holidays on the Continent - France, Italy (including Venice and Rome) and Greece. Ernest's paintings of castles and churches were architecturally perfect. Travel was important and his visits to art galleries and exhibitions always stimulated him.

Ernest was a great artist and a great man. His last series of six paintings was a panoramic tribute to Dartmoor, which meant so much to him. He died in October, 1995.

Throughout their life together there ran a thread very important to them and they worked together for peace. When they met for the first time on their voyage from Africa to England they were drawn to each other by their concern for solving world problems through peace, not violence. Kit had been a dedicated member of the Anglican Pacifist Fellowship for some time. Ernest had been reading Aldous Huxley's Perennial Philosophy on the voyage and that, together with their discussions on the subject, convinced him that he should accept the ethic of non-violence and he became utterly committed to peace work. This deep commitment cemented their relationship.

When Kit and Ernest returned to England after their marriage they took an active part in the growing Peace movement. It was a great bond between them and they joined pilgrimages to Hyde Park, Canterbury Cathedral, and Aldermaston. Ernest drove his camper van, filled with food, and collected marchers en route. There was a very deep camaraderie amongst these dedicated people and their lives were greatly enriched by the movement. His work for peace evolved from his gifts as an artist and his search for harmony.

"We all miss Ernest and are grateful for his inspired years of dedication to peace."
R. Mallone

"Ernest radiated friendliness and I pay tribute to him as a man of peace who made a valuable contribution to the peace campaign and to the life of the Anglican Pacifist Fellowship. His fine pictures live on as a memorial."
Dr Philip Dransfield November 1996

"I found the combination of generous hospitality, lively conversation and tenacious exploration of the arguments immensely enriching......"
The Revd. Sidney Hinkes November 1996

In London, Ernest Knight has exhibited with the Royal Society of Oil Painters, The Royal Society of Marine Artists and the Lord Mayor of London's Award Exhibition.

His paintings have also been exhibited in various parts of England, Canada, Europe and Africa and reflect a magnificent record of his extensive travels.

Ernest Knight was the grandson of Ernest Griset, a well-known Victorian artist and illustrator.

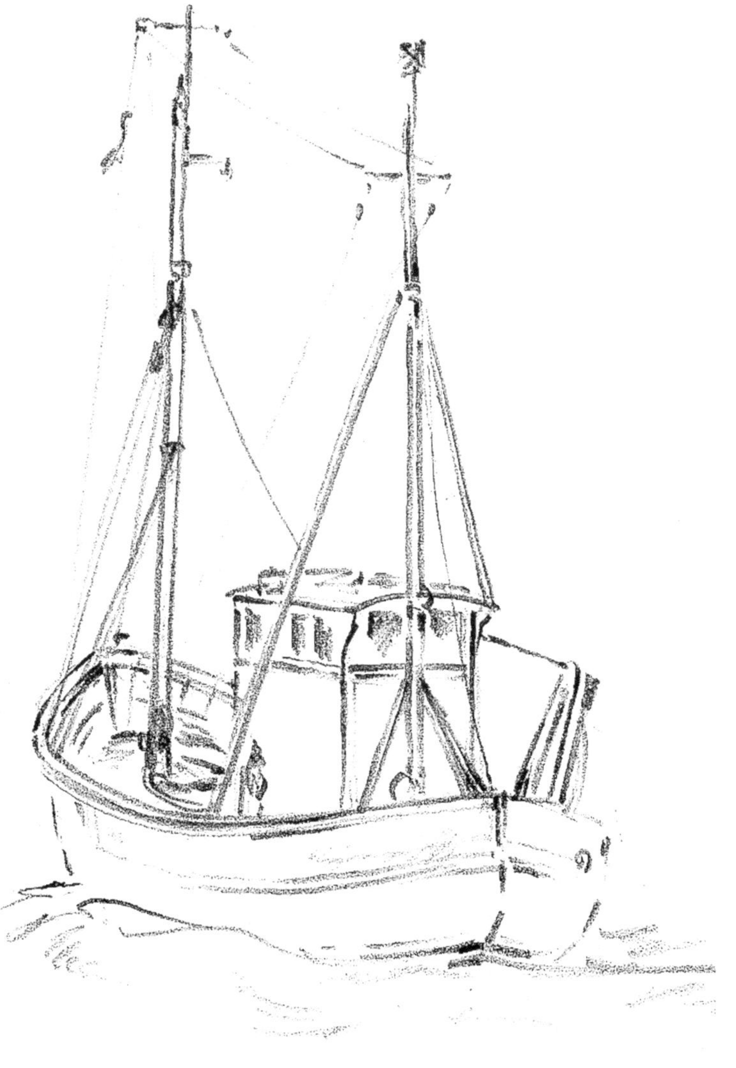

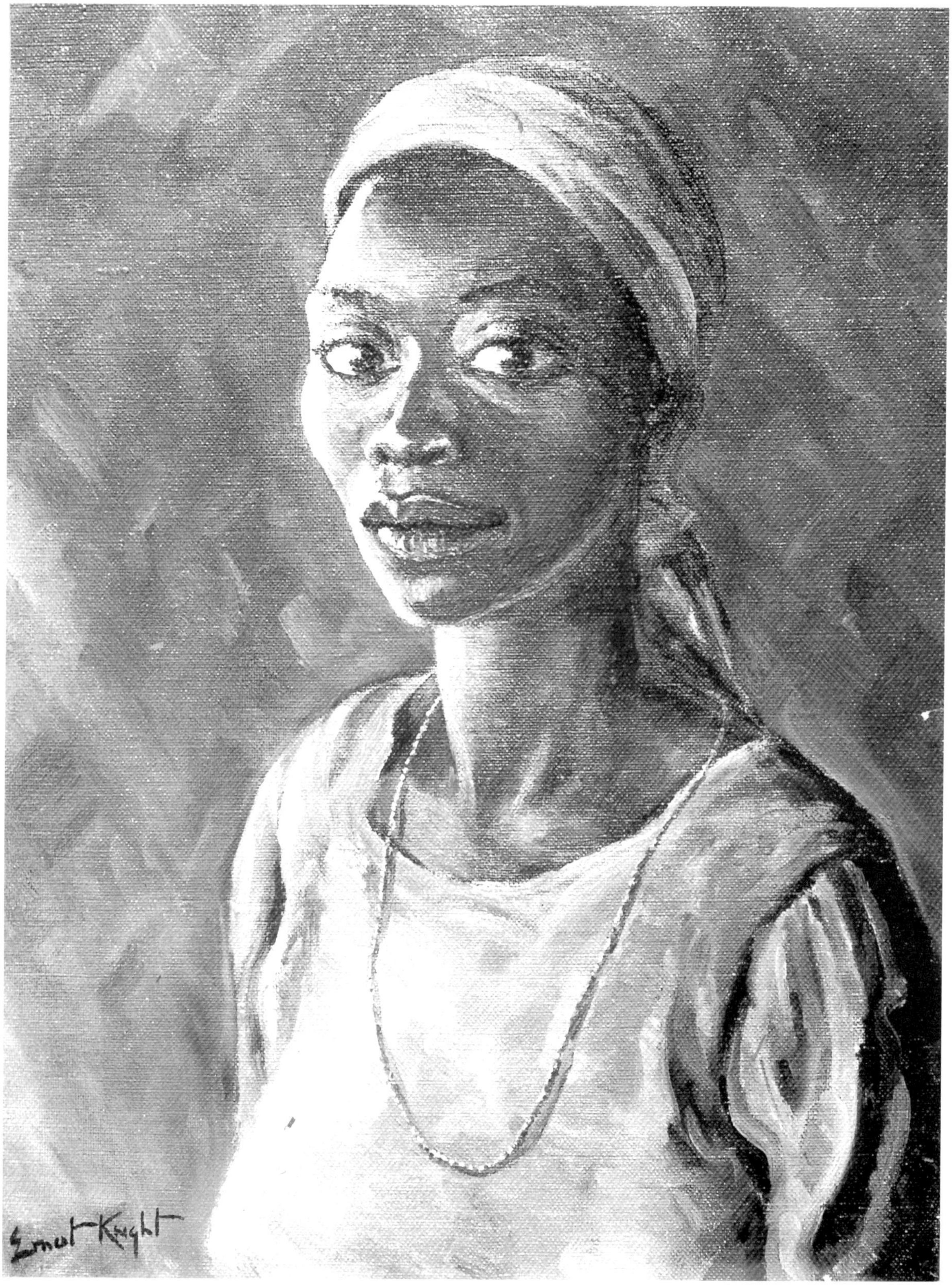

African Girl, Northern Rhodesia. 15 cm x 41 cm.

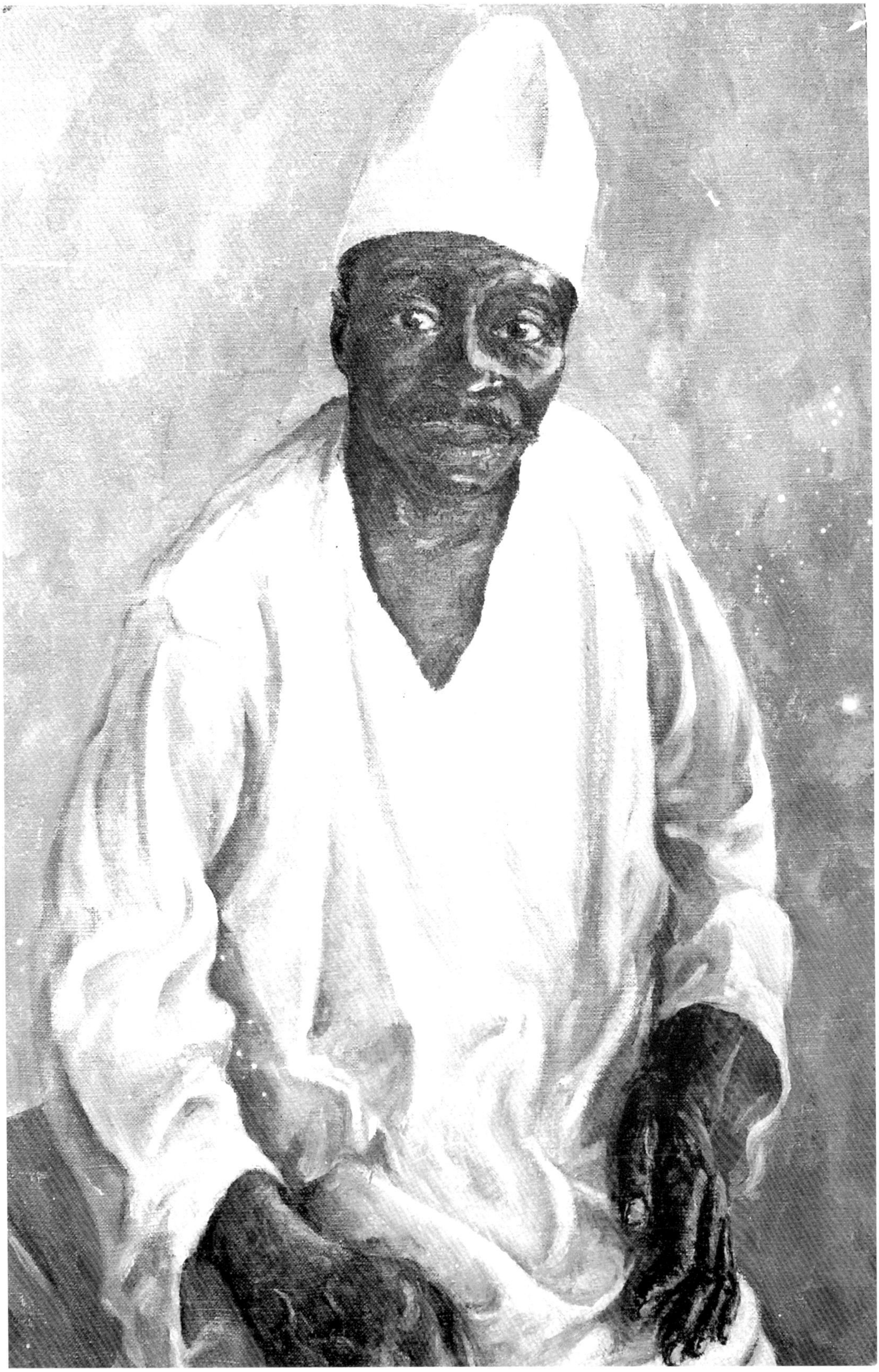

Moslem Woodcarver, Central Africa.

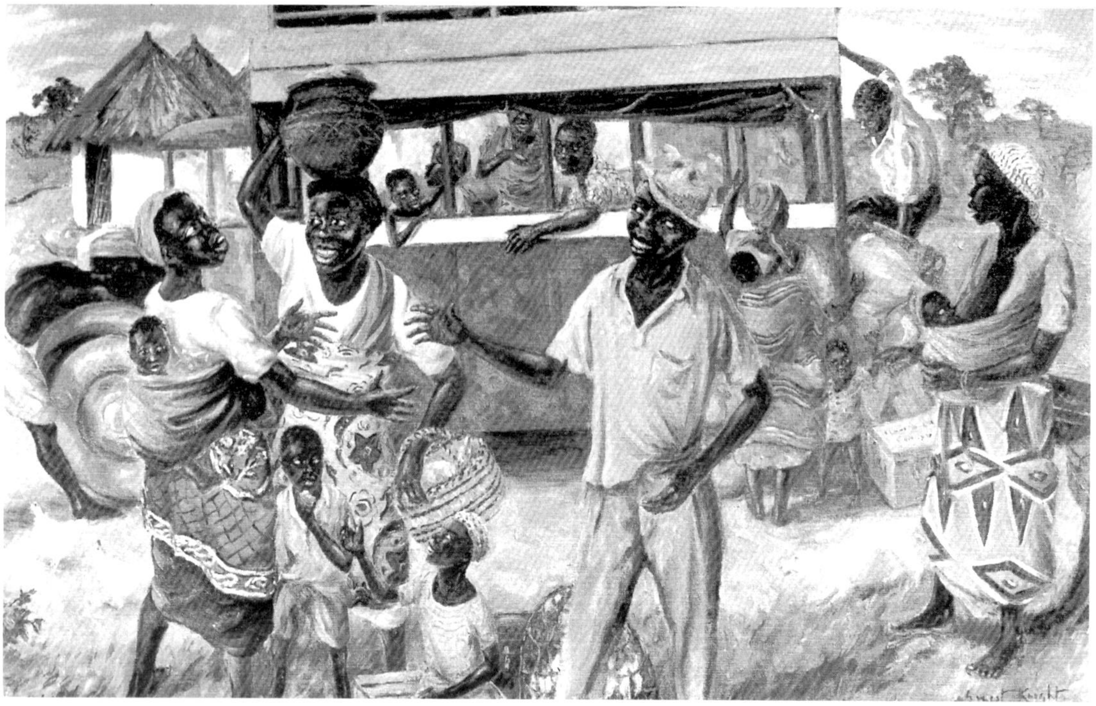

Bus Stop, Northern Rhodesia.

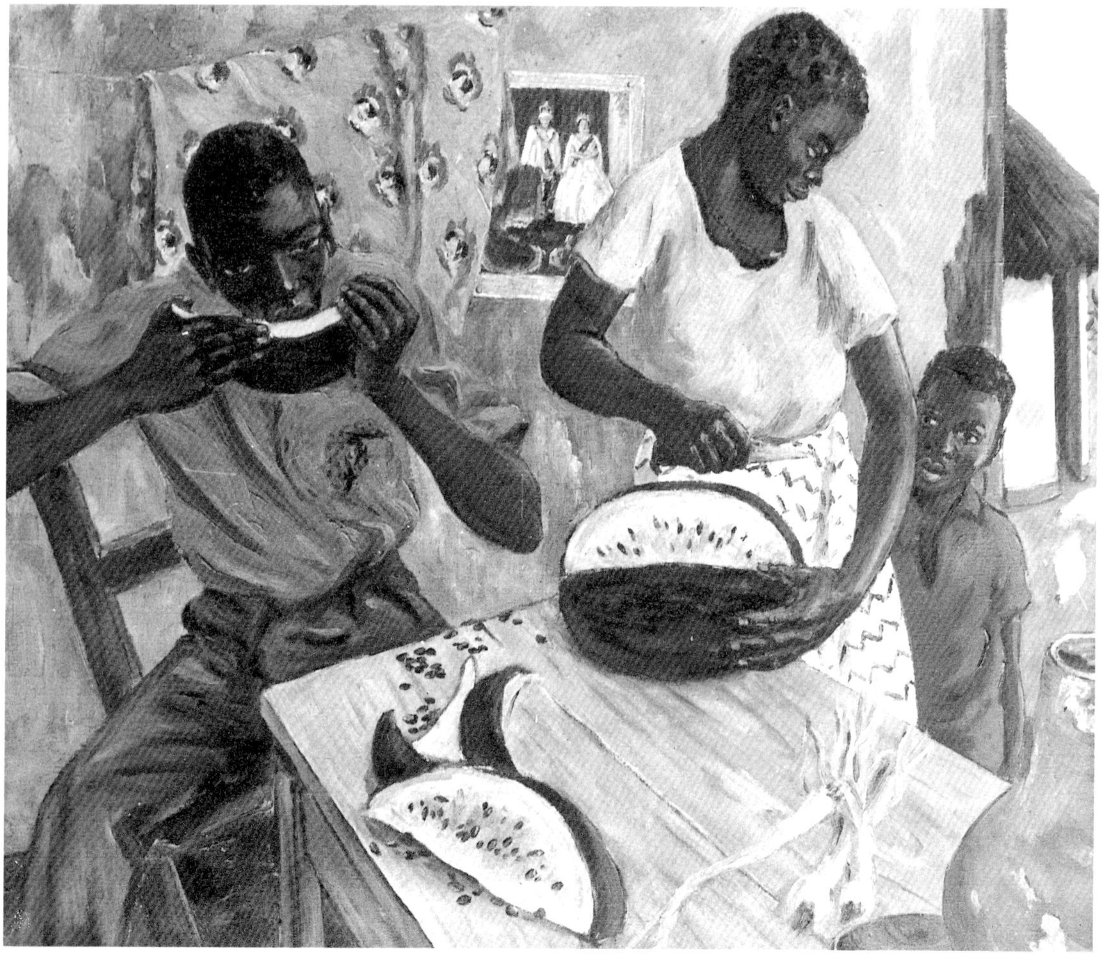

The Melon Eaters, Lusaka, Northern Rhodesia.

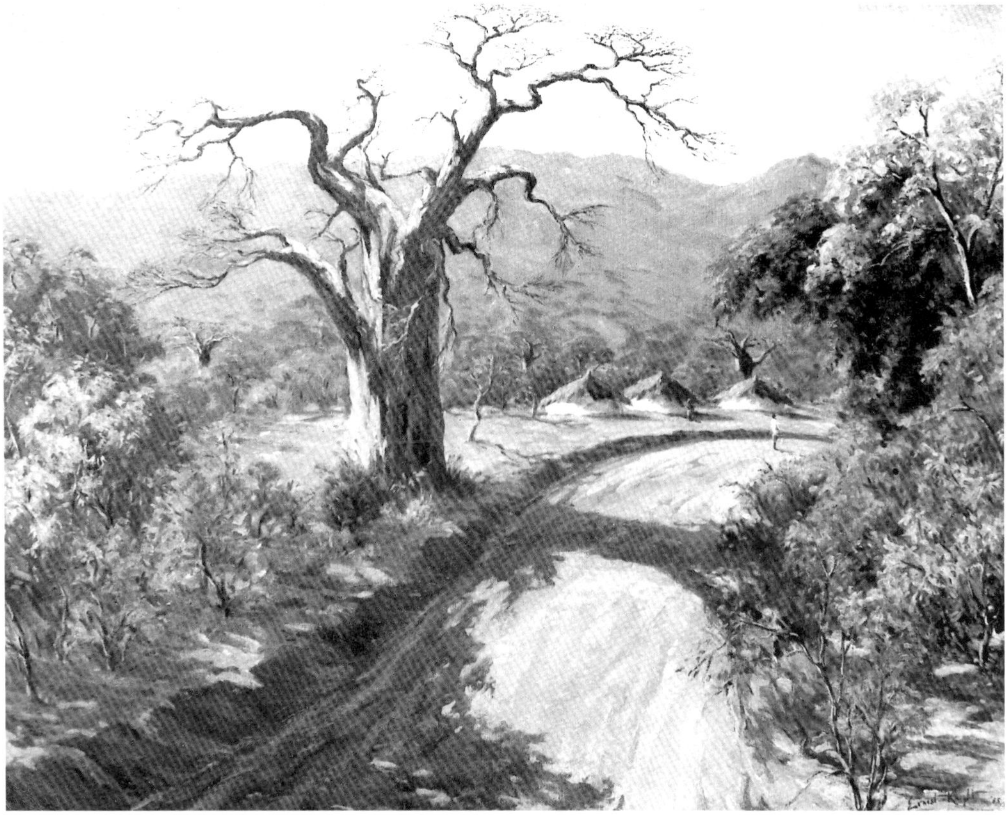

Chirundu Landscape, Northern Rhodesia. 127 cm x 102 cm.

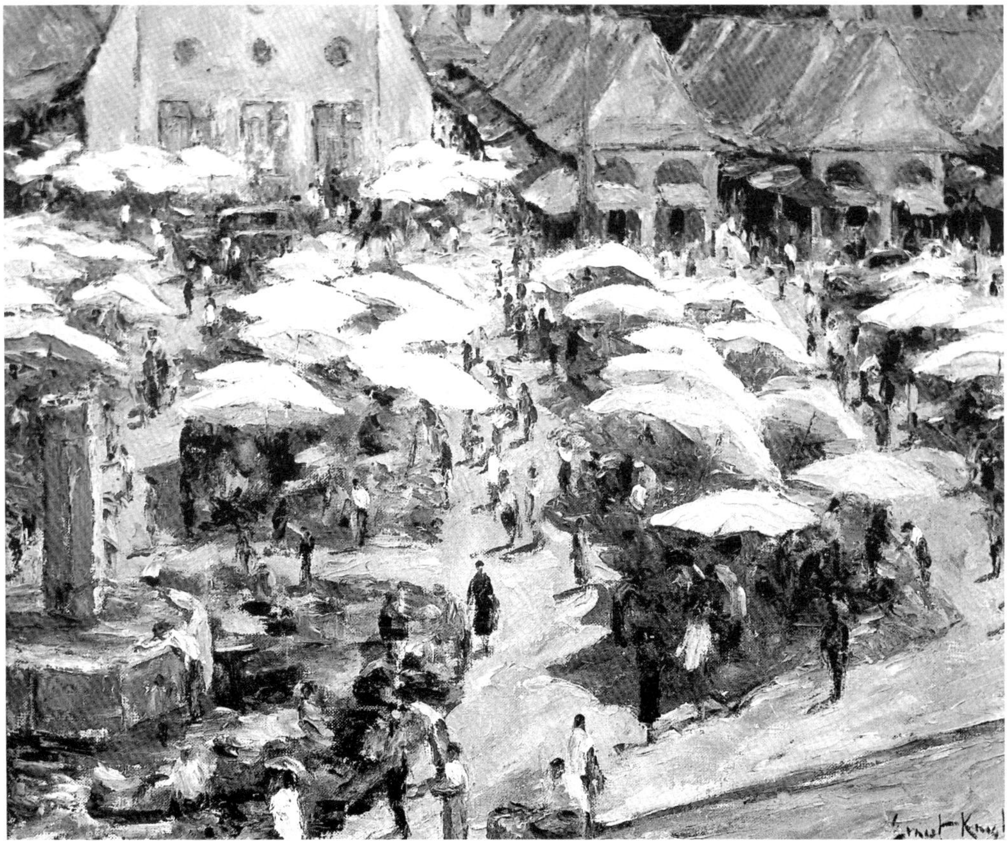

The Market, Tananarive Madagascar.

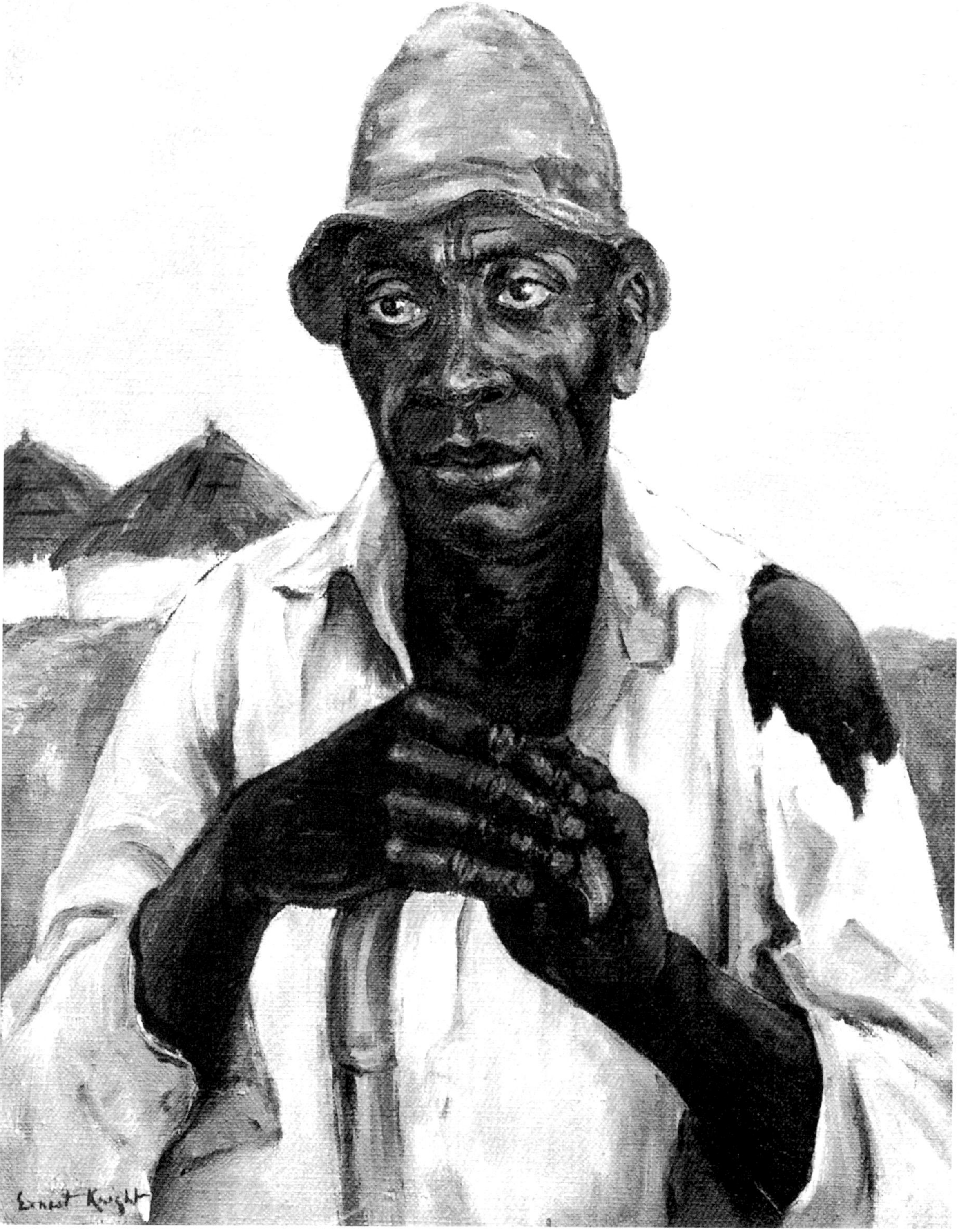

Old African, Northern Rhodesia.

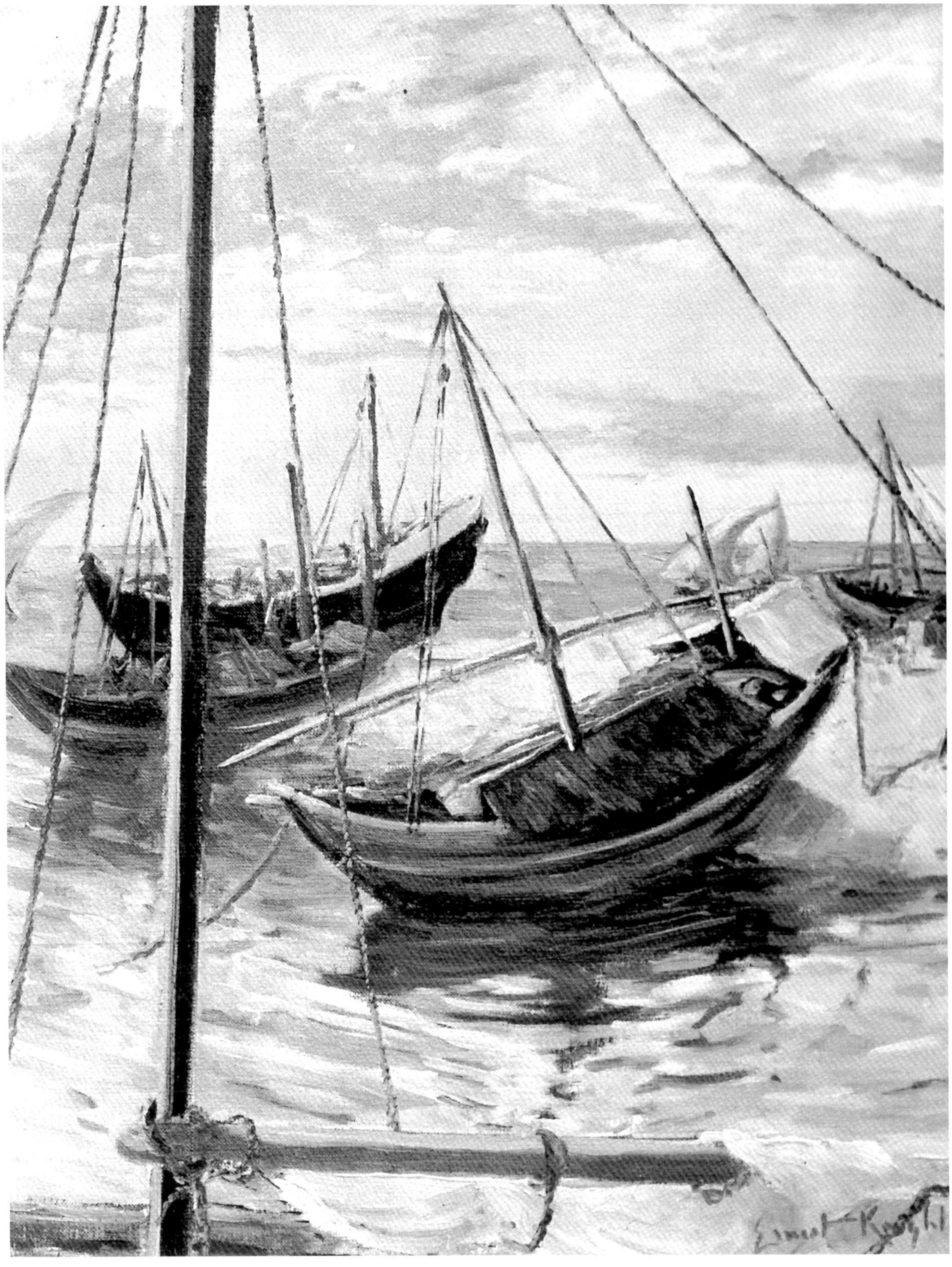

Fishing Boats, Madagascar.

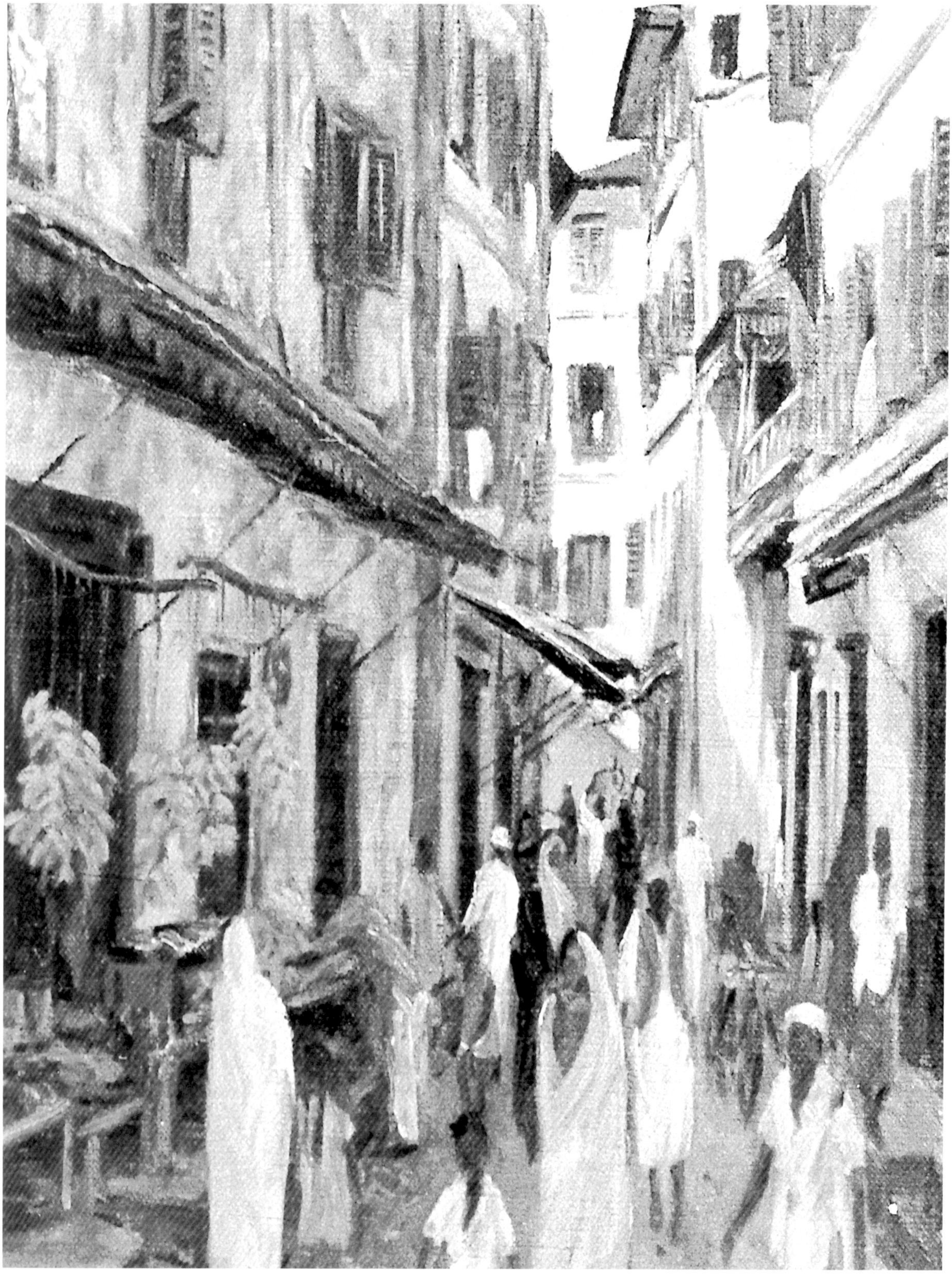

Street Scene, Zanzibar.

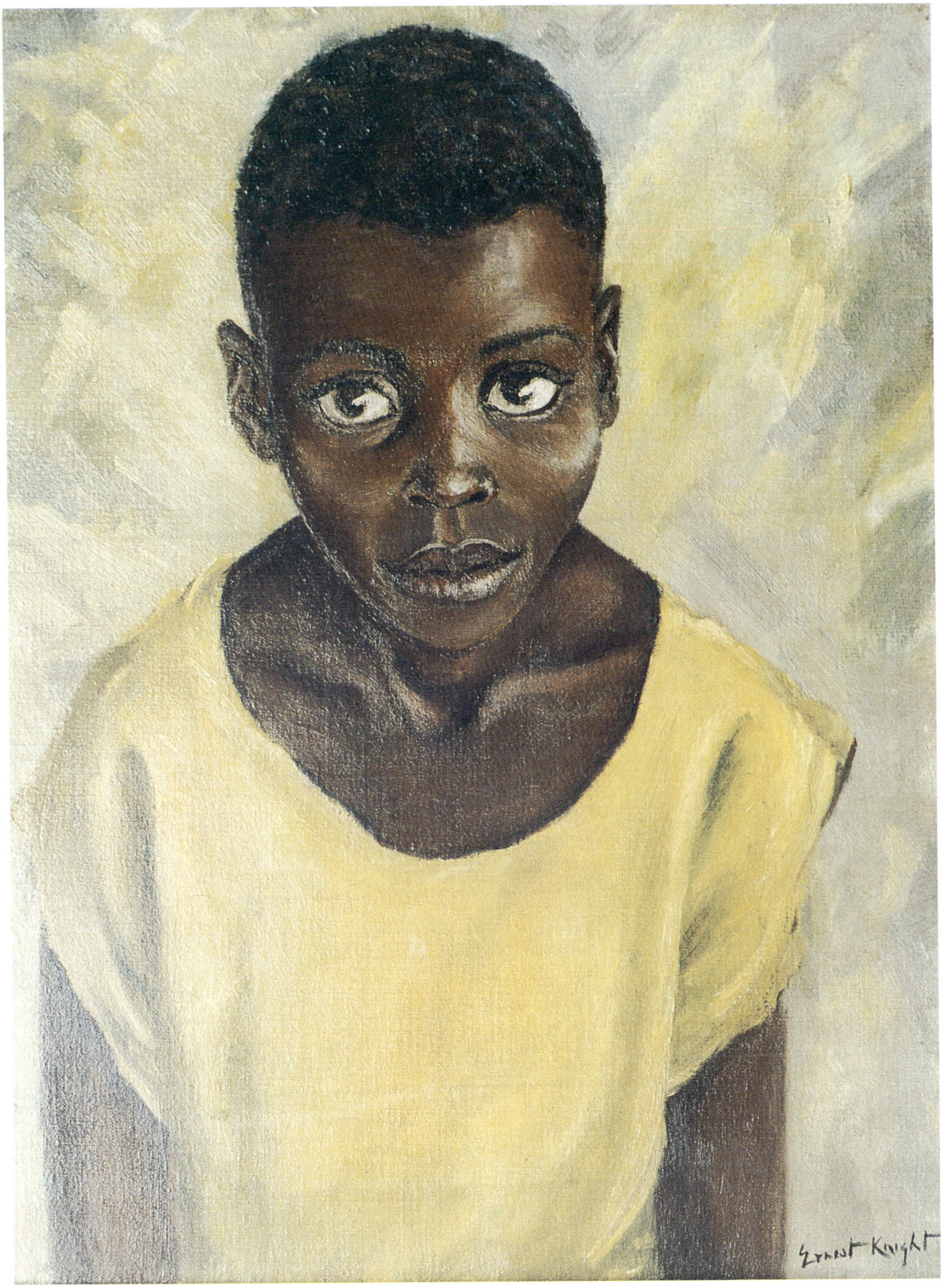

African Child, Kapepwe, Northern Rhodesia. Oil on Canvas. 41 cm x 51 cm. Plate 1.

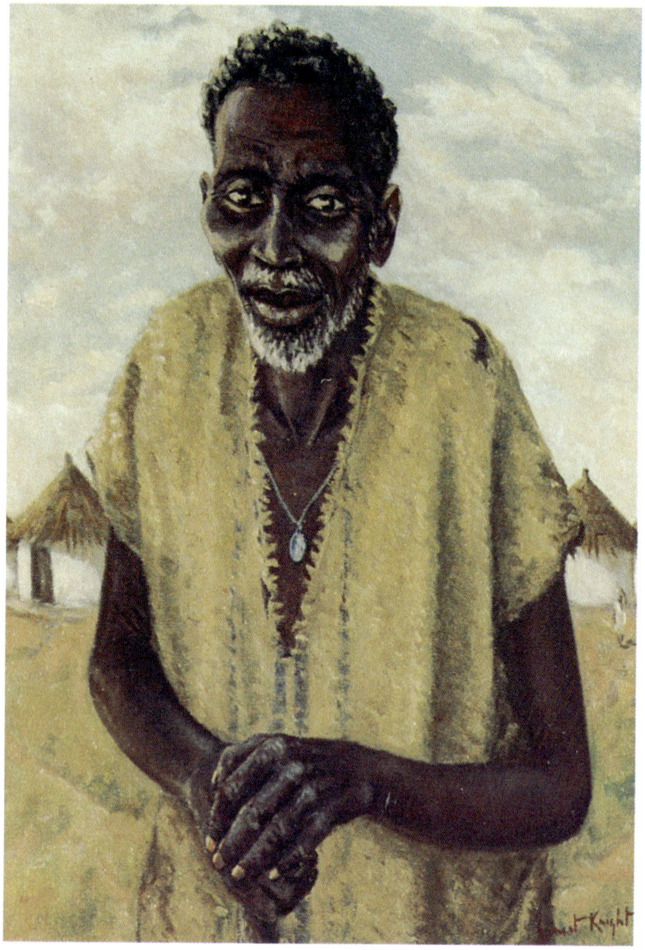

Old Man, Tanganyika. Oil on Canvas. Plate 2.

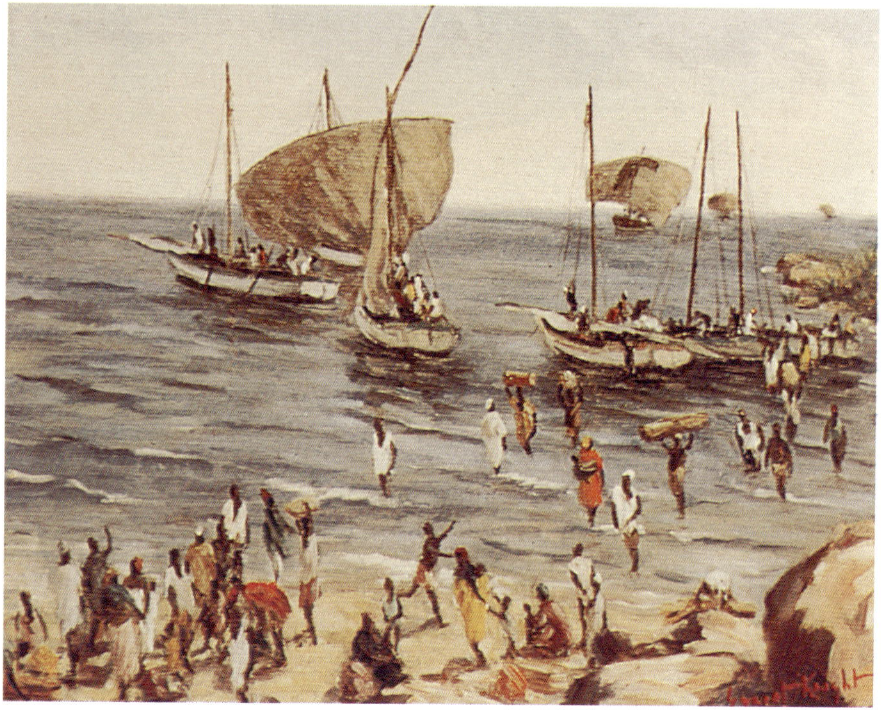

Fishermen, Lake Nyasa. Oil on Canvas. Plate 3.

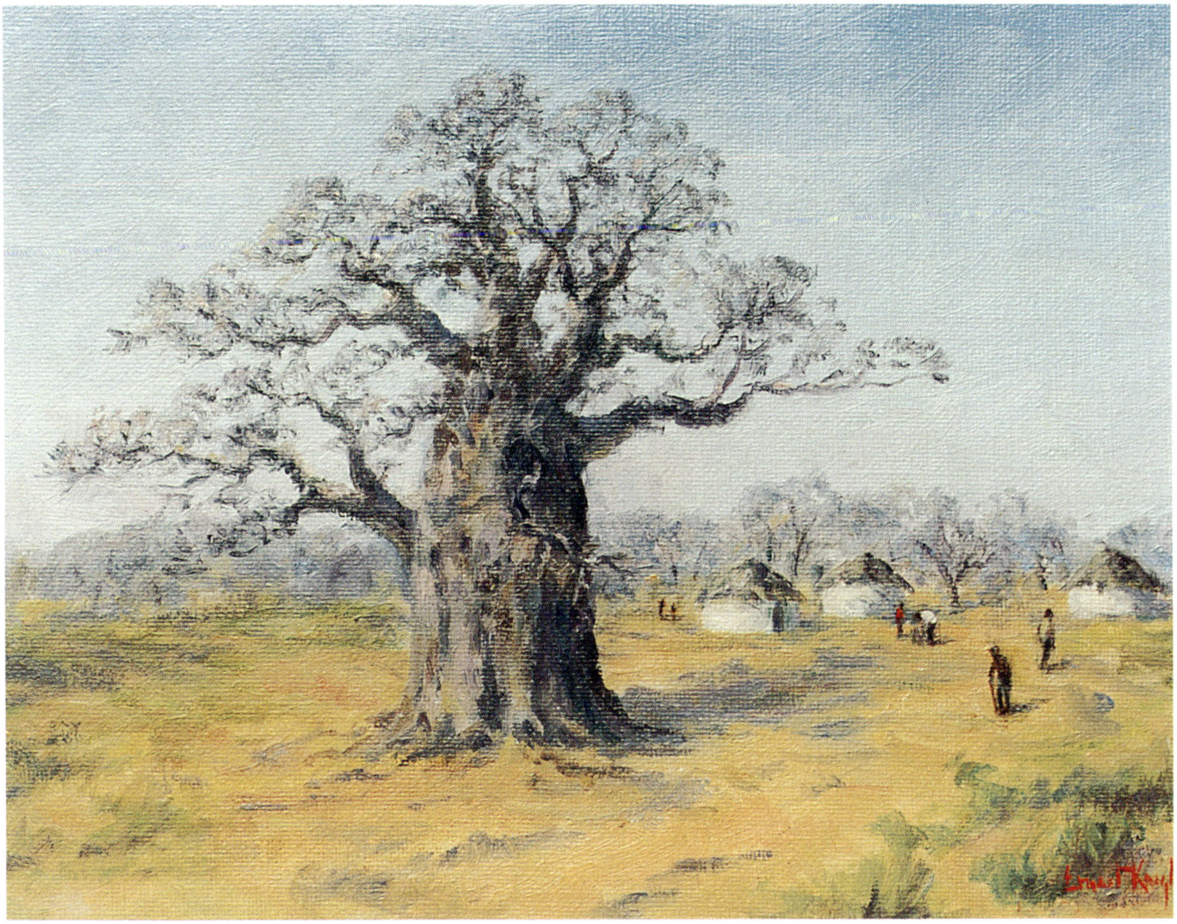

The Baobab Tree. Oil on Canvas. 41 cm x 31 cm. Plate 4.

The Baobab tree is the giant of the African bush. It can grow up to seventy feet high and when it has shed its leaves it looks so ungraceful that it is called the 'upside-down tree'.

It is very generous to the Africans who live in the bush. It offers food, shelter, clothing and a final resting place.

The fibrous bark is stripped off in large sheets then pounded and woven into blankets and mats. The bark will regrow. During the short period when it is in leaf, a tasty relish is made from its foliage. The seeds taken from the hard oval pod are covered in a white powder - cream of tartar - and provides a rich source of Vitamin C. The seeds are also pounded to make a porridge and salt is provided from the burned wood of the tree.

Bush fires may burn out the centre of the huge trunk of the tree and this offers shelter for up to twenty travellers. The hollow branches retain water and bees store honey there. The hollow trunk may also provide a burial place and thorn bushes are stacked against the entrance to stop marauding animals.

The trees tower above all others and are often struck by lightening, making them look even more grotesque, yet they have their own individual beauty and are revered by the Africans.

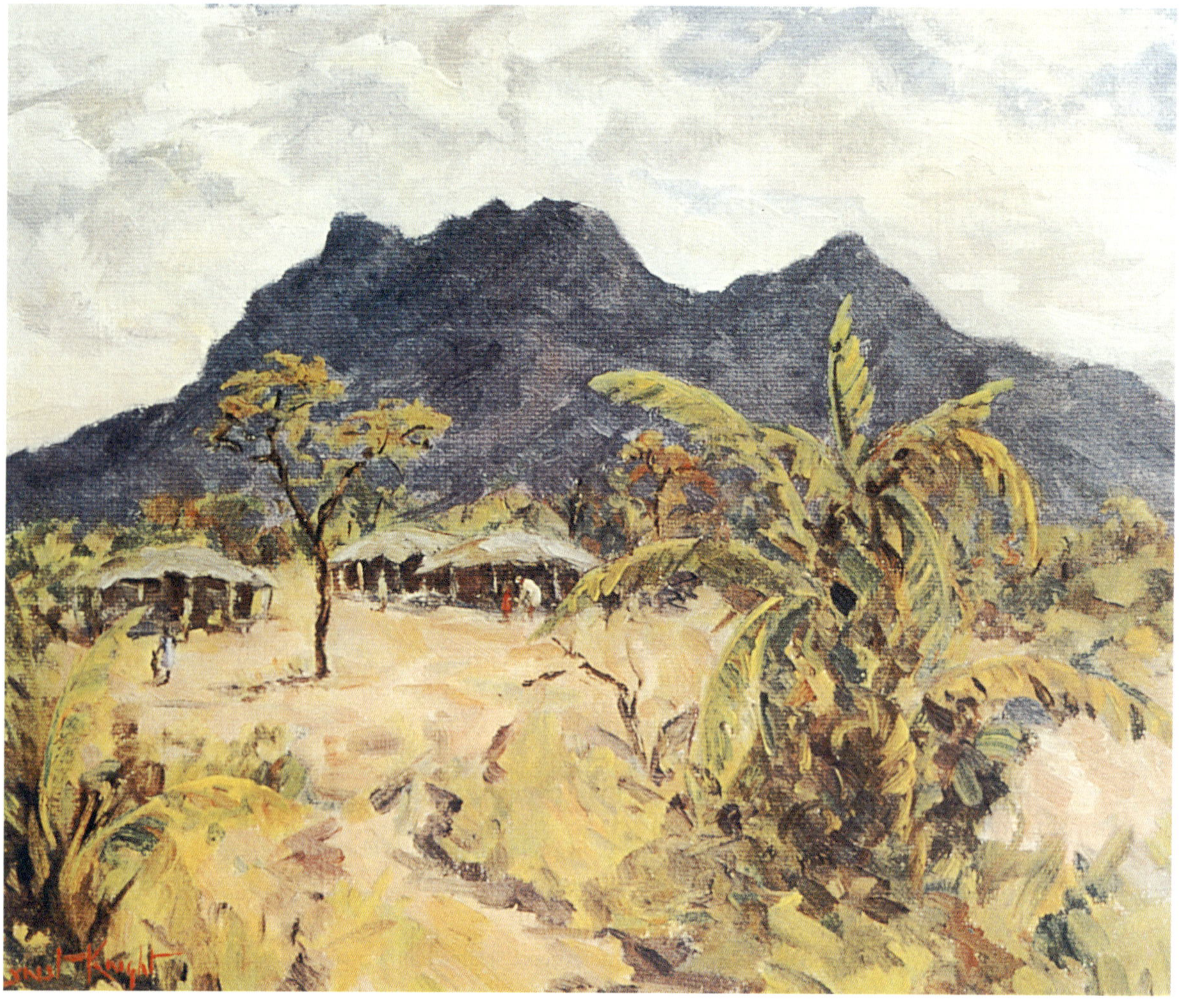

Village, Nyasaland. Oil on Canvas. Plate 5.

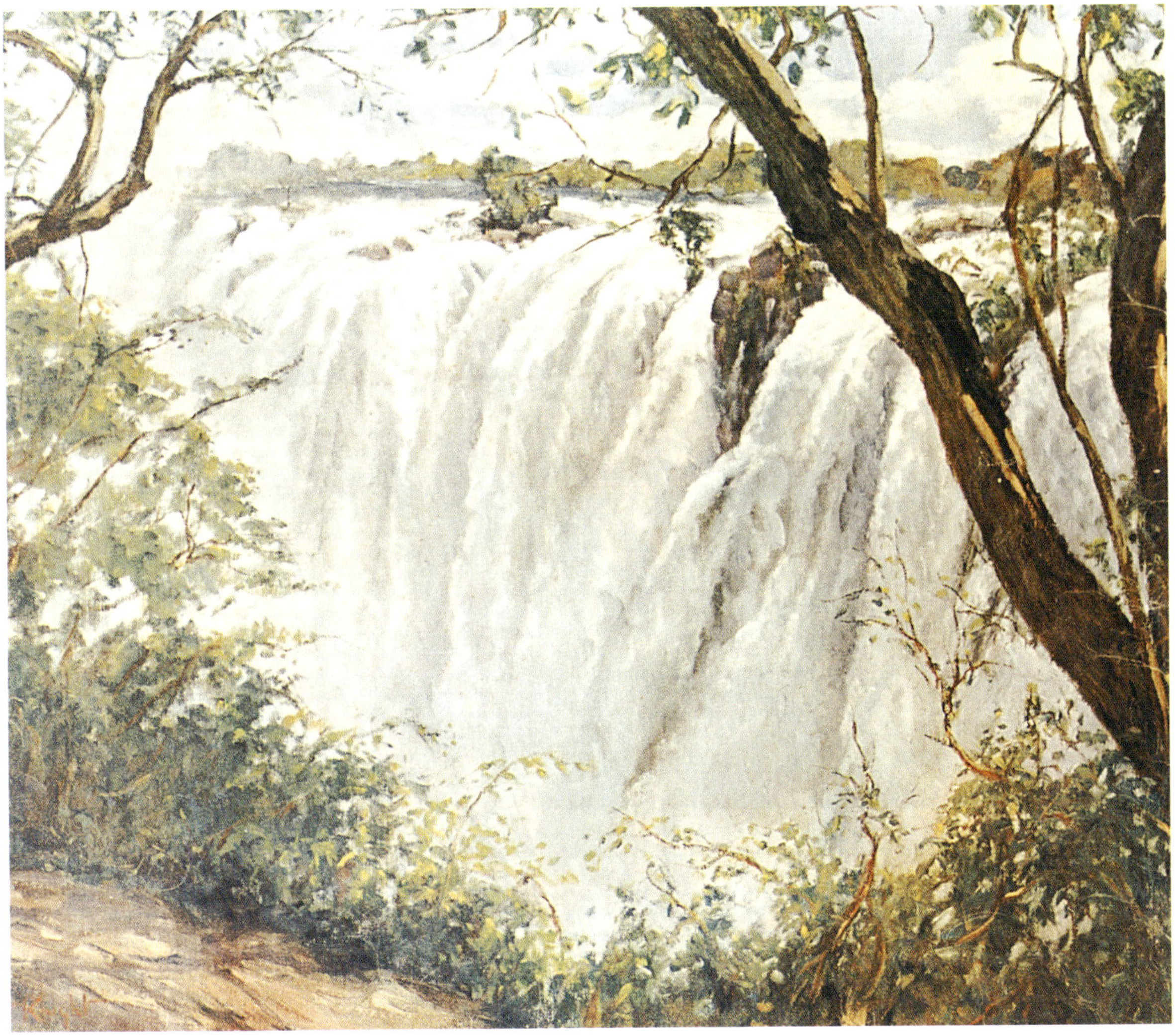

Victoria Falls, Northern Rhodesia. Oil on Canvas. Plate 6.

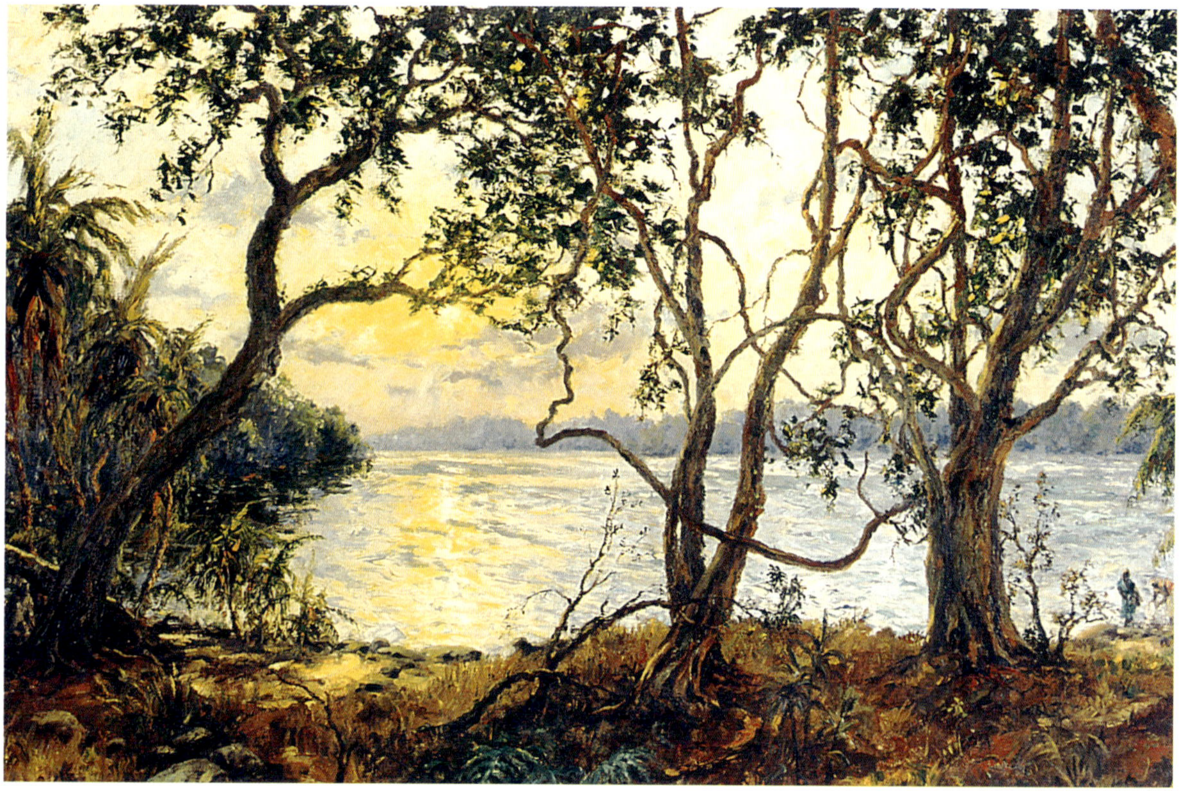

The Zambesi River above Victoria Falls, Northern Rhodesia. 212 cm x 122 cm. Plate 7.

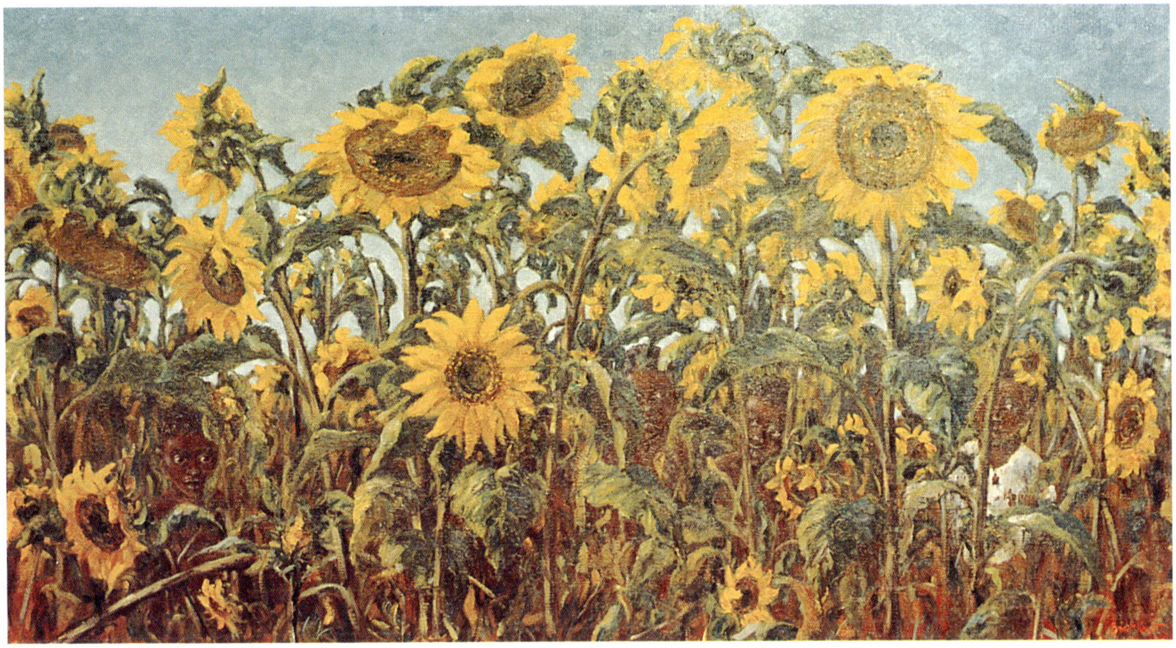

Sunflowers and Children, Northern Rhodesia. Oil on Canvas. Plate 8.

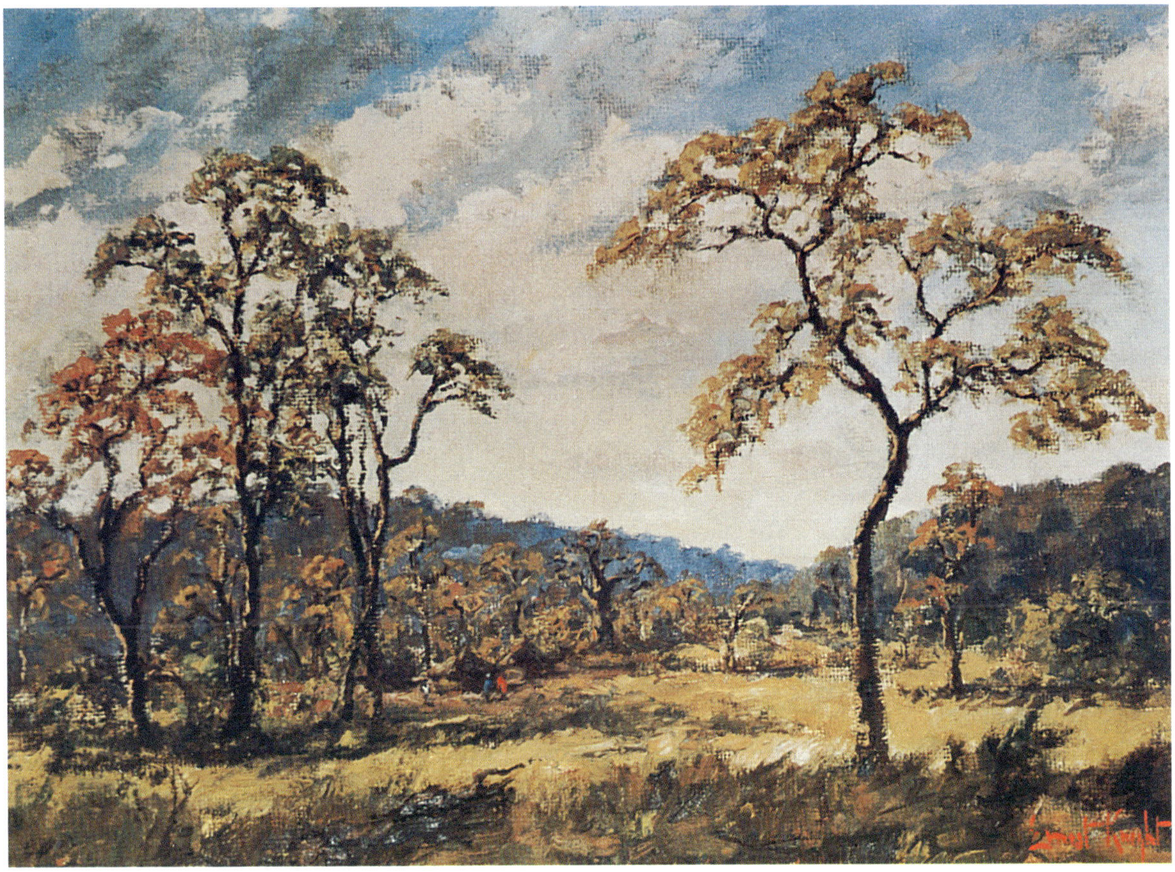

The Bush, Northern Rhodesia. Oil on Canvas. Plate 9.

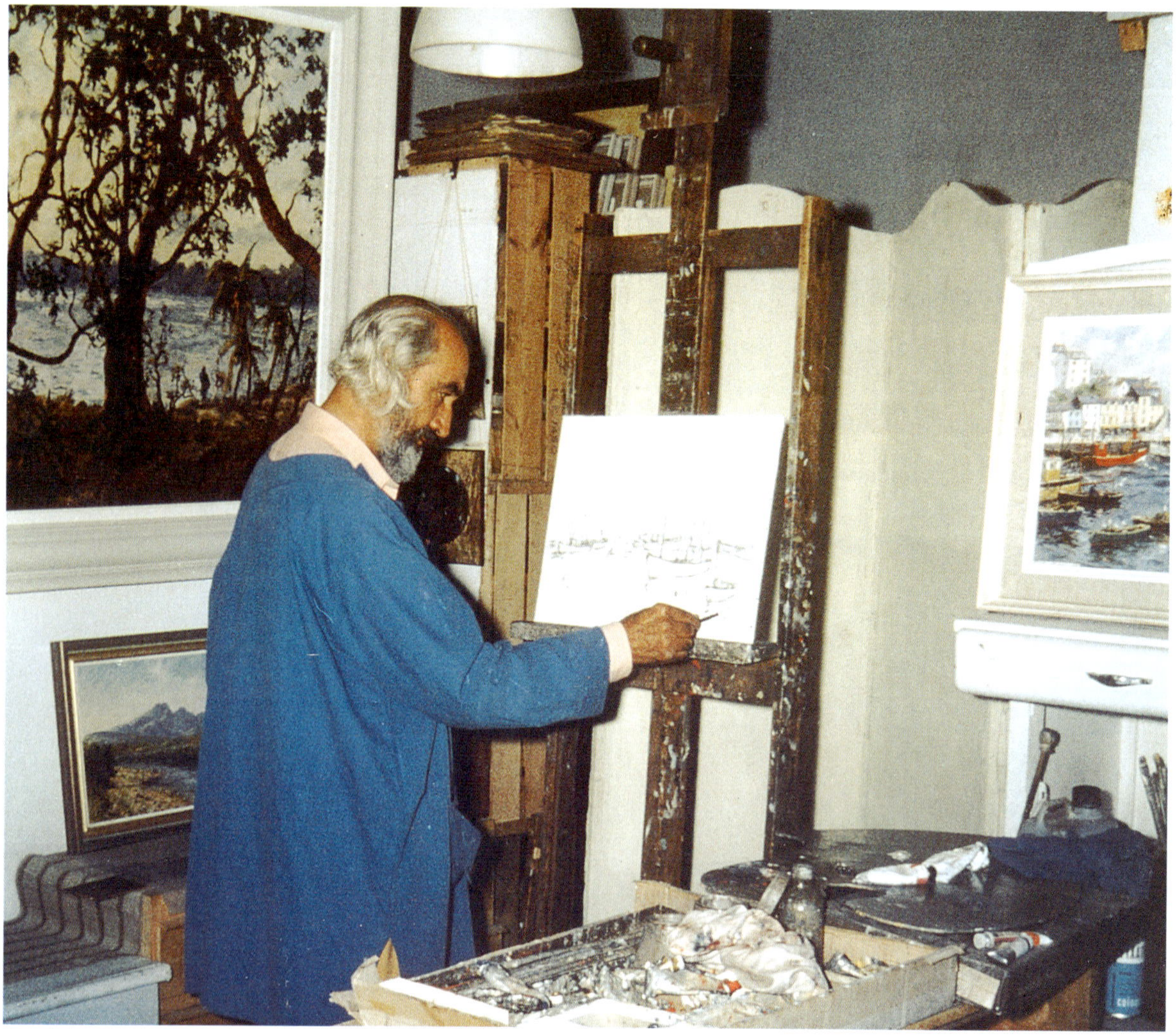

The Studio, Torcroft, Brixham. Plate 10.

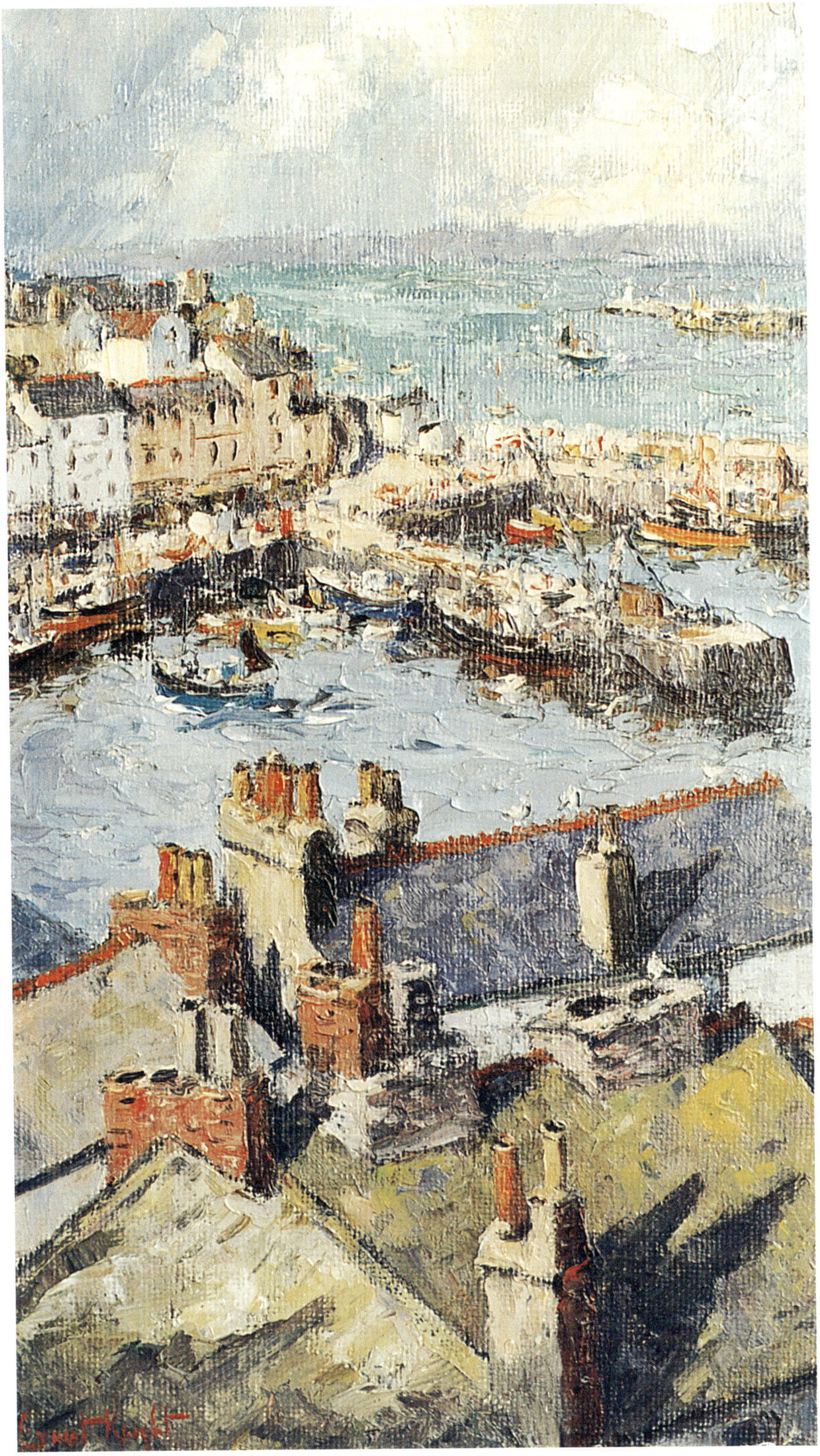

View of Brixham Harbour from Torcroft. 33 cm x 52 cm. Oil on Canvas. Plate 11.

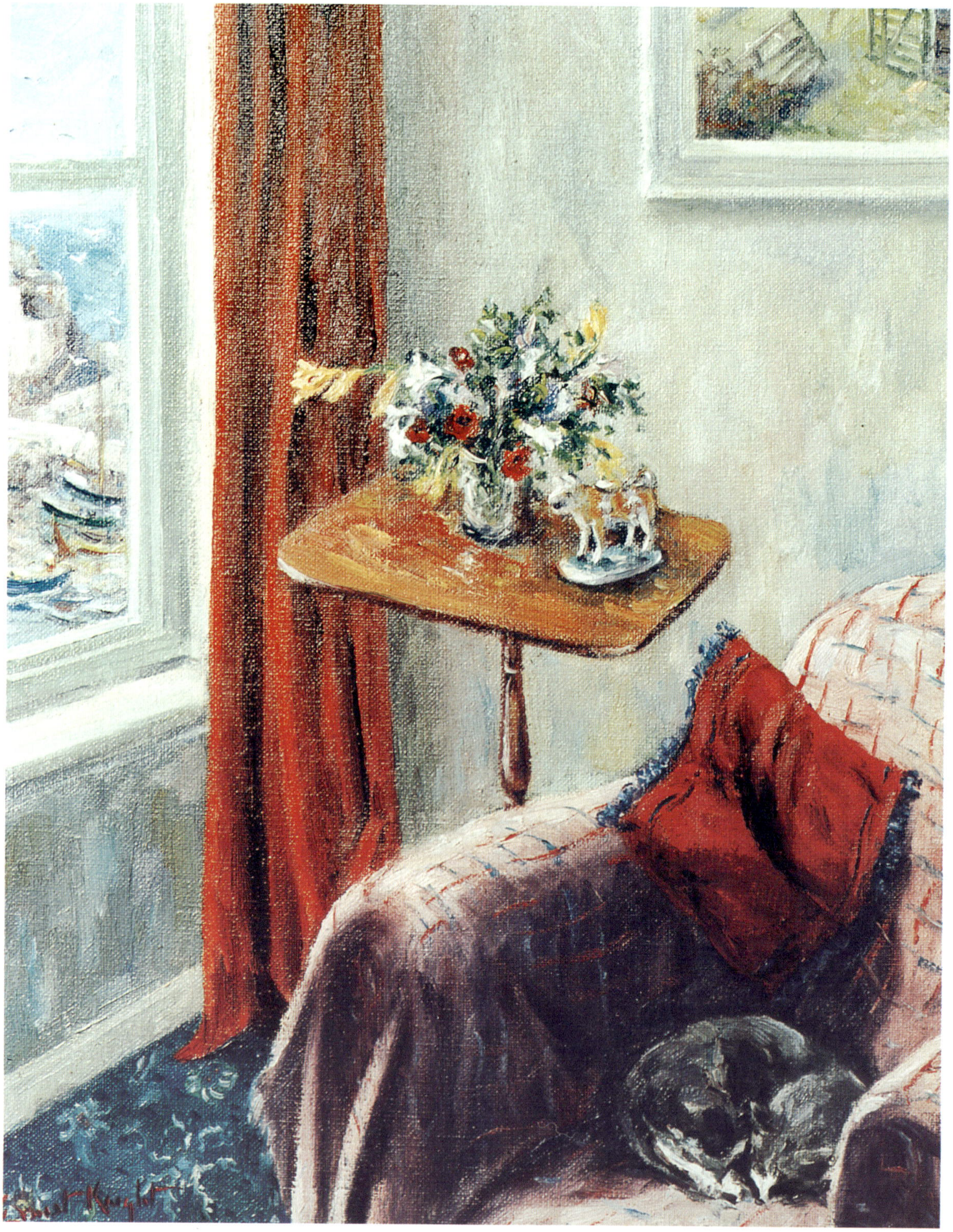

The Sitting Room, Torcroft, Brixham. Oil on Canvas. 38 cm x 49 cm. Plate 12.

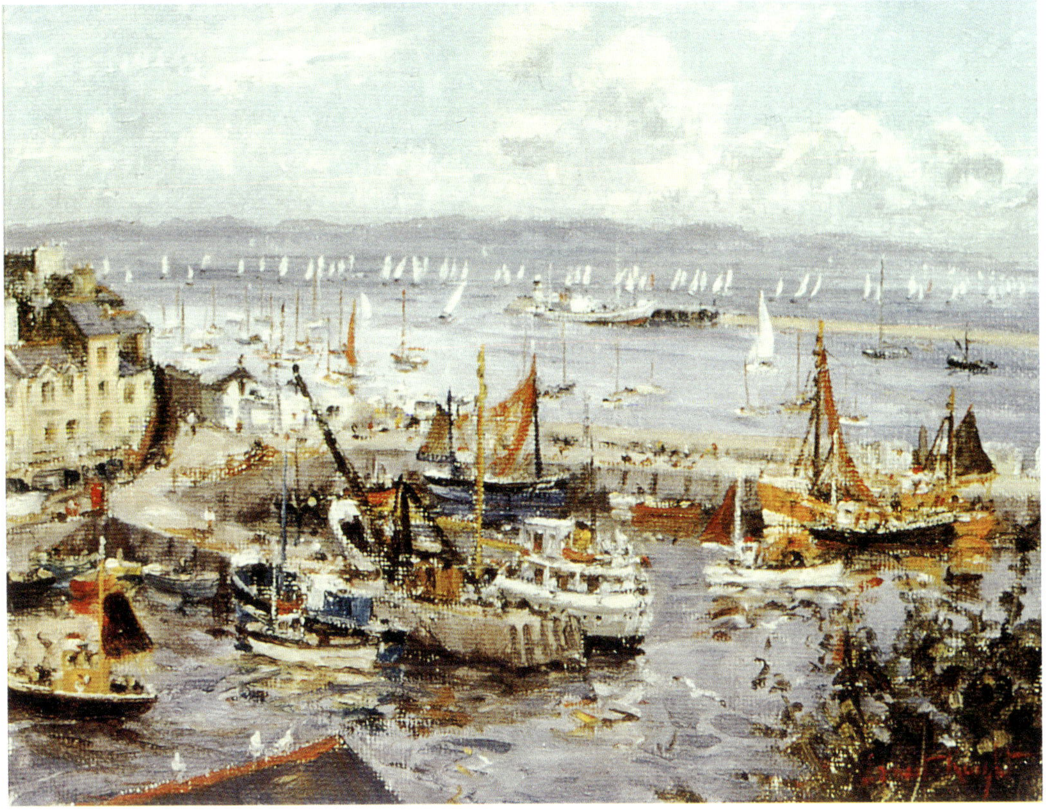

Torbay Regatta, Brixham, Devon. Plate 13.

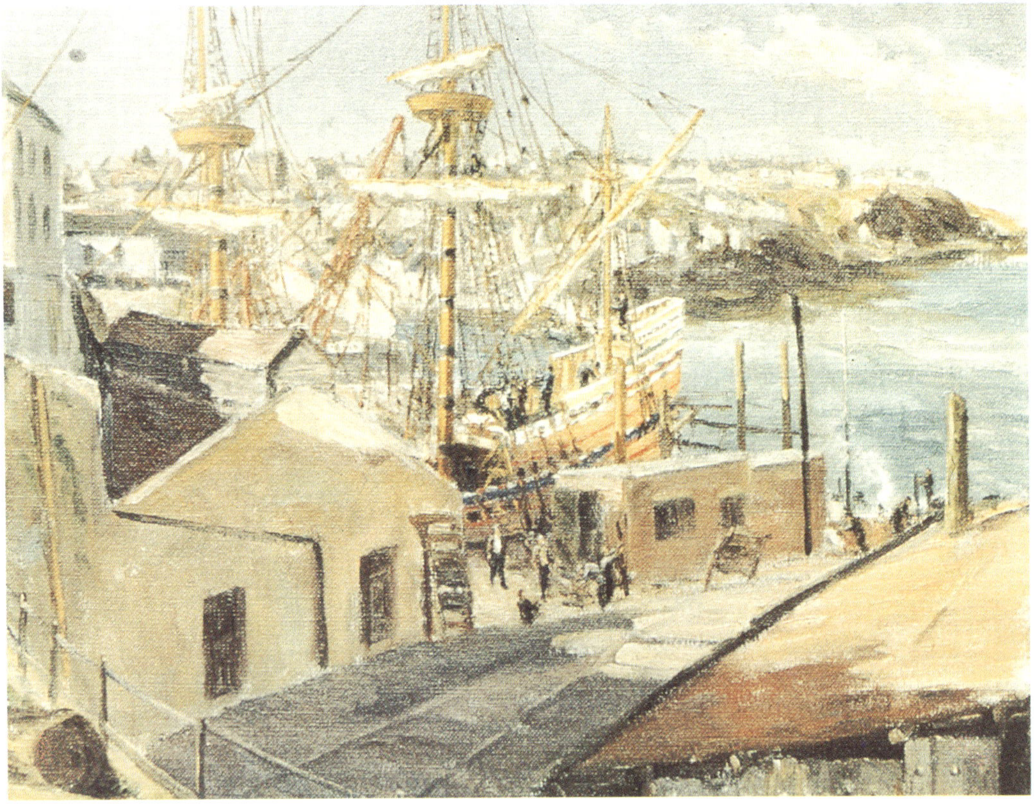

Building of Mayflower II, Brixham Harbour. Plate 14.

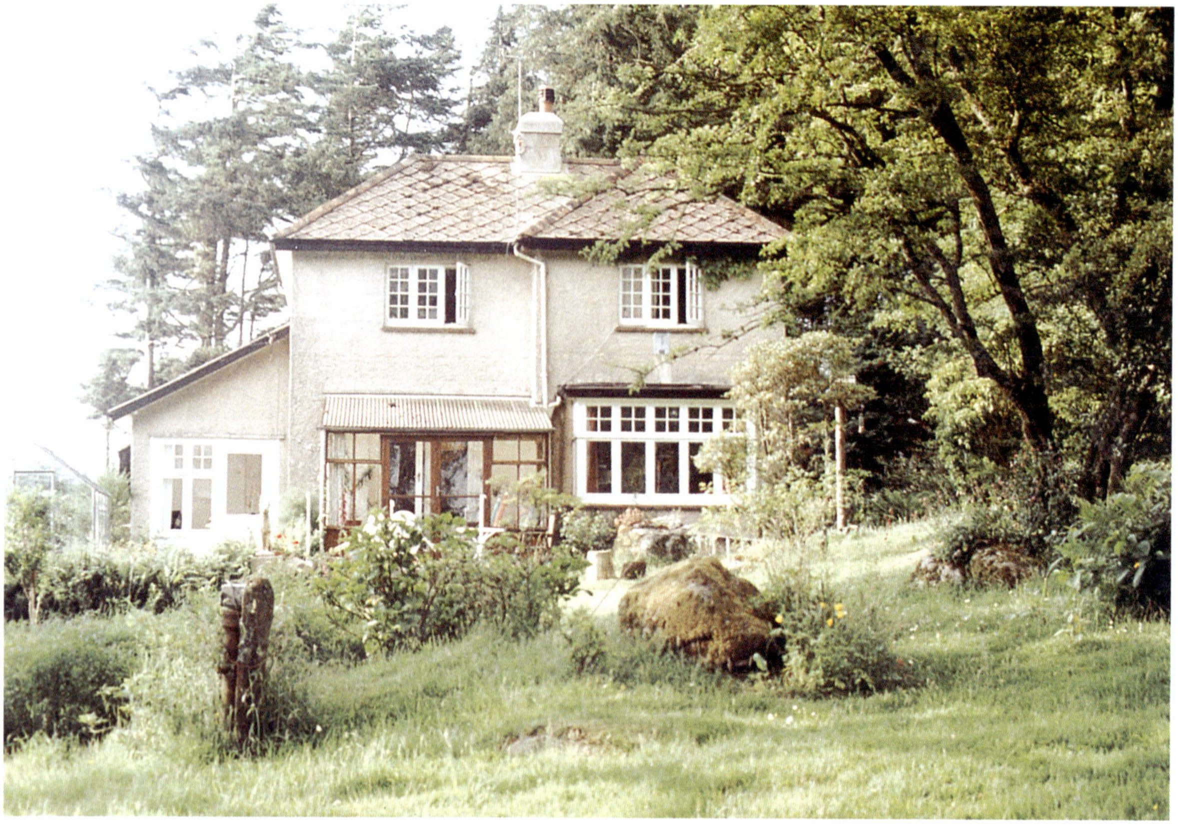

Torcroft, Widecombe-in-the-Moor. Plate 15.

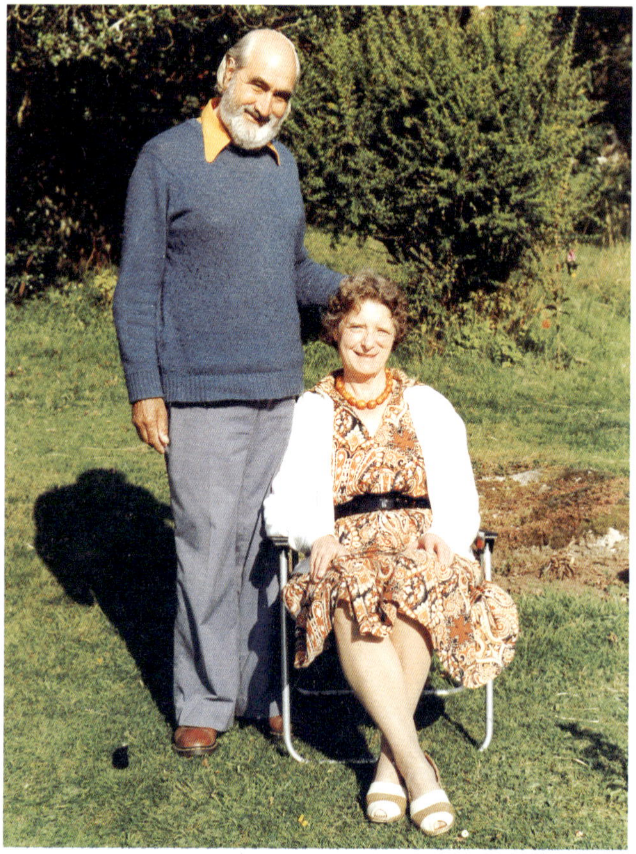

Kit and Ernest at Torcroft, Widecombe. Plate 16.

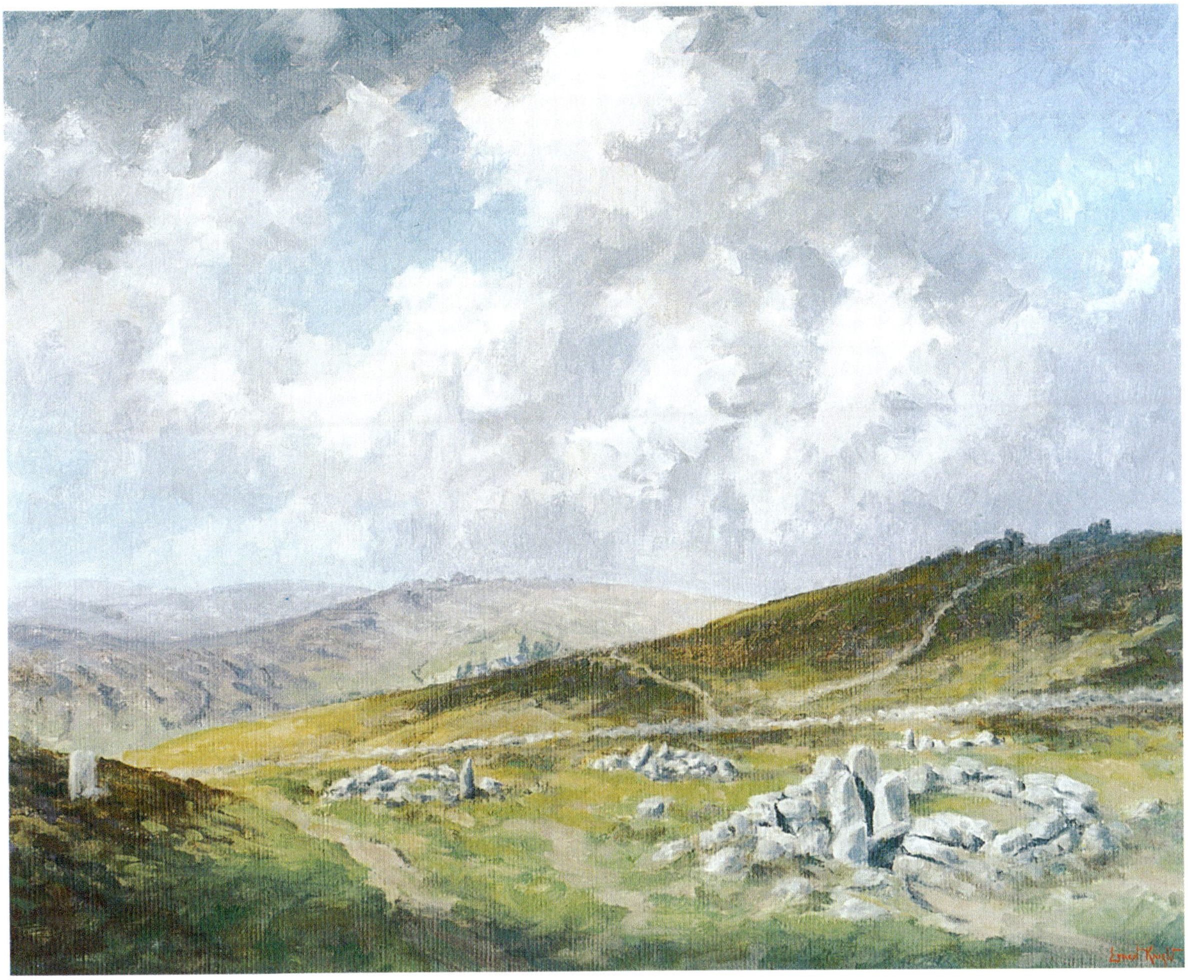

Grimpound, Dartmoor. Oil on Canvas. 76 cm x 61 cm. Plate 17.

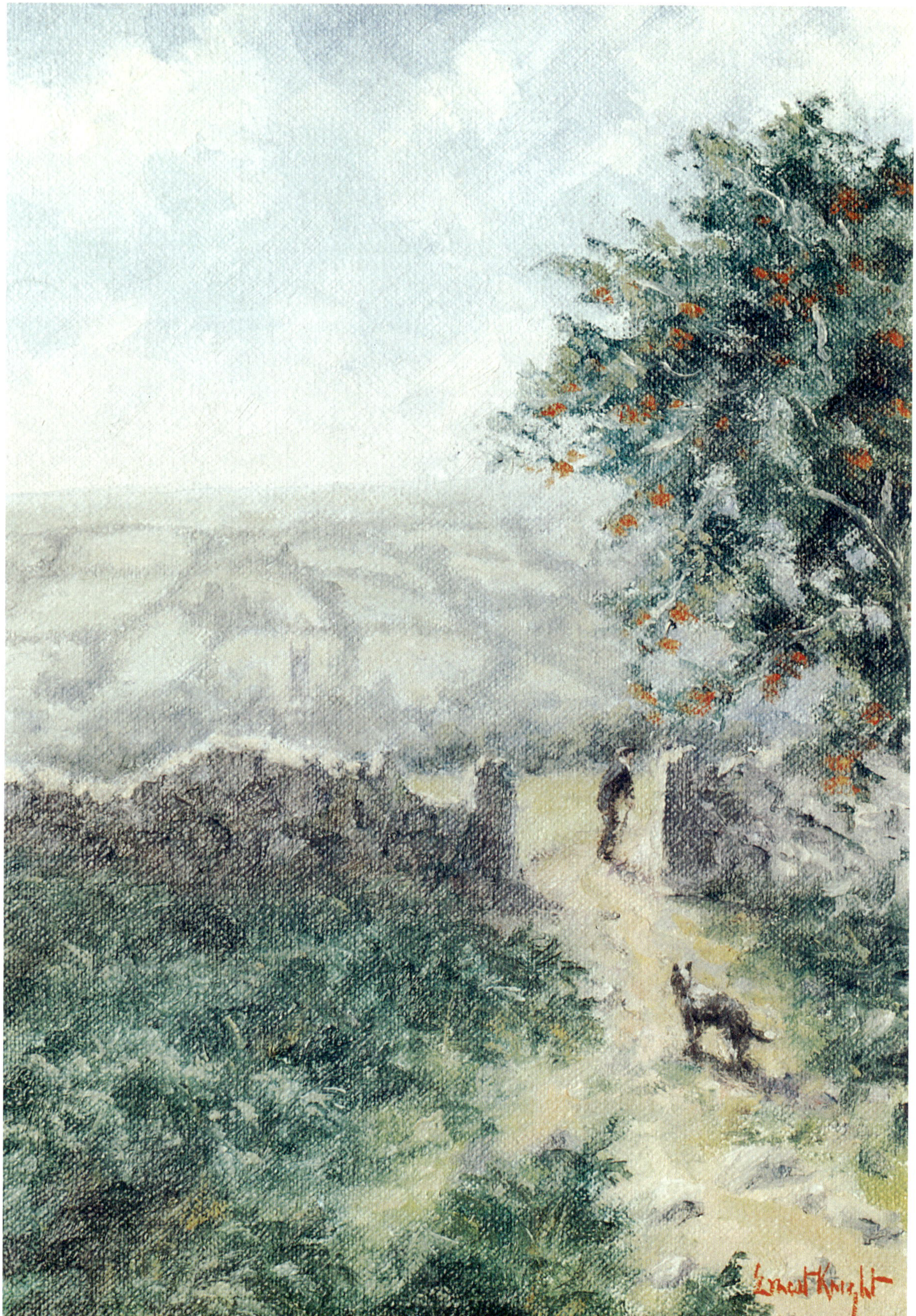

Gate onto the Moor from Torcroft. Oil on Canvas. 24cm x 34.5 cm. Plate 18.

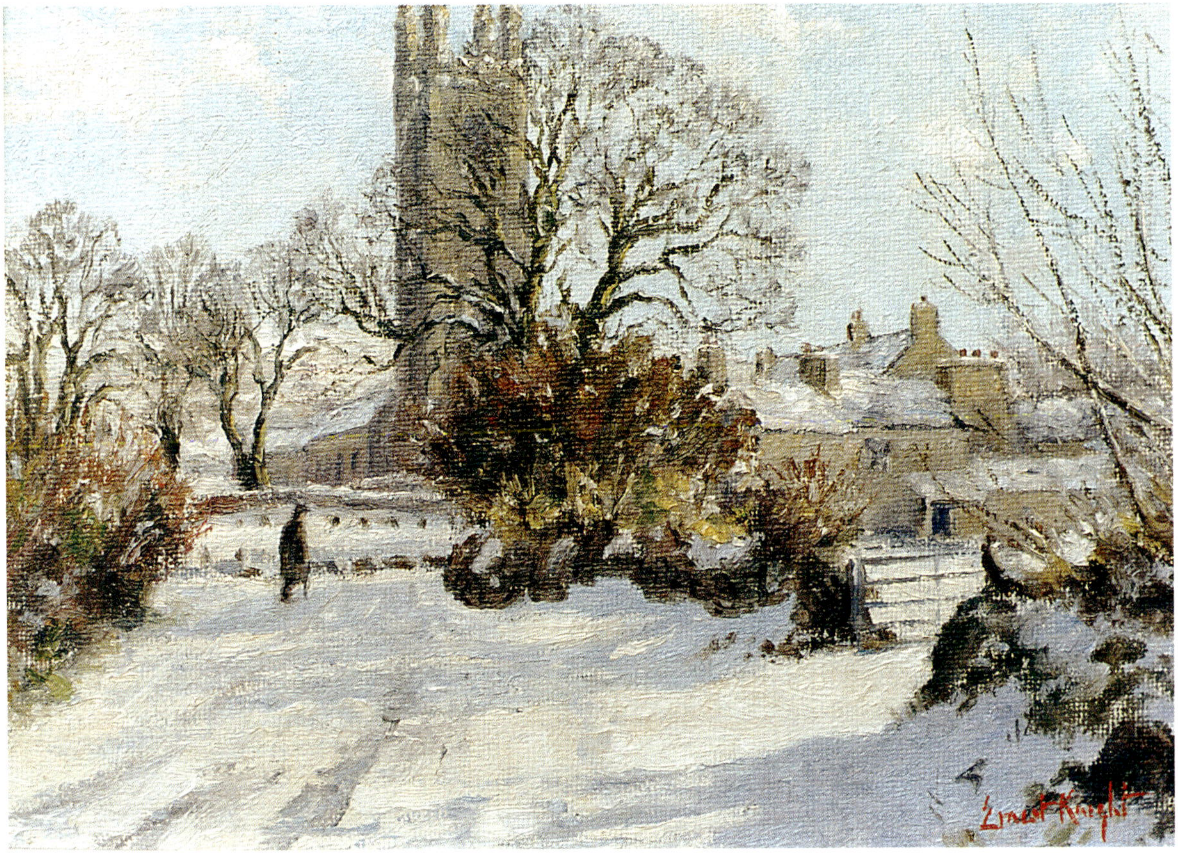

Widecombe-in-the-Moor Winter 1979. Oil on Canvas. 41 cm x 31 cm. Plate 19.

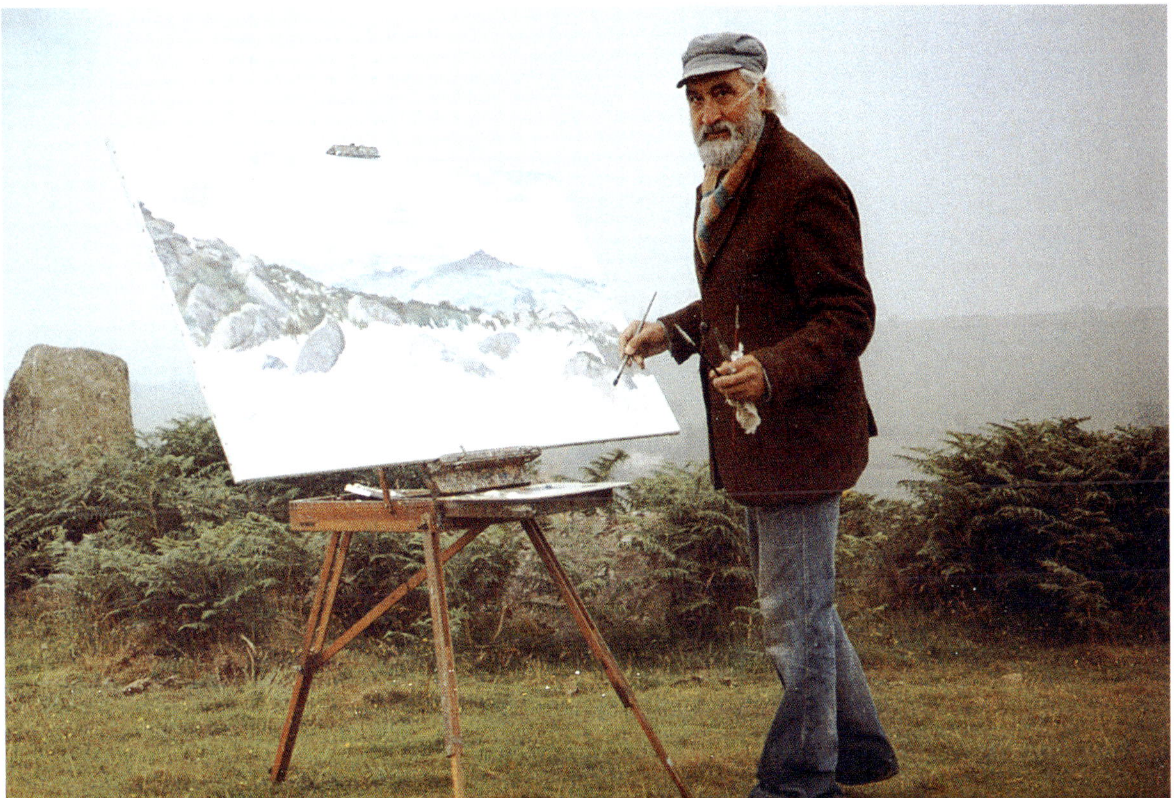

Ernest Painting on Dartmoor. Oil on Canvas. Plate 20.

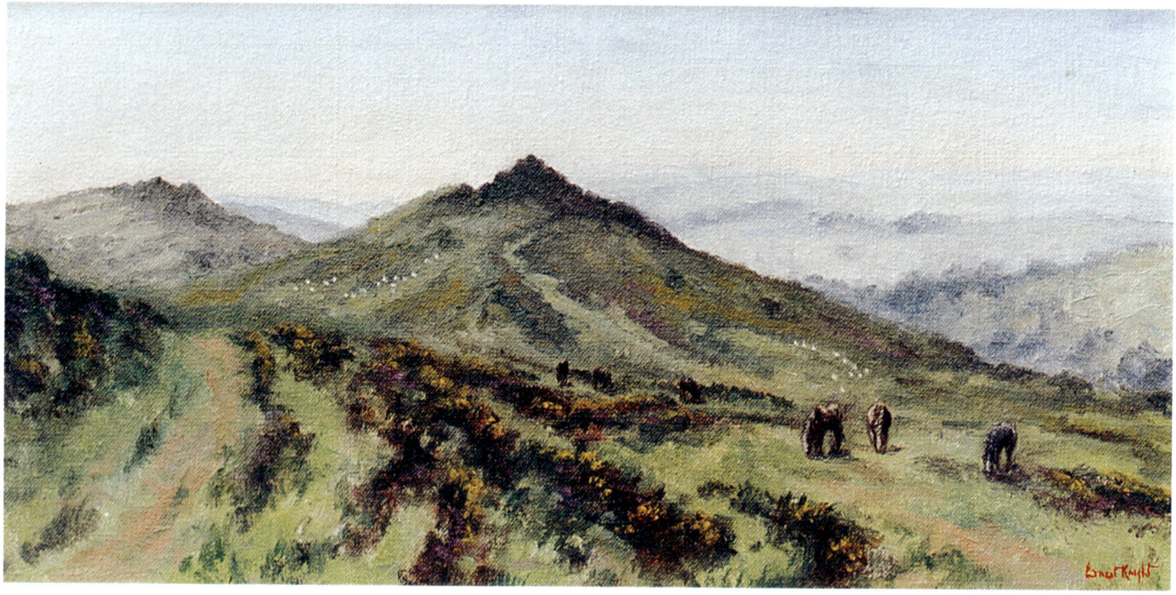

Sharp Tor, Dartmoor. Oil on Canvas. 61 cm x 30.5 cm. Plate 21.

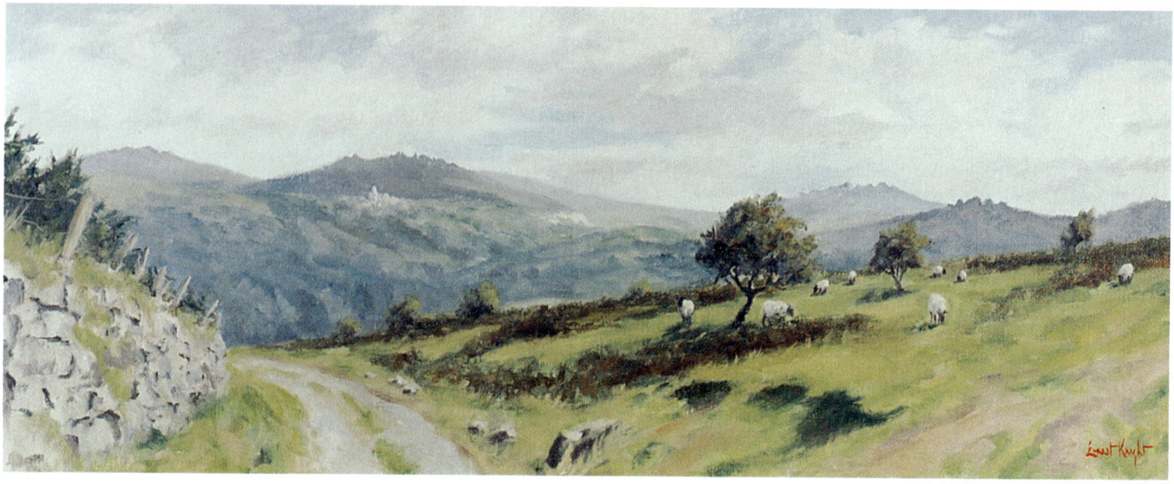

Combestone Tor, Dartmoor. Oil on Canvas. 75.5 cm x 30 cm. Plate 22.

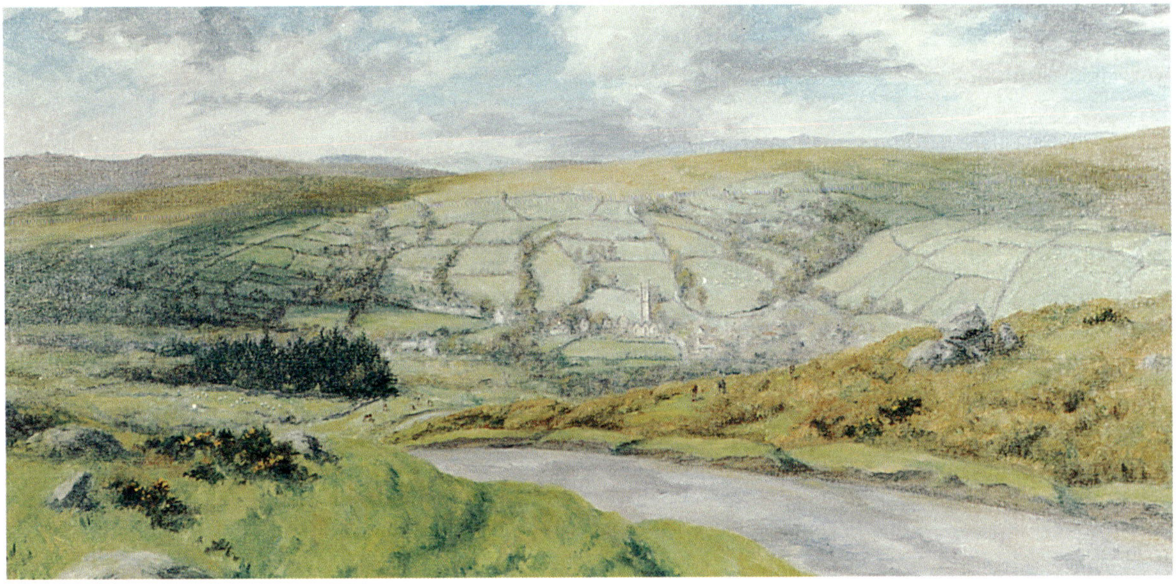

Road to Widecombe, Dartmoor. Oil on Canvas. 112cm x 60 cm. Plate 23.
Donated by Kit Knight to the Parish Church, Widecombe.

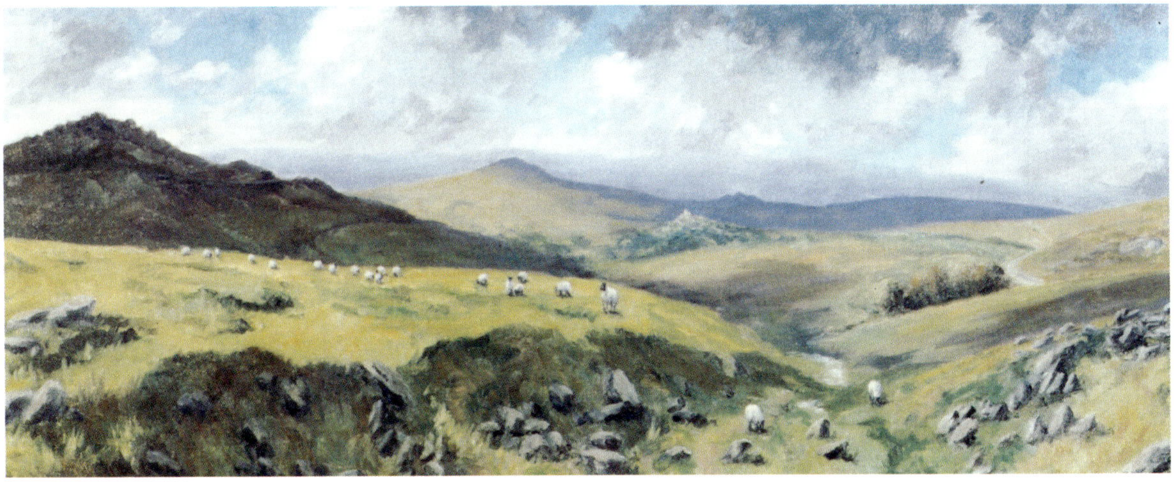

Kings's Tor, Vixen Tor, Pew Tor, Central Dartmoor. Oil on Canvas. 156cm x 41 cm. Plate 24.
Donated by Kit Knight to the Dartmoor National Park Authority, Princetown, Dartmoor.

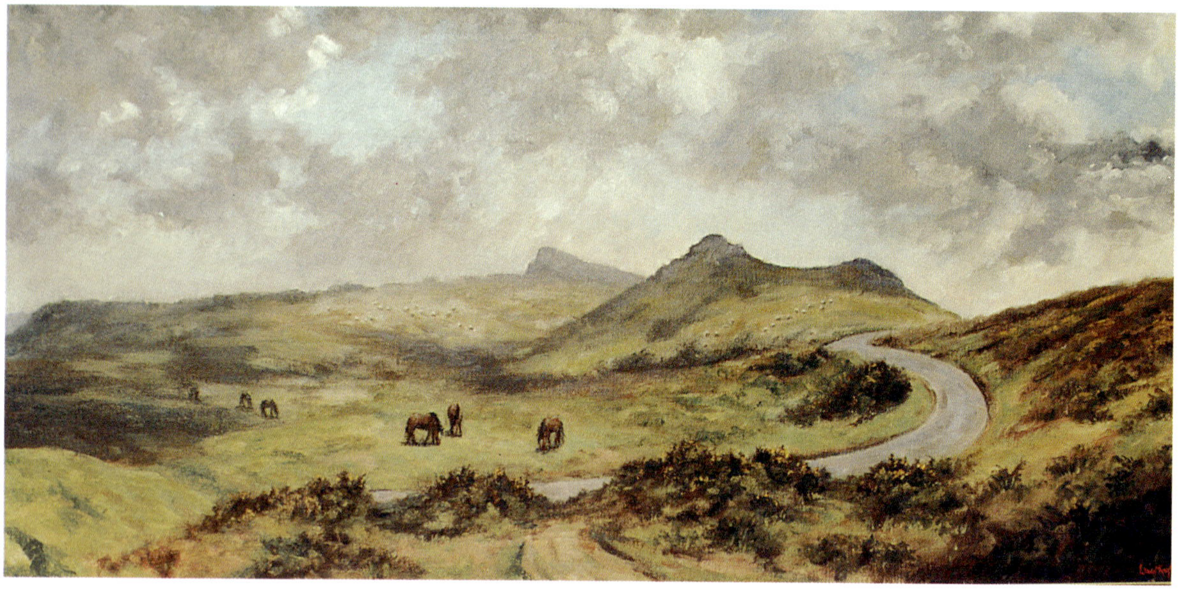

Rippon Tor, Dartmoor. Oil on Canvas. 122 cm x 62 cm. Plate 25.

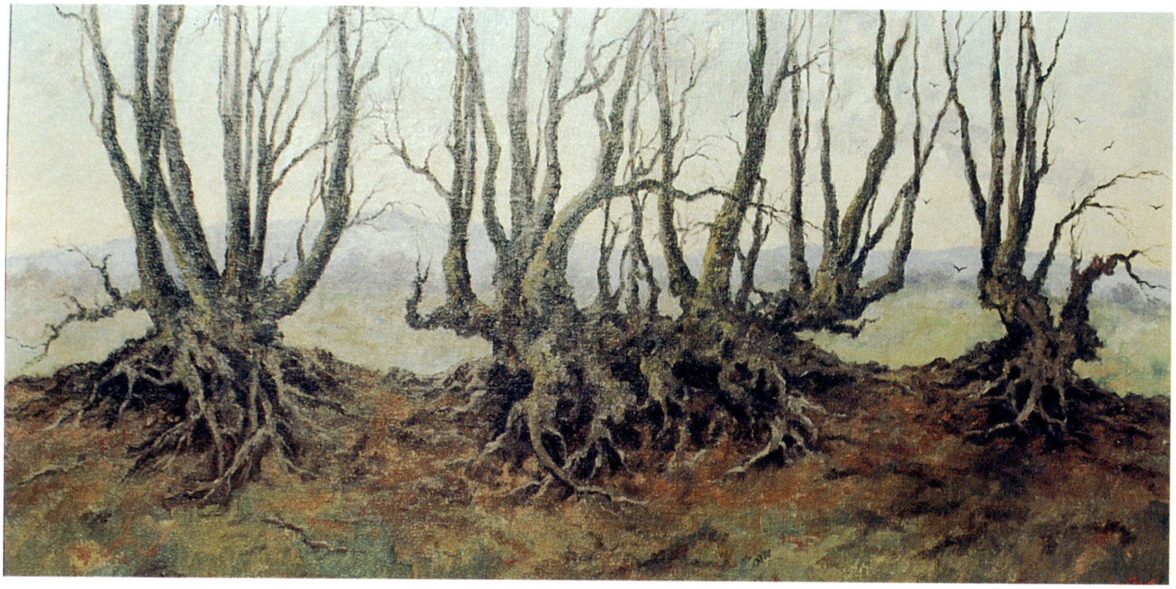

Beech Roots, Dartmoor. Oil on Canvas. 119.5 cm x 58.5 cm. Plate 26.

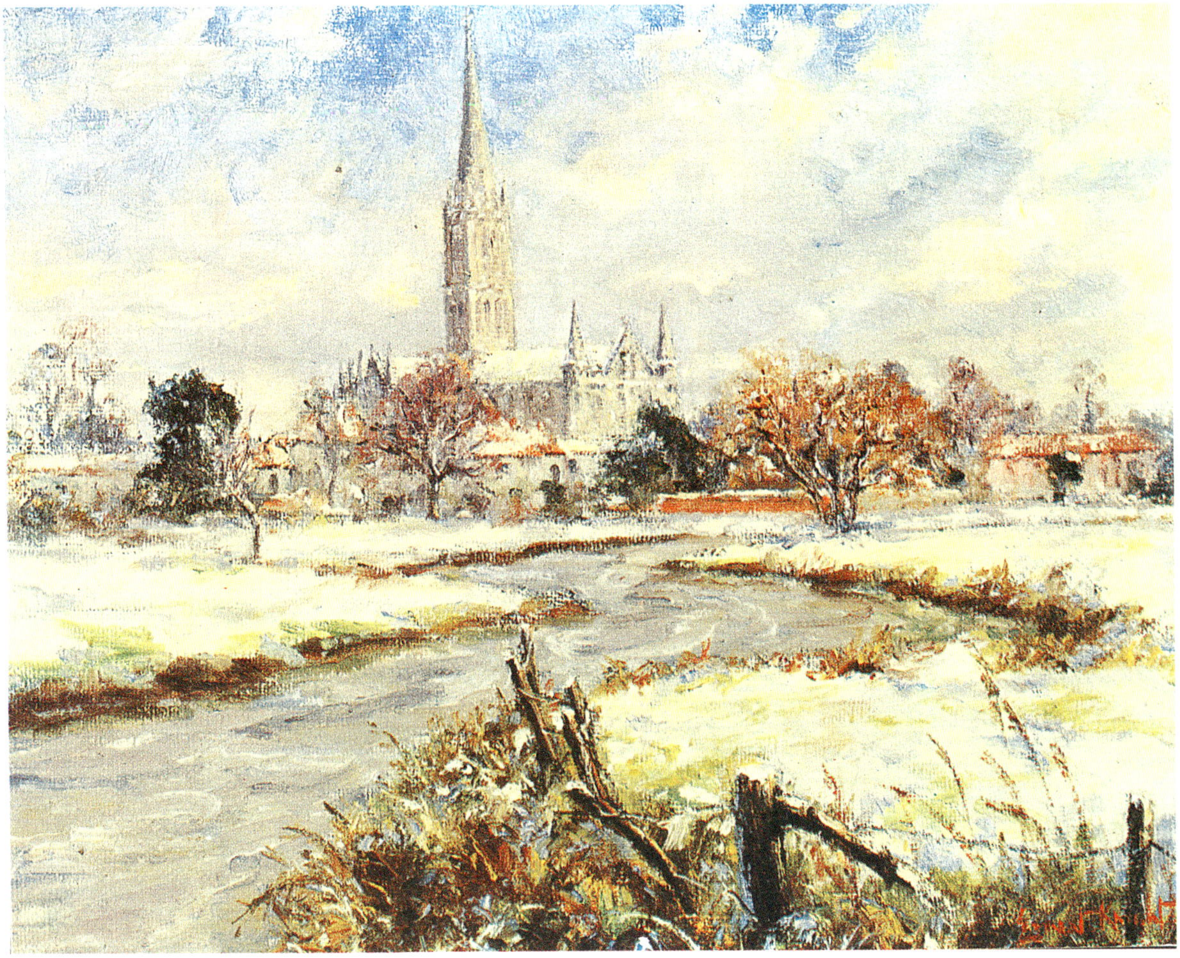

Salisbury Cathedral. Oil on Canvas. Plate 27.

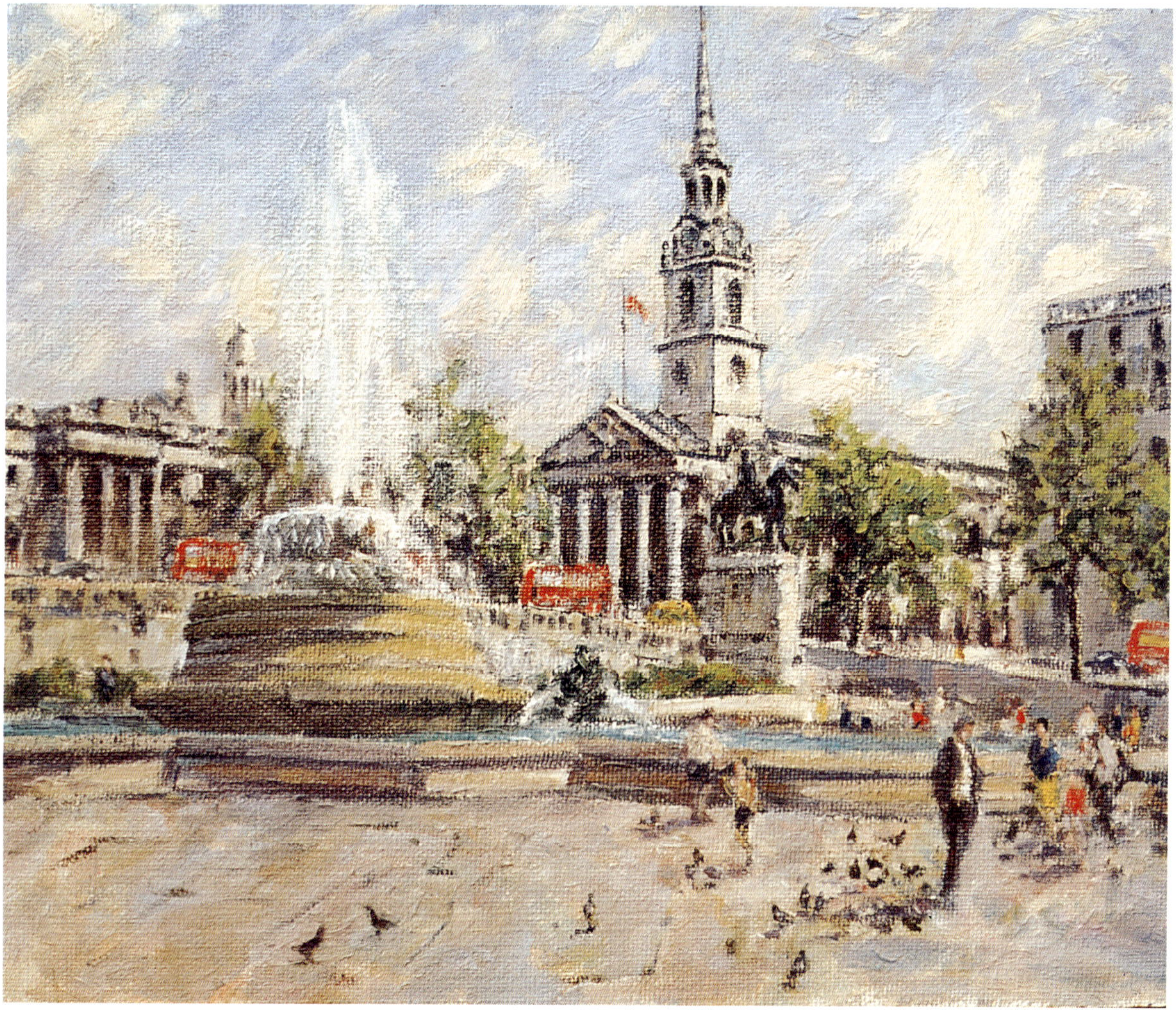

Trafalgar Square, London. Oil on Board. 51 cm x 41 cm. Plate 28.

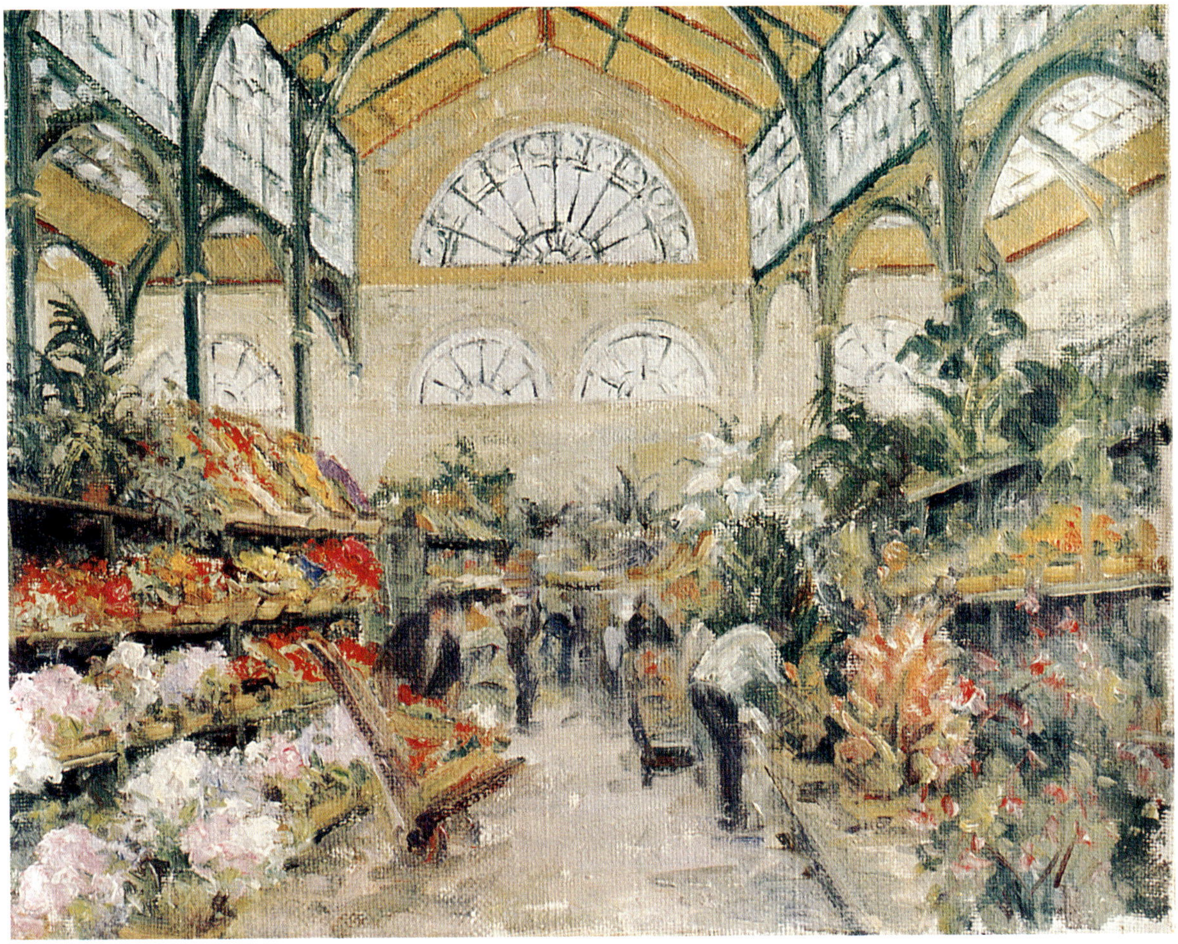

Covent Garden Market, London. Oil on Canvas. 51 cm x 40 cm. Plate 29.

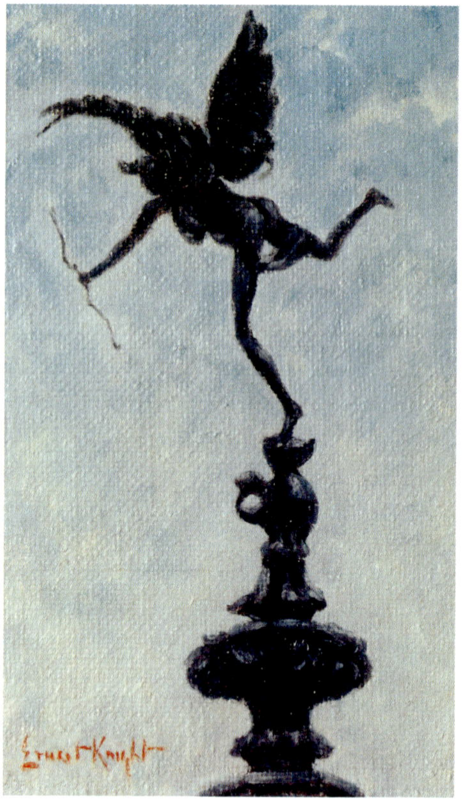

Eros, London. Oil on Board. 18 cm x 30.5 cm. Plate 30.

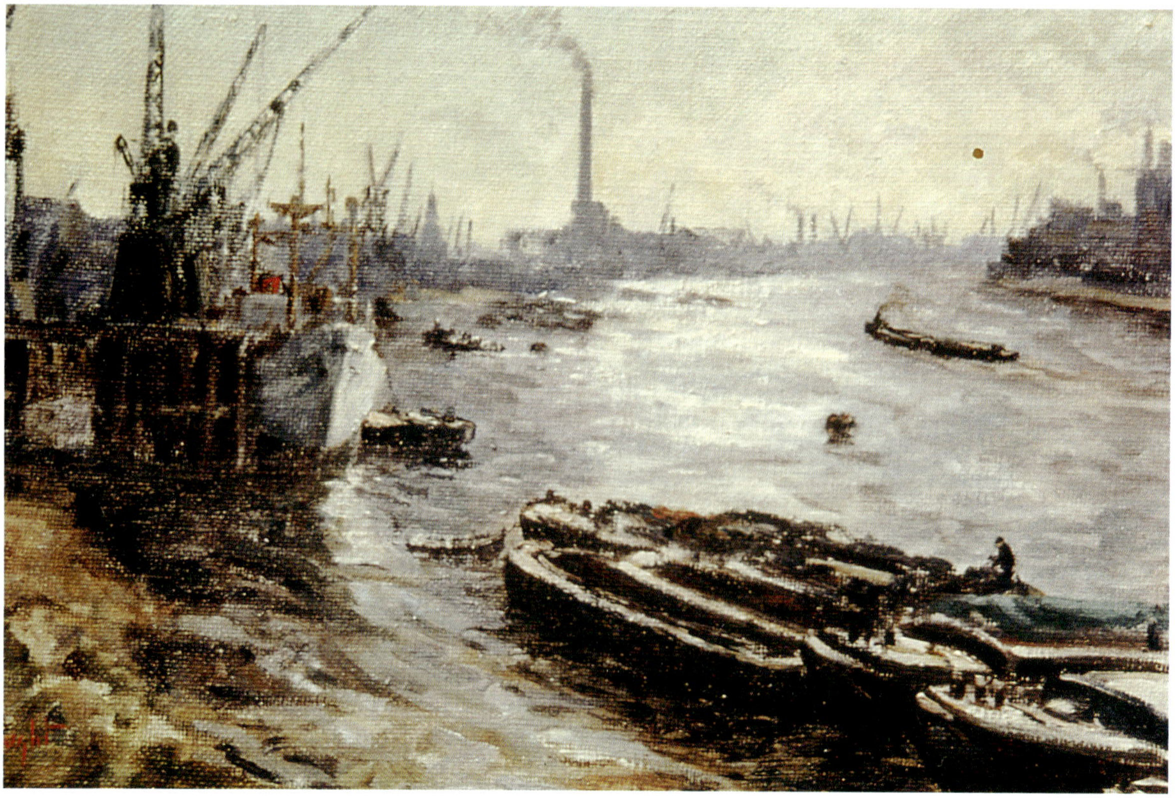

Wapping, London. Oil on Canvas. Plate 31.

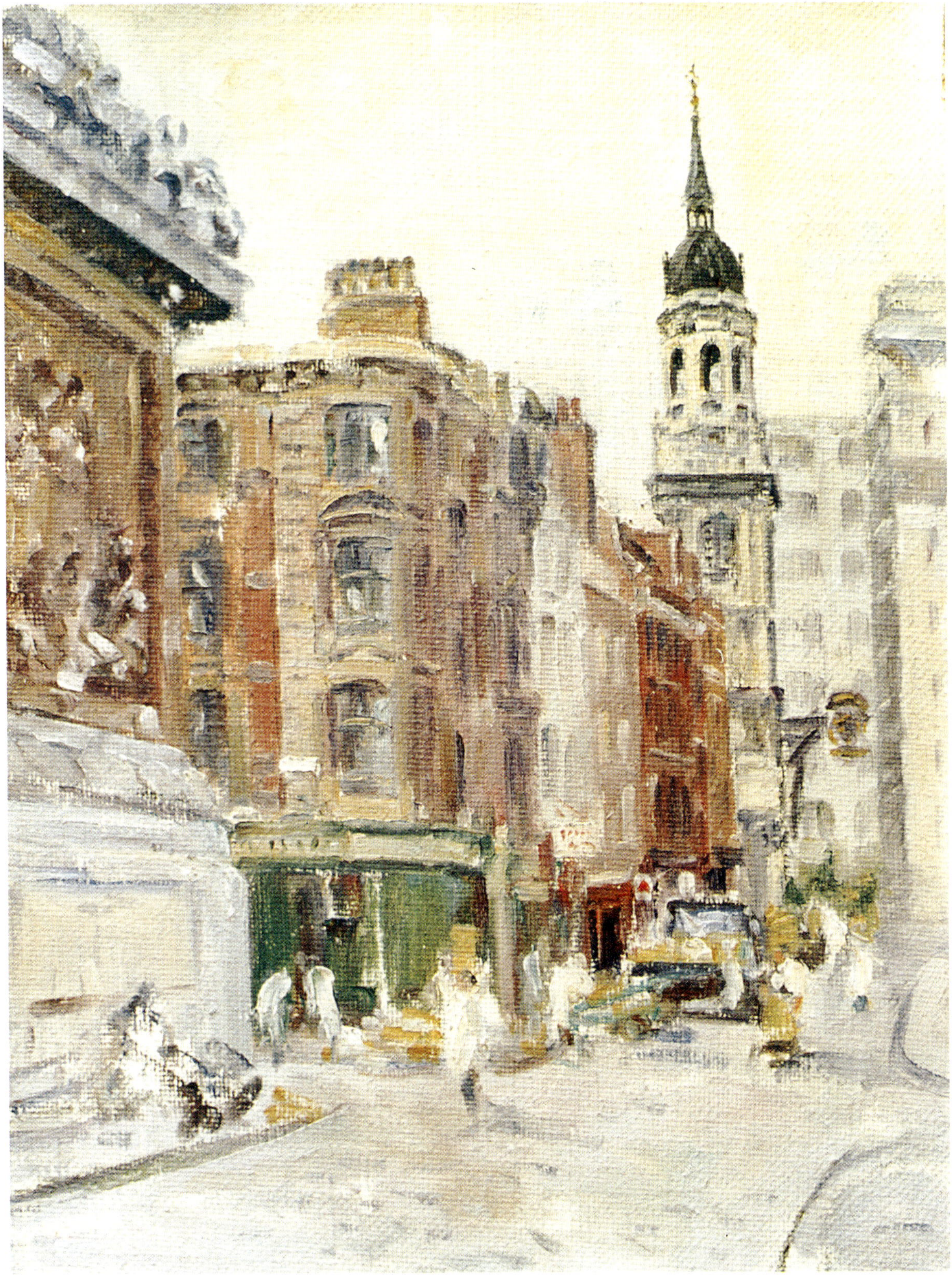

City, London. Oil on Canvas (unfinished). 14 cm x 18 cm. Plate 32.

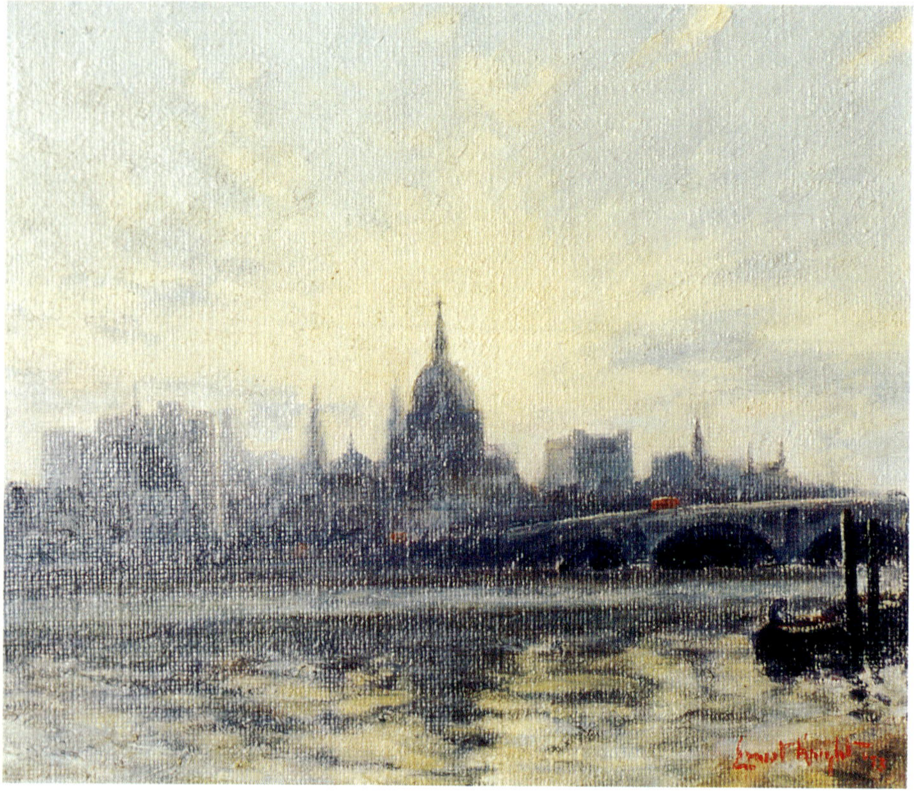

St. Paul's Cathedral, London, Sunrise. Oil on Canvas. 29 cm x 27 cm. Plate 33.

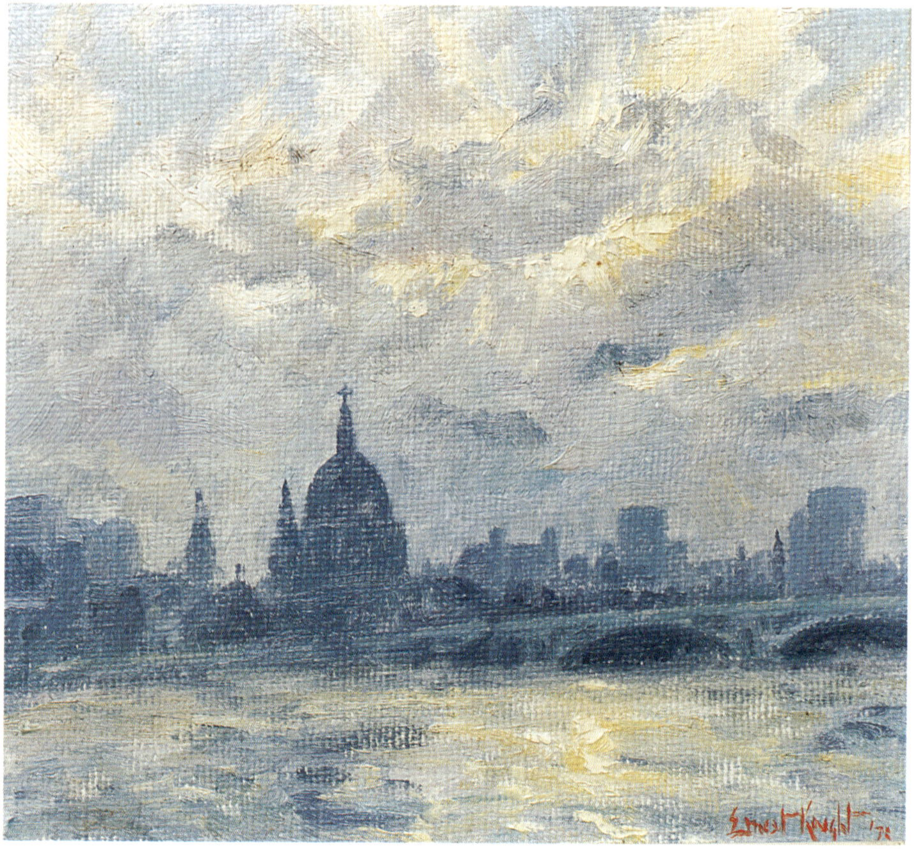

St. Paul's Cathedral, London, Evening. Oil on Canvas. 29 cm x 27 cm. Plate 34.

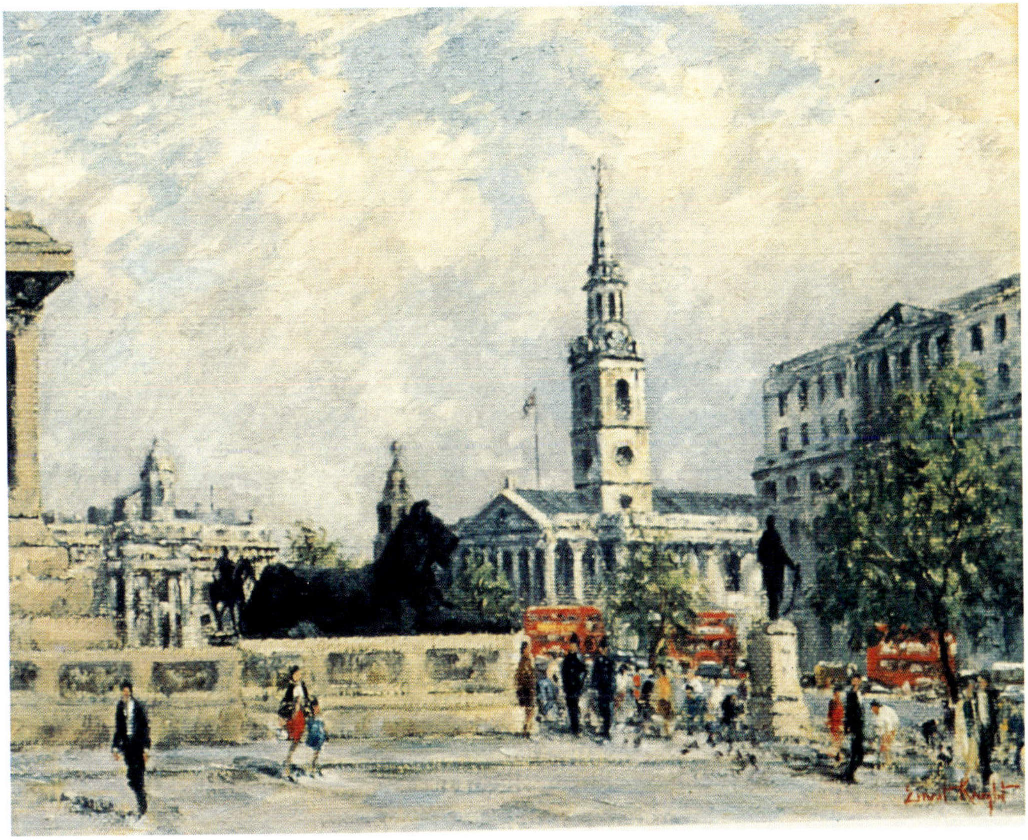

Trafalgar Square, London. Oil on Canvas. 51 cm x 41 cm. Plate 35.

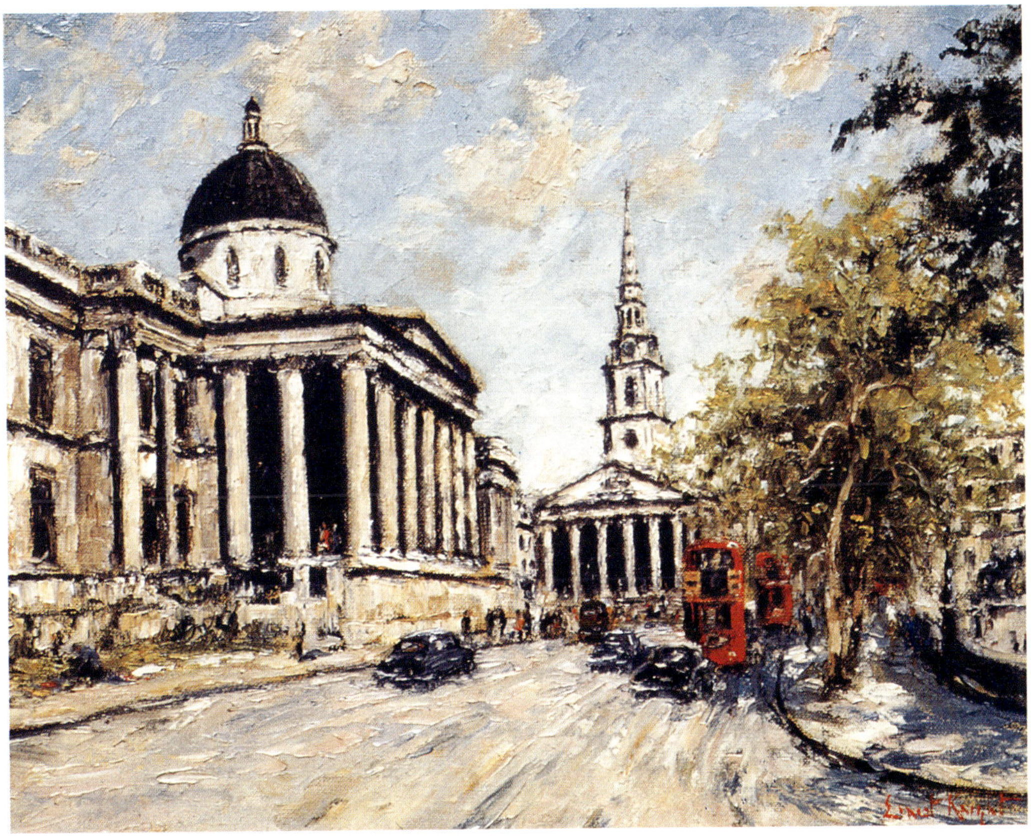

The National Gallery and St. Martin-in-the-Fields, London. Oil on Canvas. 51 cm x 41 cm. Plate 36.

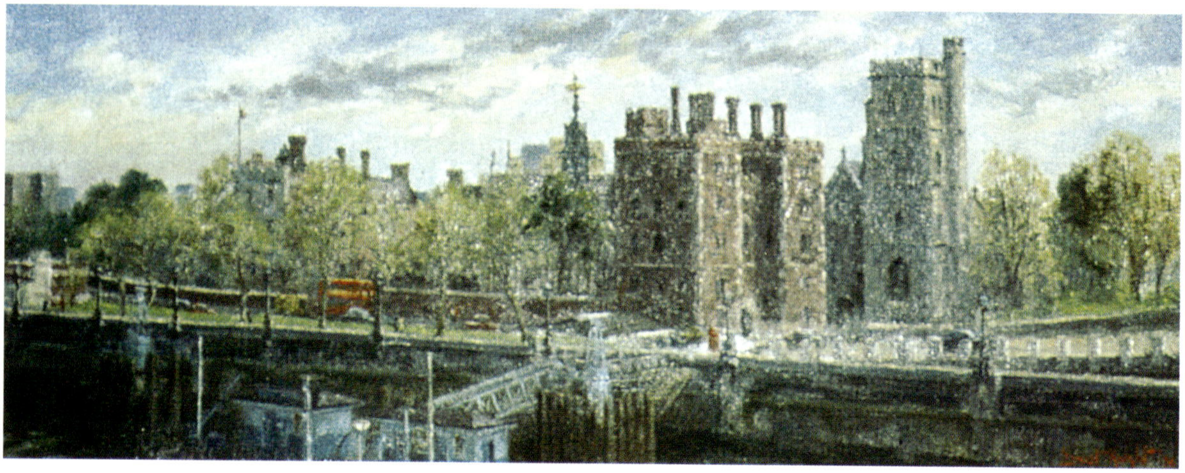

Lambeth Palace, London. Oil on Canvas. 77 cm x 31 cm. Plate 37.

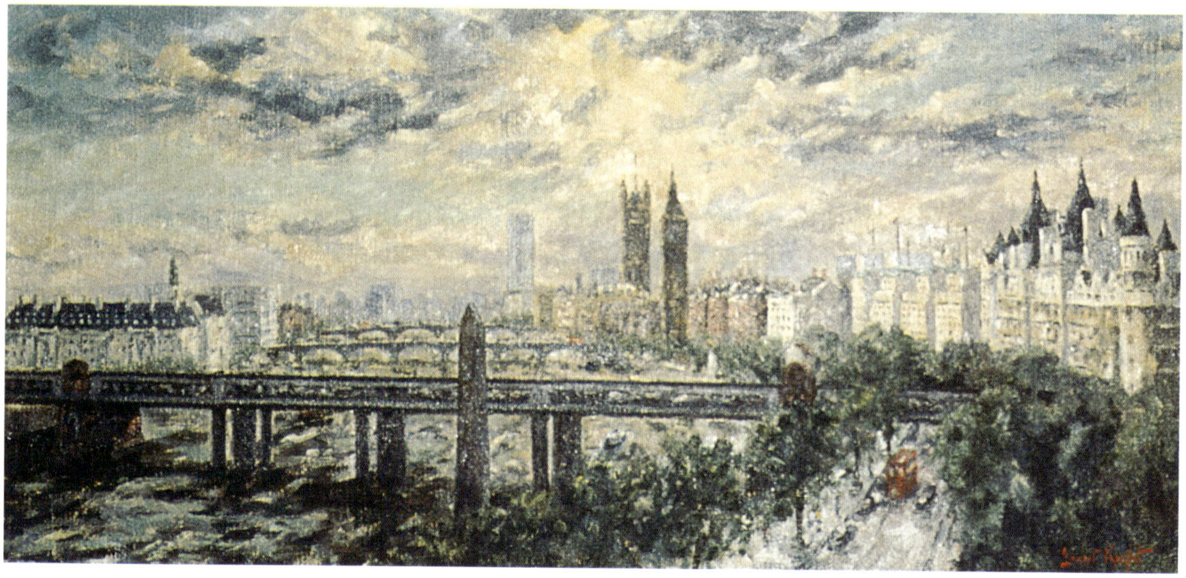

Thames View from the Savoy Hotel, London. Oil on Canvas. 85 cm x 41 cm. Plate 38.

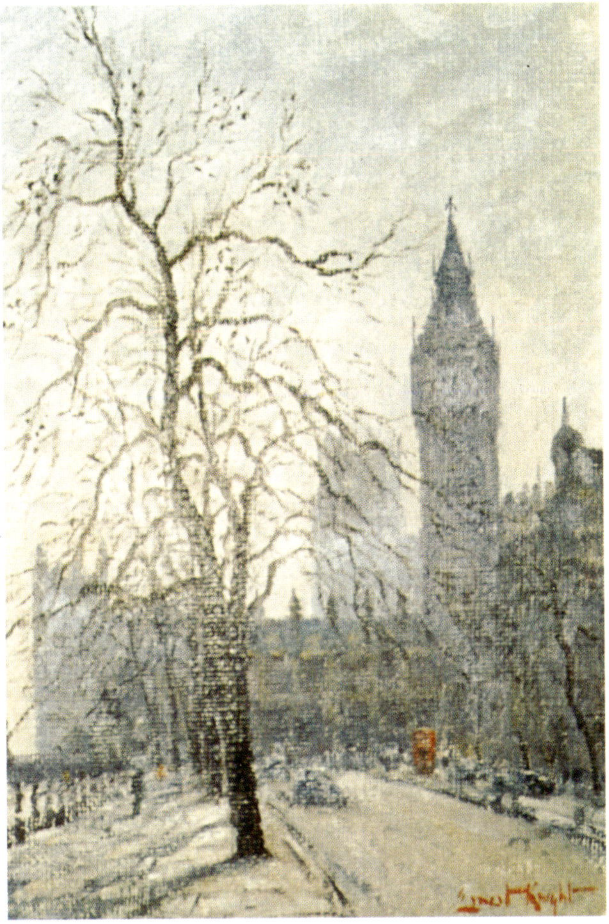

Houses of Parliament and Embankment, London. Oil on Canvas. Plate 39.

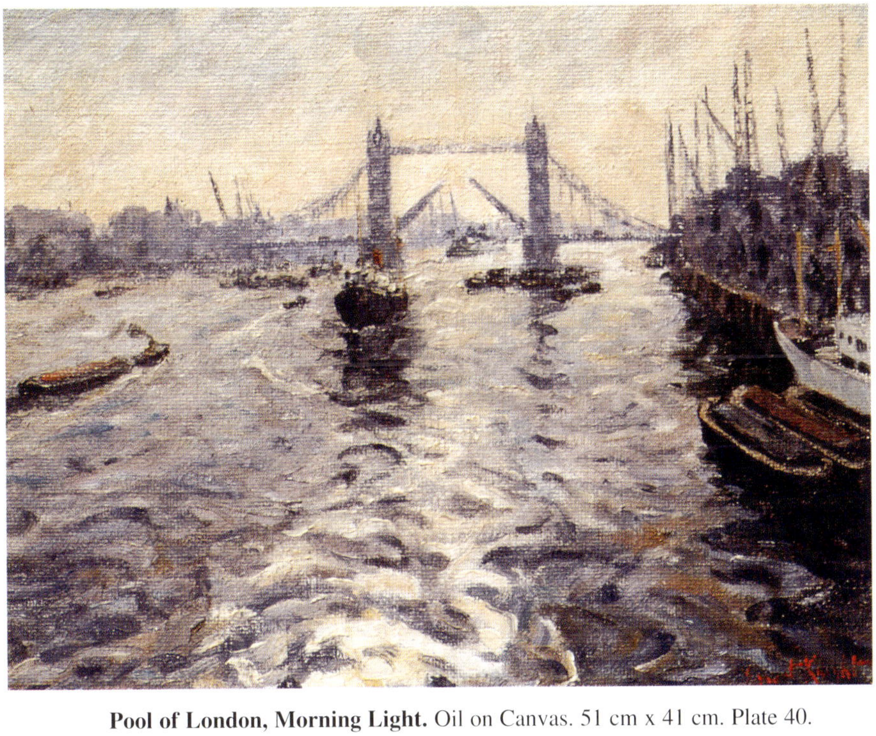

Pool of London, Morning Light. Oil on Canvas. 51 cm x 41 cm. Plate 40.

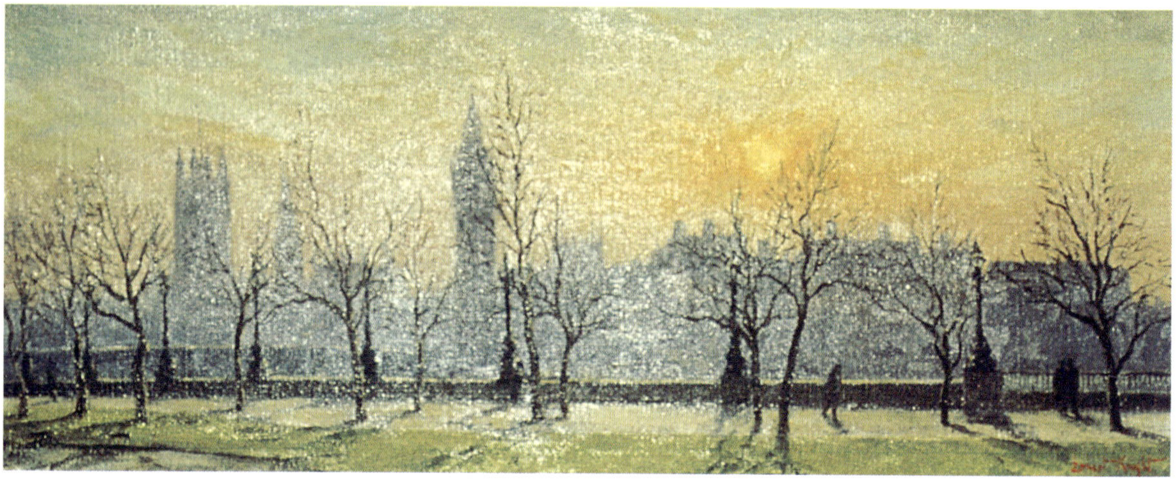

Houses of Parliament from the South Bank, London. Oil on Canvas. Plate 41.

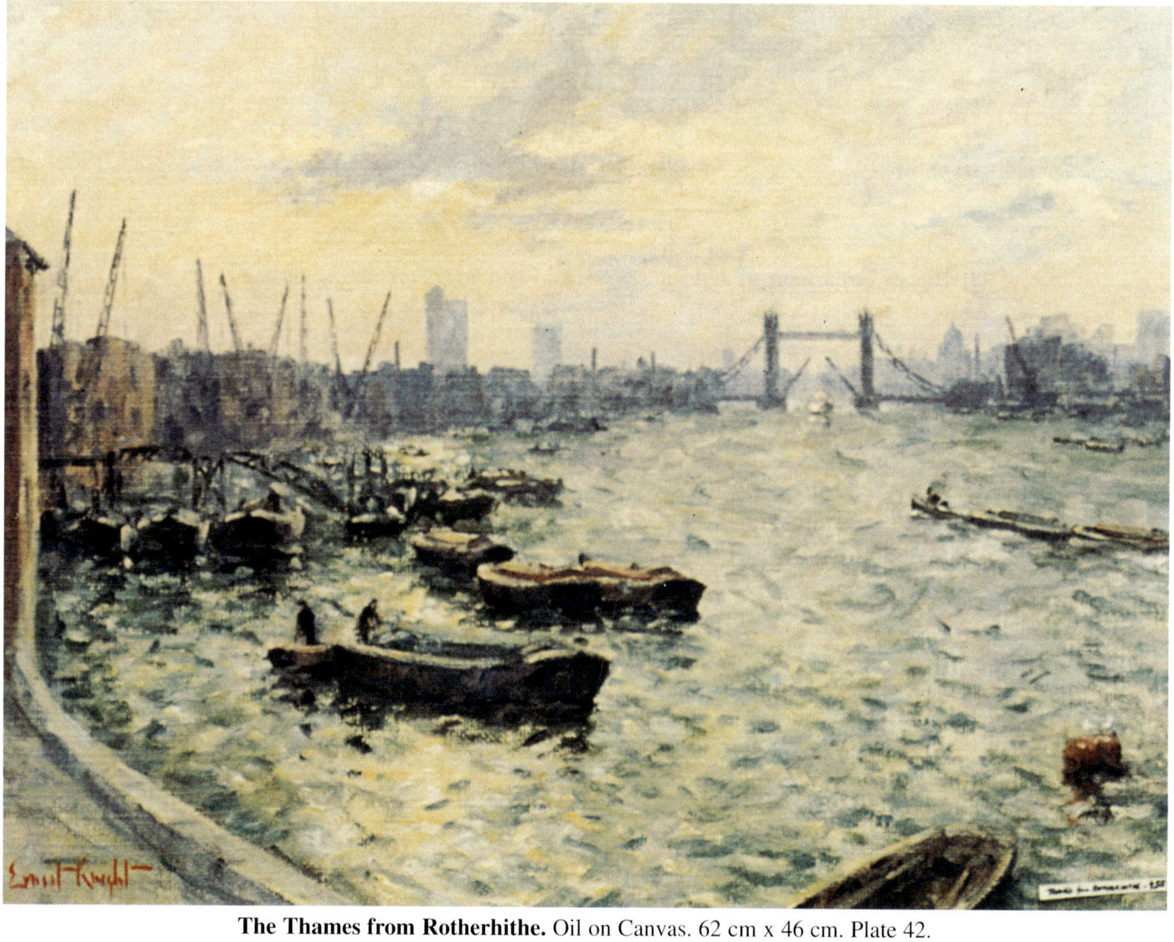

The Thames from Rotherhithe. Oil on Canvas. 62 cm x 46 cm. Plate 42.

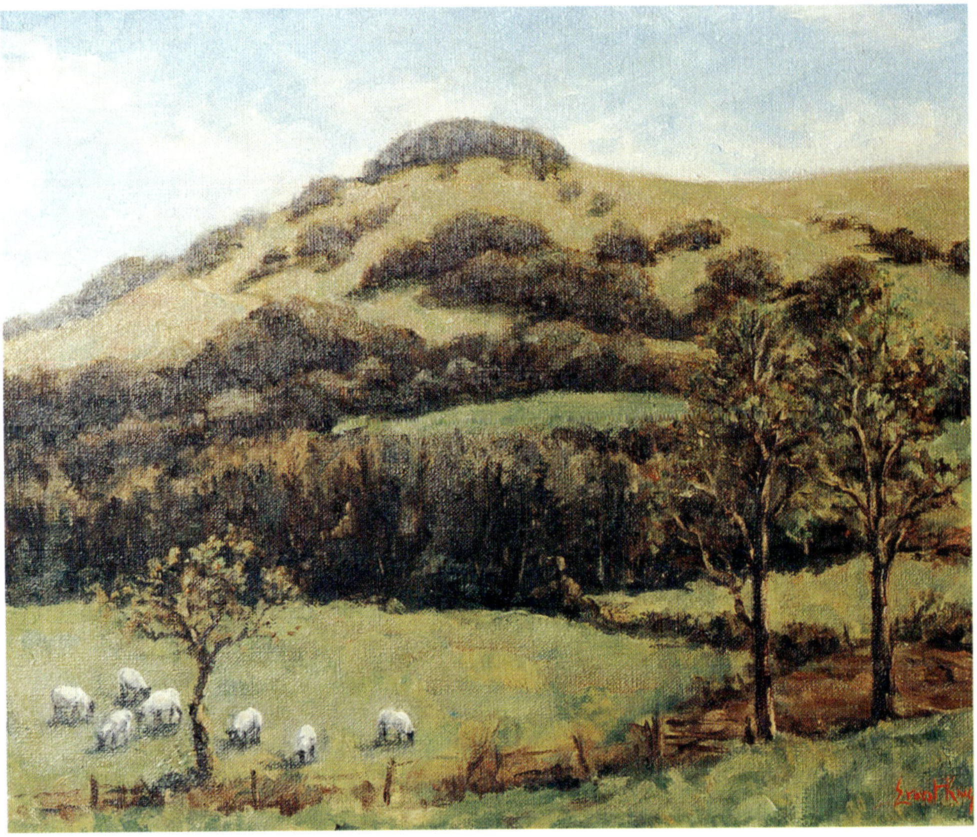

Chanctonbury Ring, Sussex. Oil on Canvas. 49.5 cm x 39.5 cm. Plate 43.

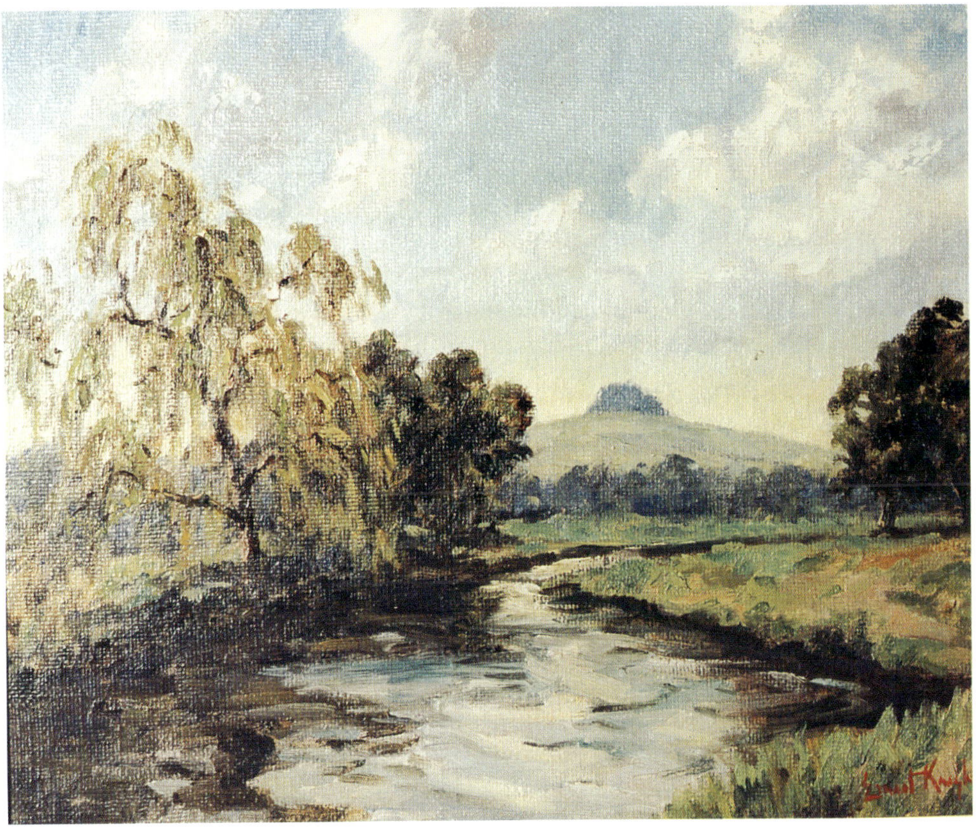

River Itchen and St. Catherines Hill, Winchester. Oil on Canvas. 49 cm x 39.5 cm. Plate 44.

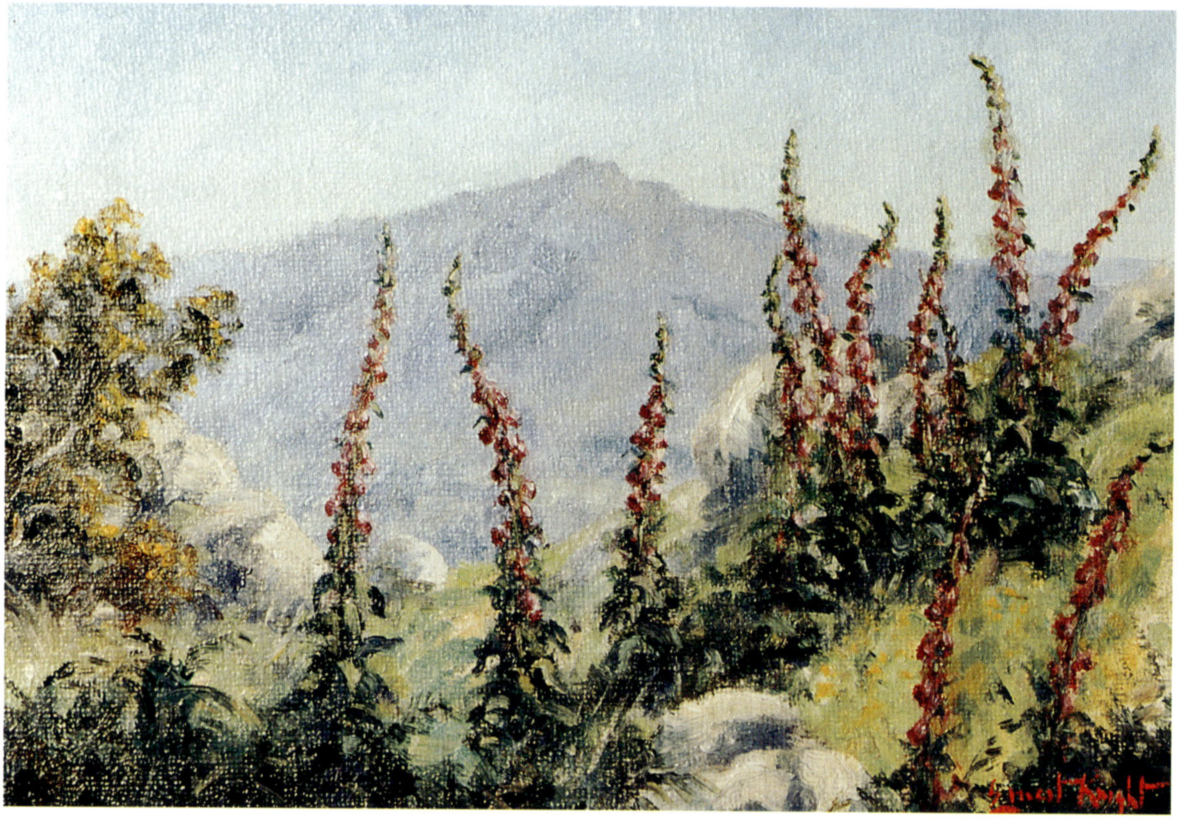

Foxgloves, Dartmoor. Oil on Canvas. 38.5 cm x 29 cm. Plate 45.

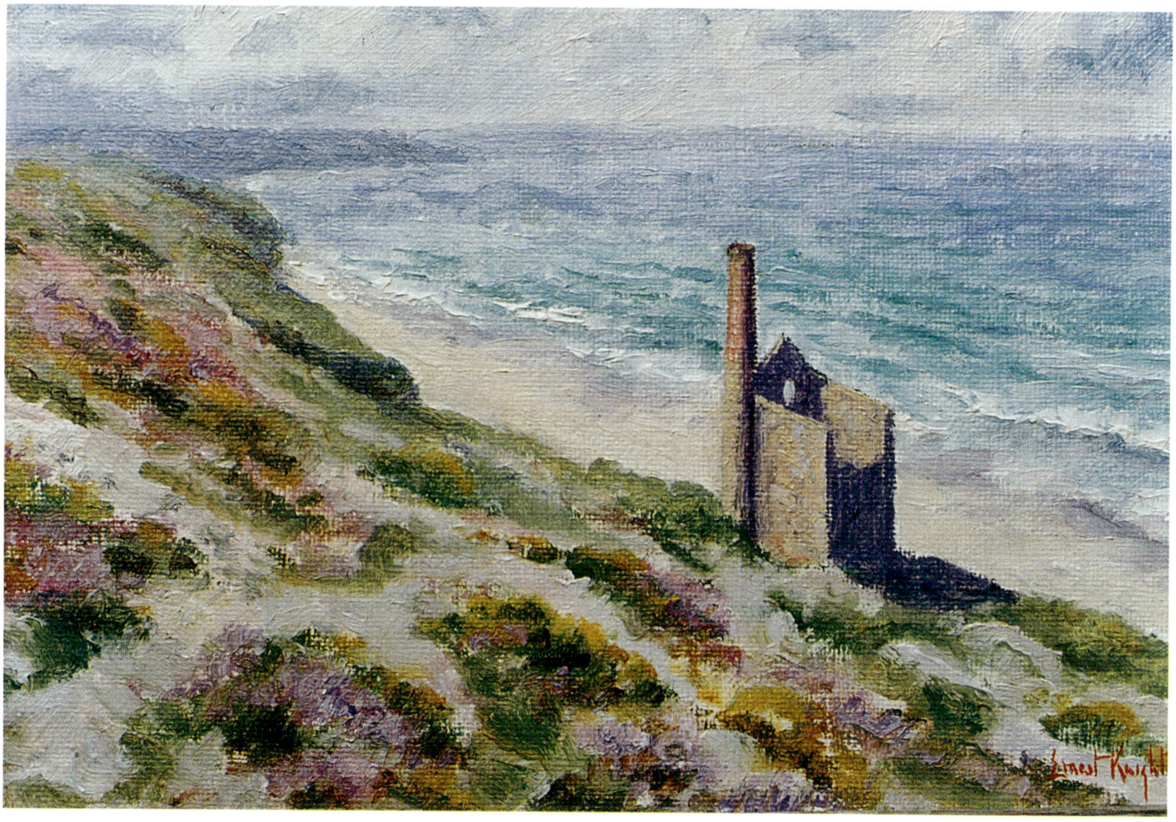

Wheal Coates, St. Agnes, Cornwall. Oil on Canvas. 36 cm x 25 cm. Plate 46.

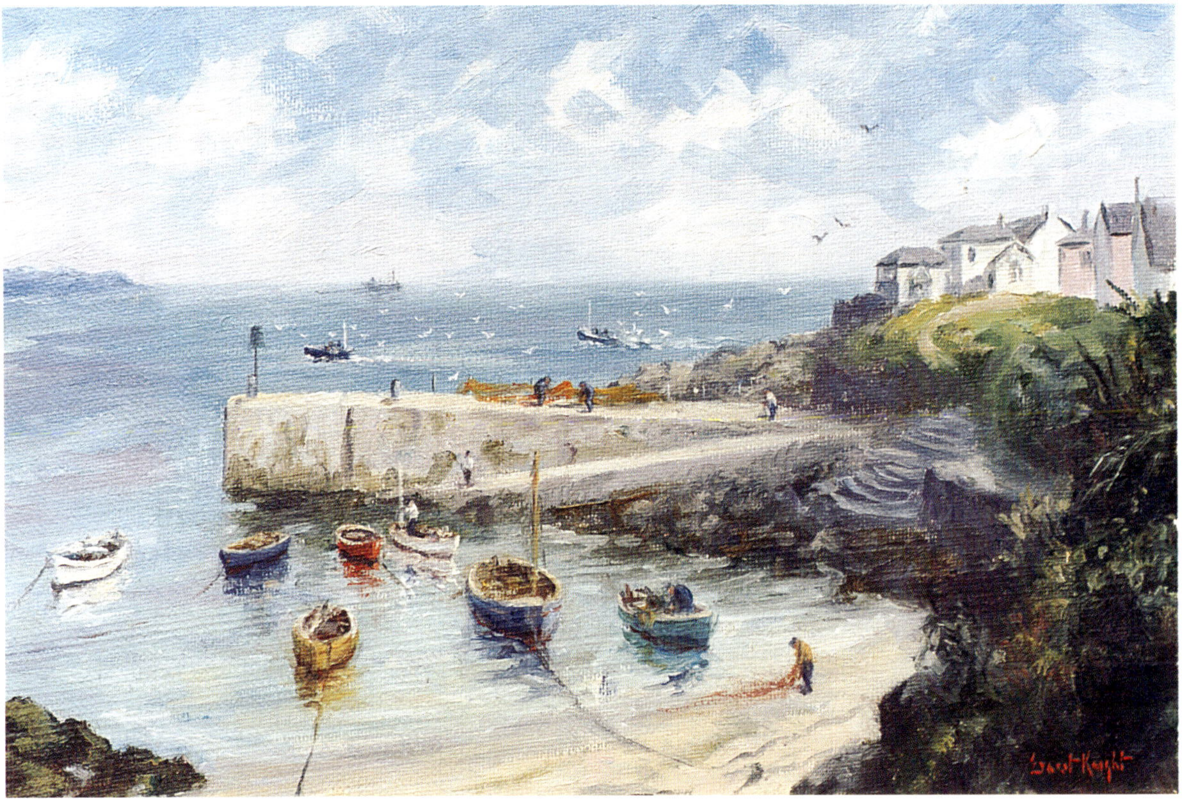

Portscatho, Cornwall. Oil on Canvas. 46 cm x 30.5 cm. Plate 47.

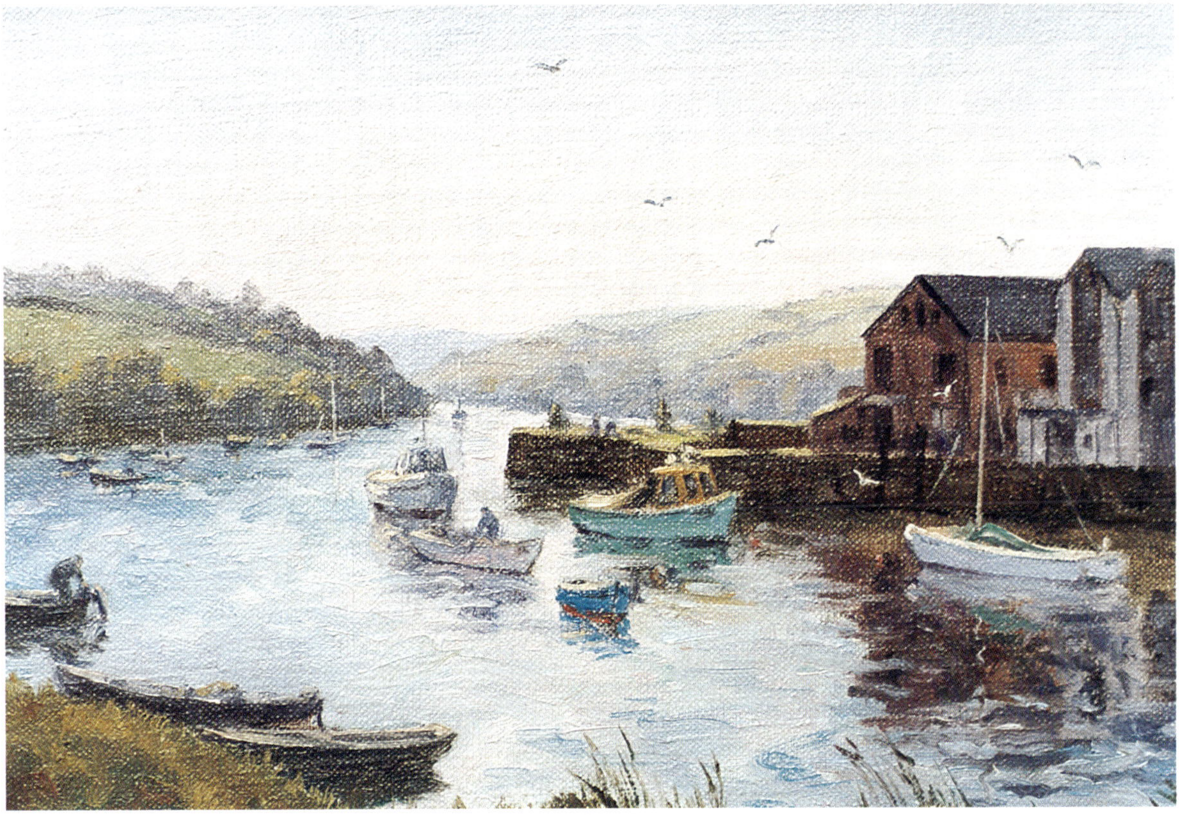

Salcombe Estuary, Devon. Oil on Canvas. 46 cm x 30.5 cm. Plate 48.

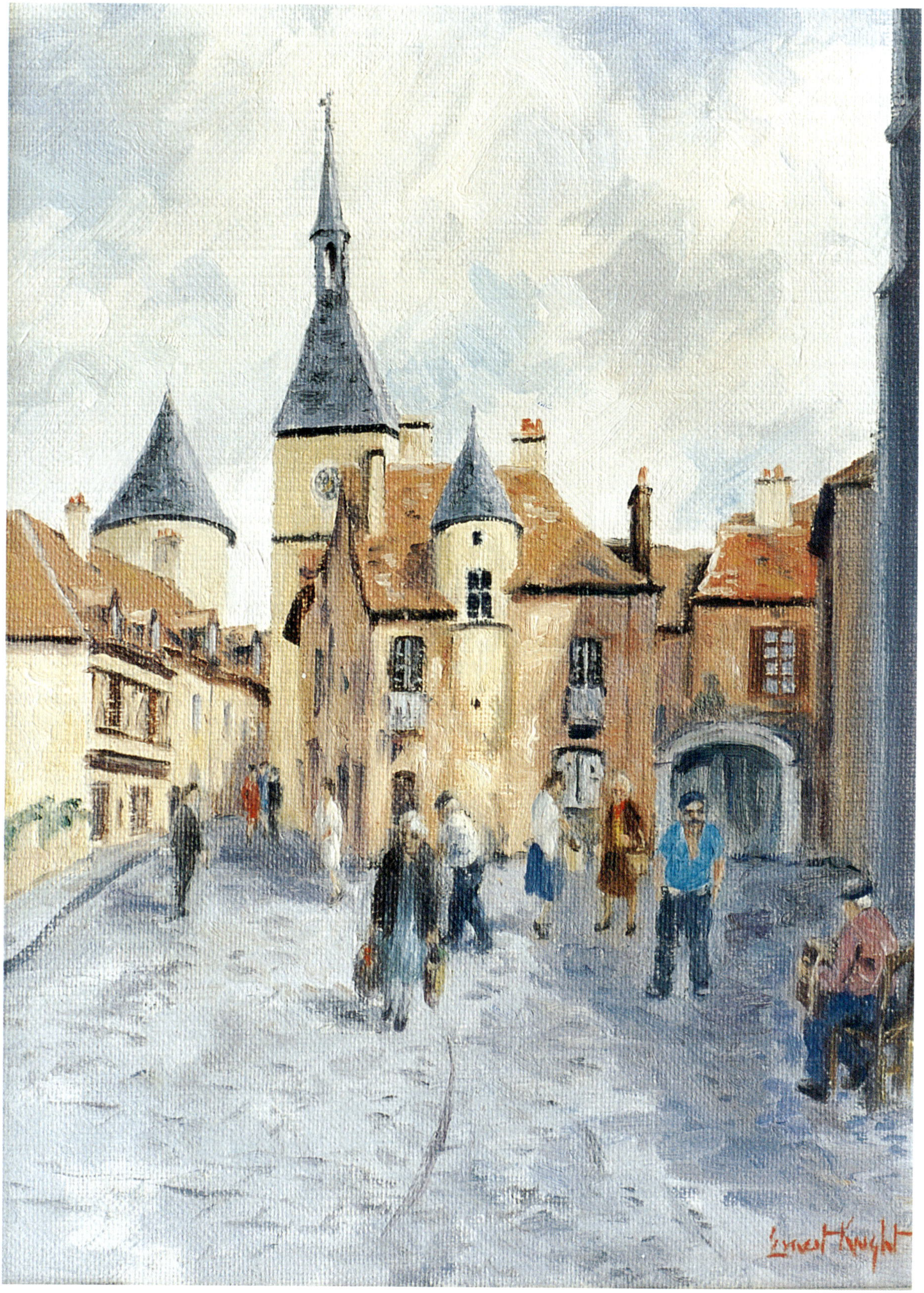

Avalon, Burgundy. Oil on Canvas. 31 cm x 41 cm. Plate 49.

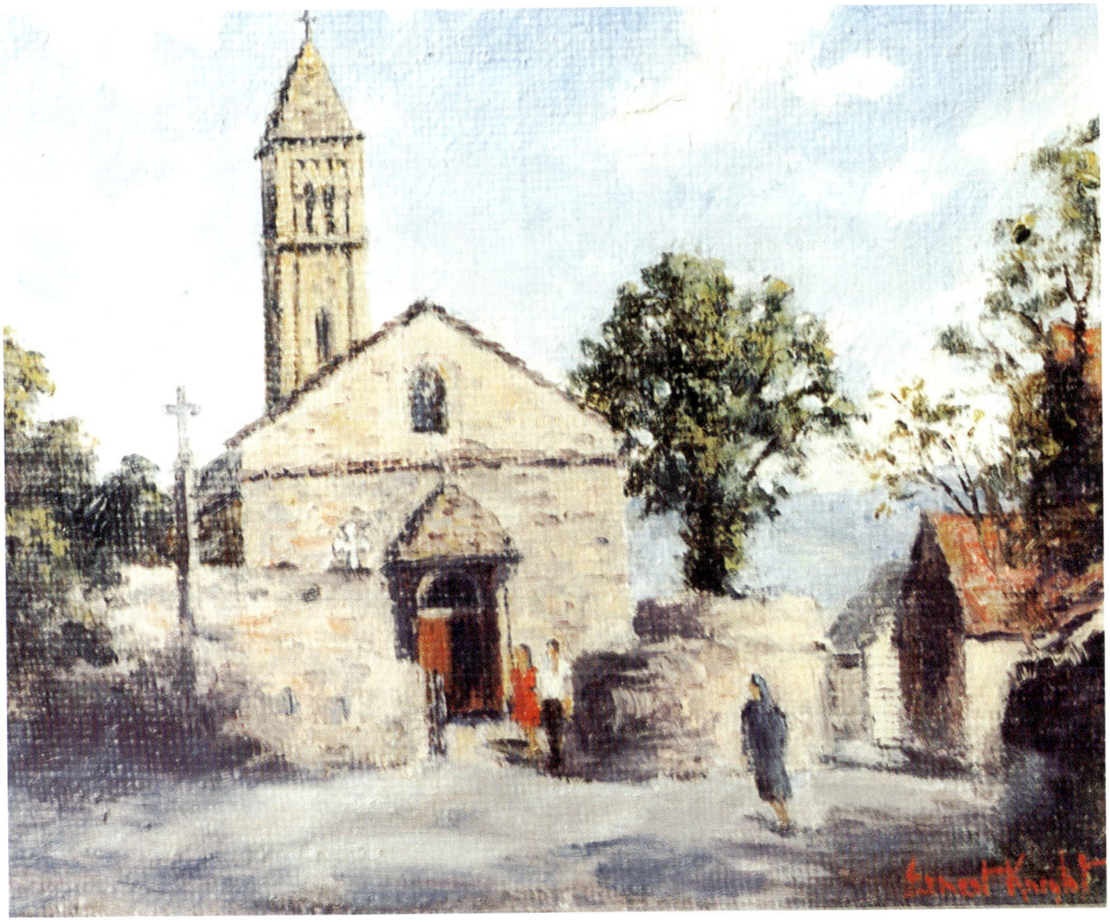

The Old Church, Taizé. Oil on Board. 28 cm x 23 cm. Plate 50.

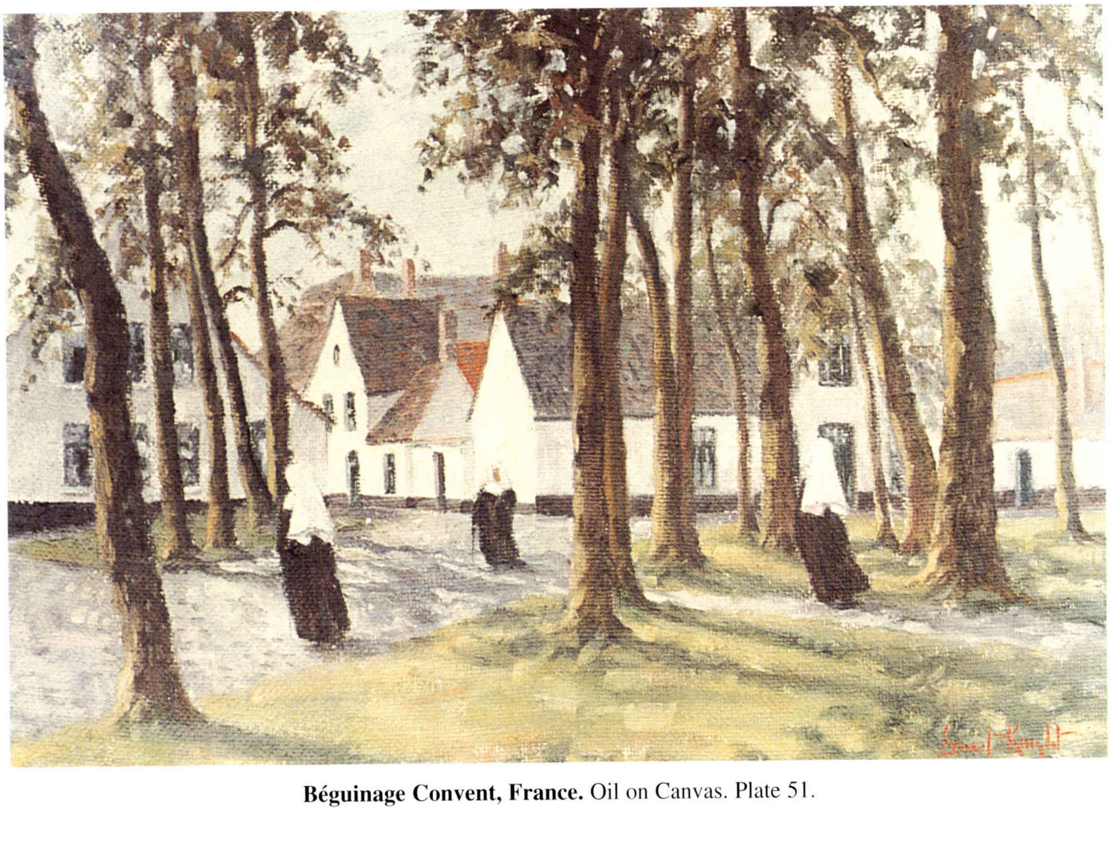

Béguinage Convent, France. Oil on Canvas. Plate 51.

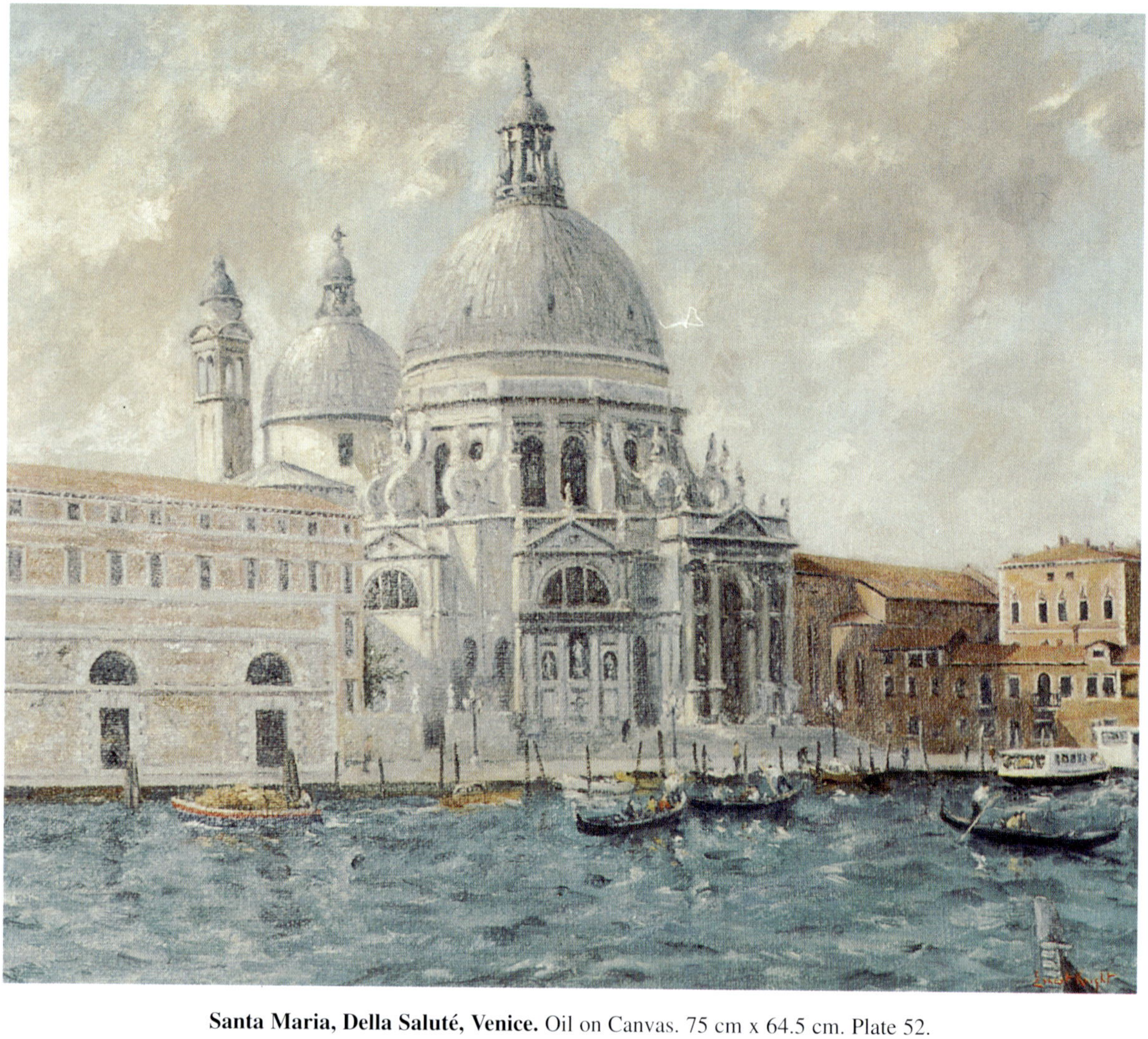

Santa Maria, Della Saluté, Venice. Oil on Canvas. 75 cm x 64.5 cm. Plate 52.

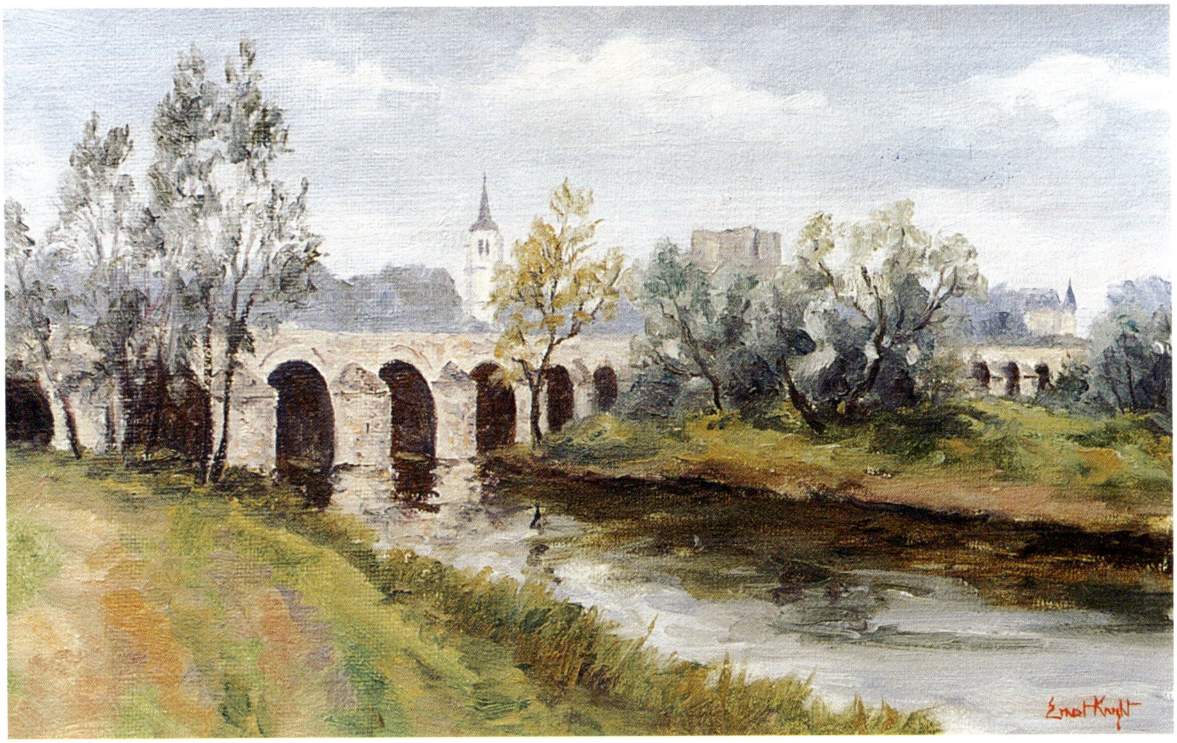

Bouginet, France. Oil on Canvas. 41 cm x 21.5 cm. Plate 53.

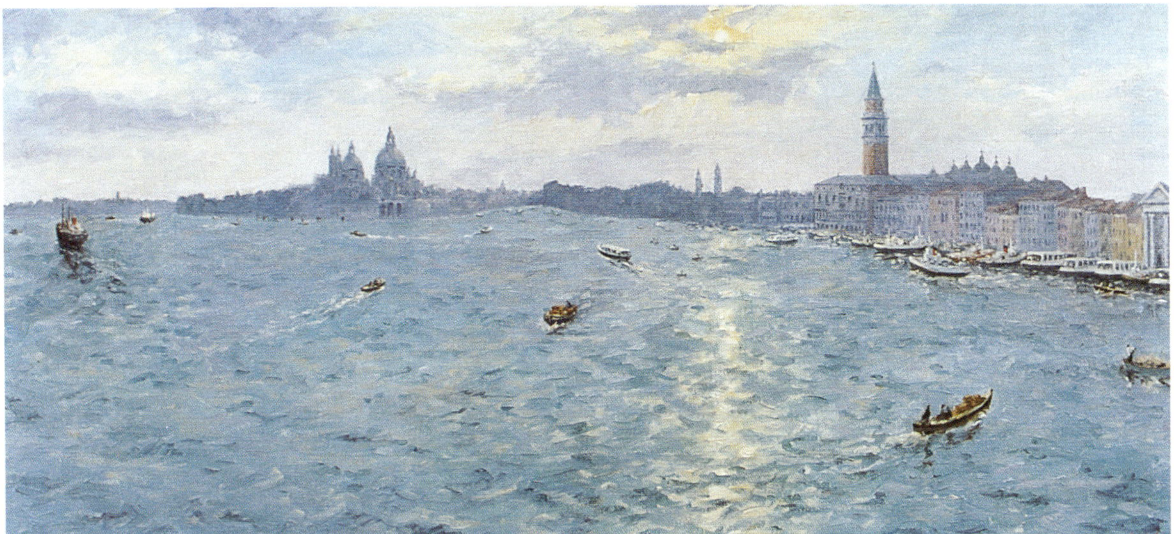

Venetian Skyline 1985. Oil on Canvas. 112 cm x 51 cm. Plate 54.

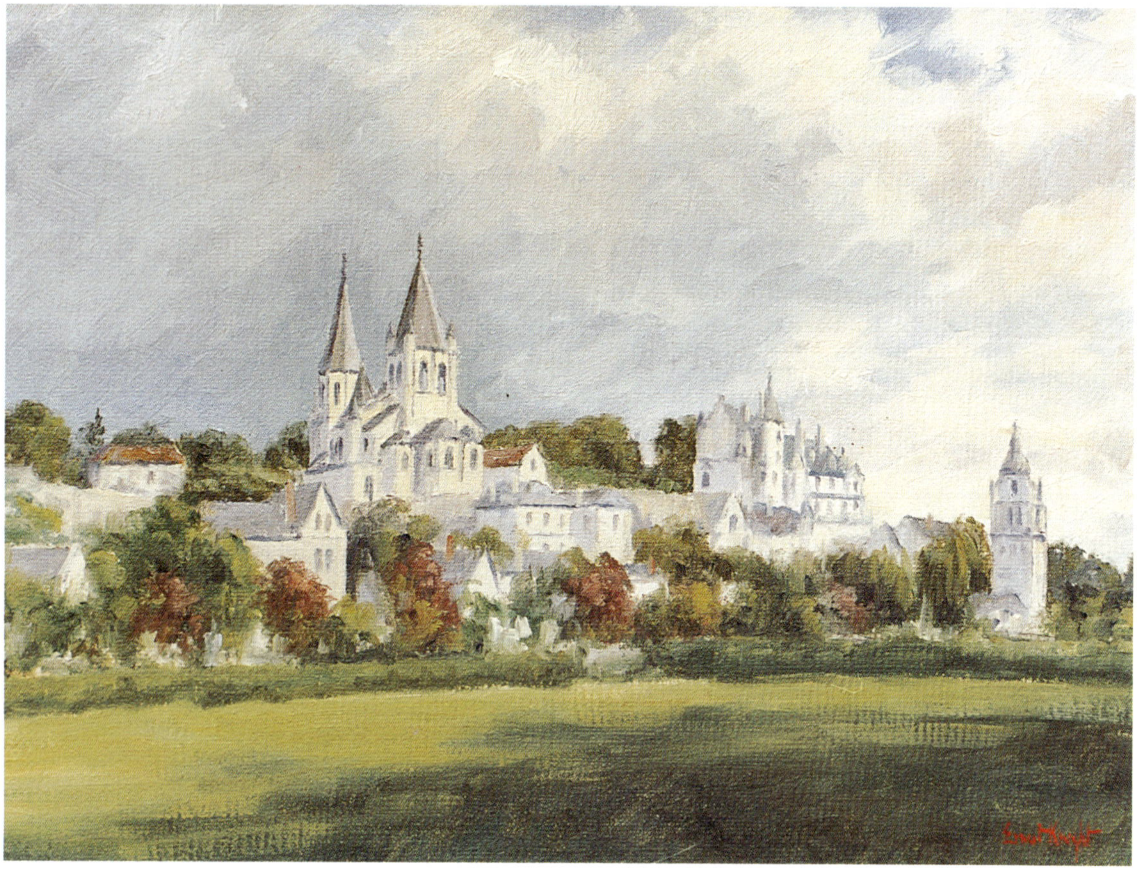

Loches, France. Oil on Canvas. 40 cm x 31 cm. Plate 55.

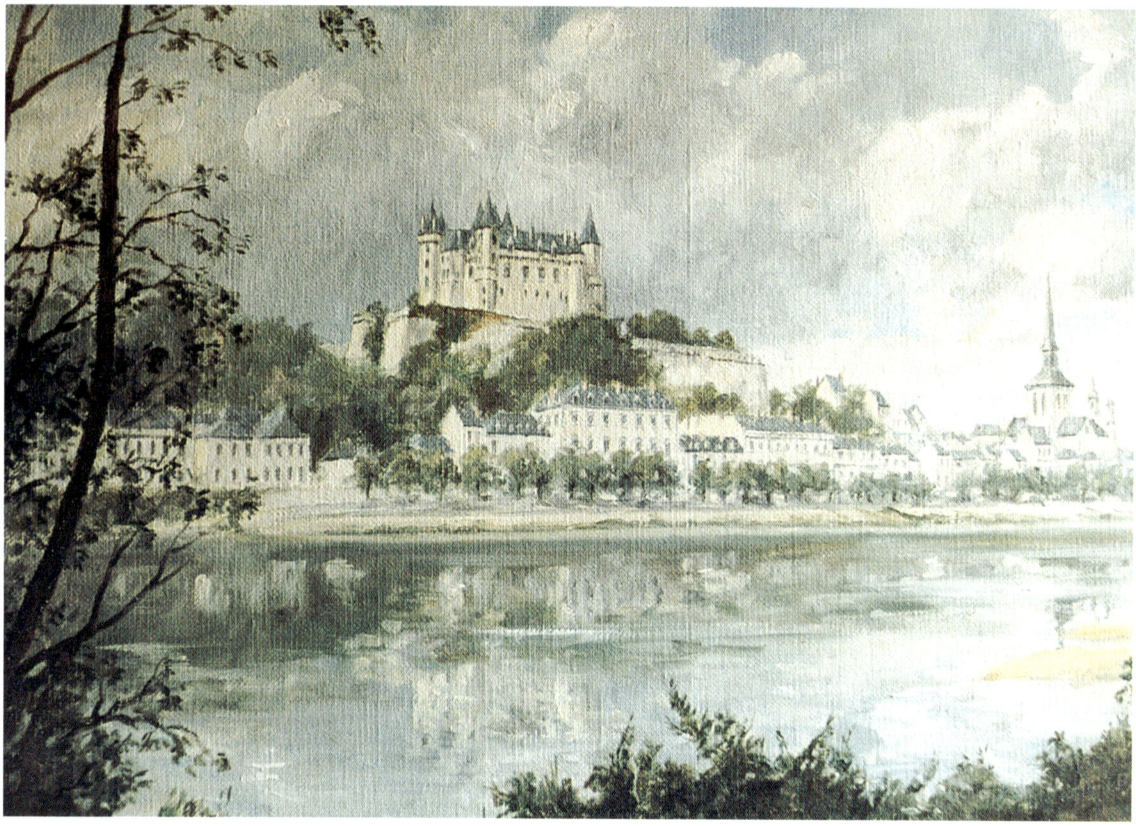

Saumur, France. Oil on Canvas. Plate 56.

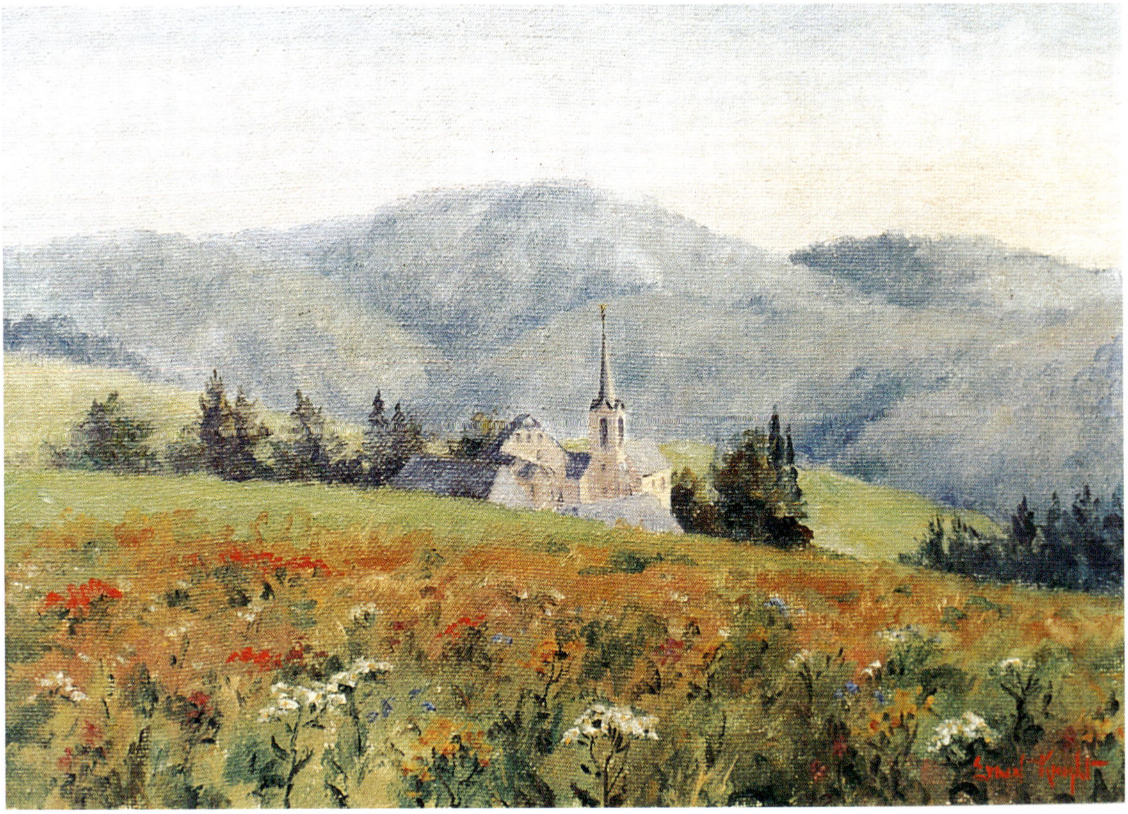

Luxembourg Landscape. Oil on Canvas. 51 cm x 36 cm. Plate 57.

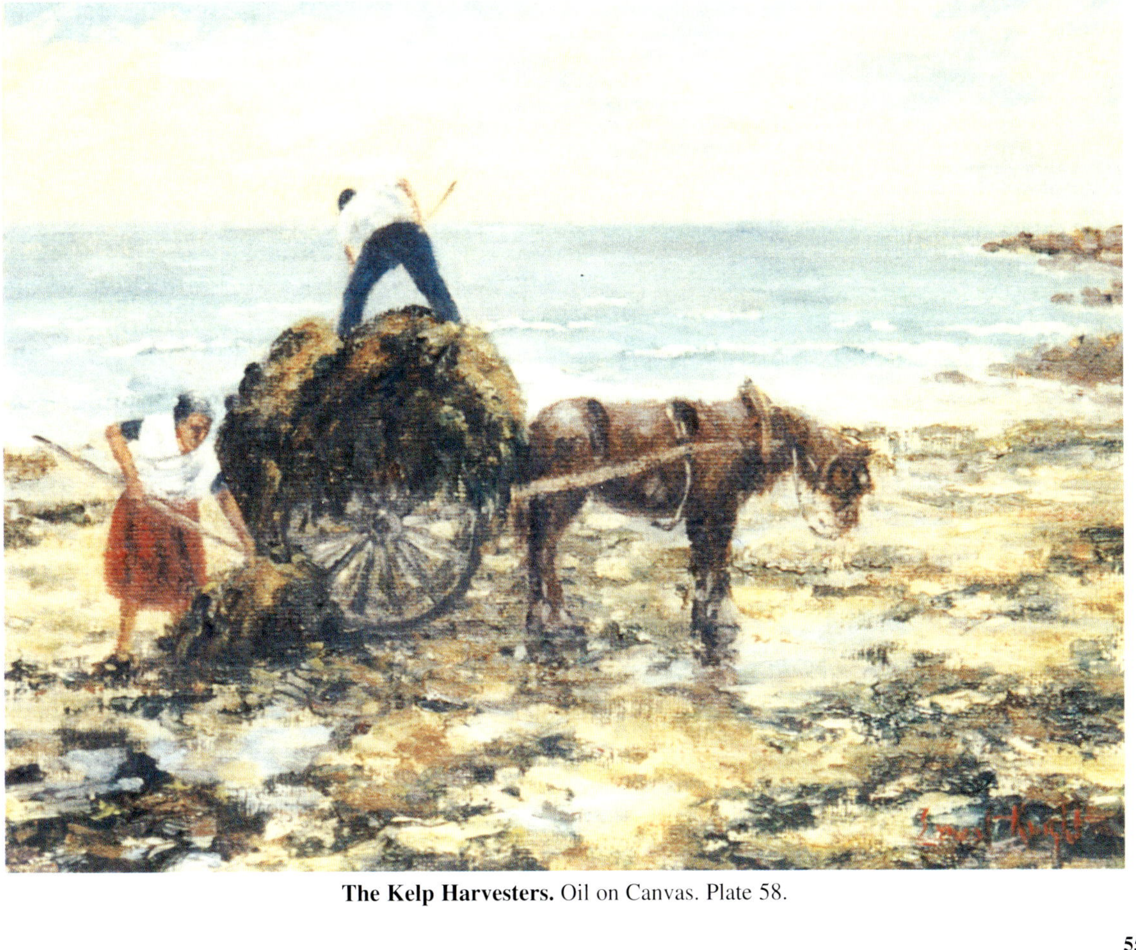

The Kelp Harvesters. Oil on Canvas. Plate 58.

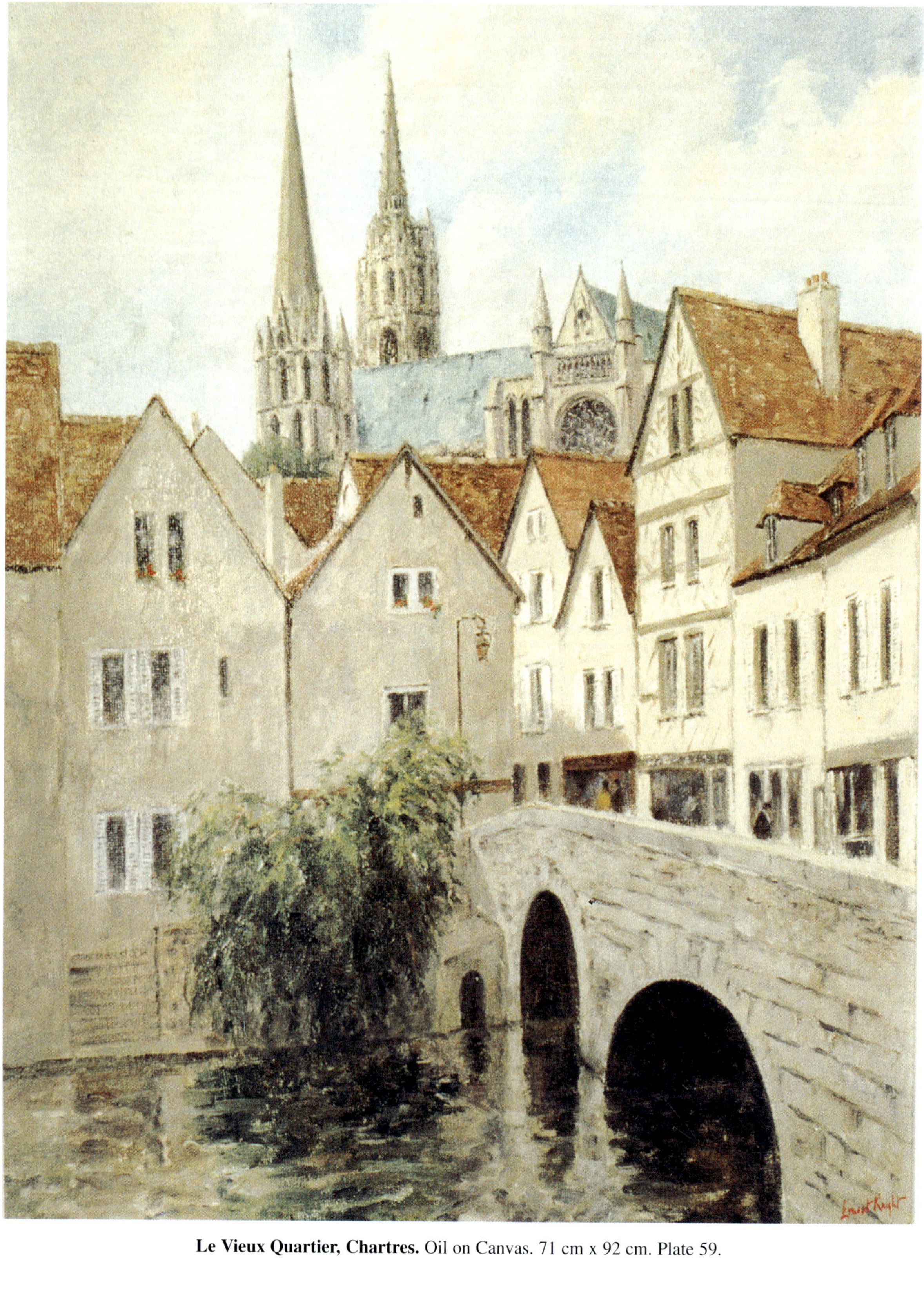

Le Vieux Quartier, Chartres. Oil on Canvas. 71 cm x 92 cm. Plate 59.

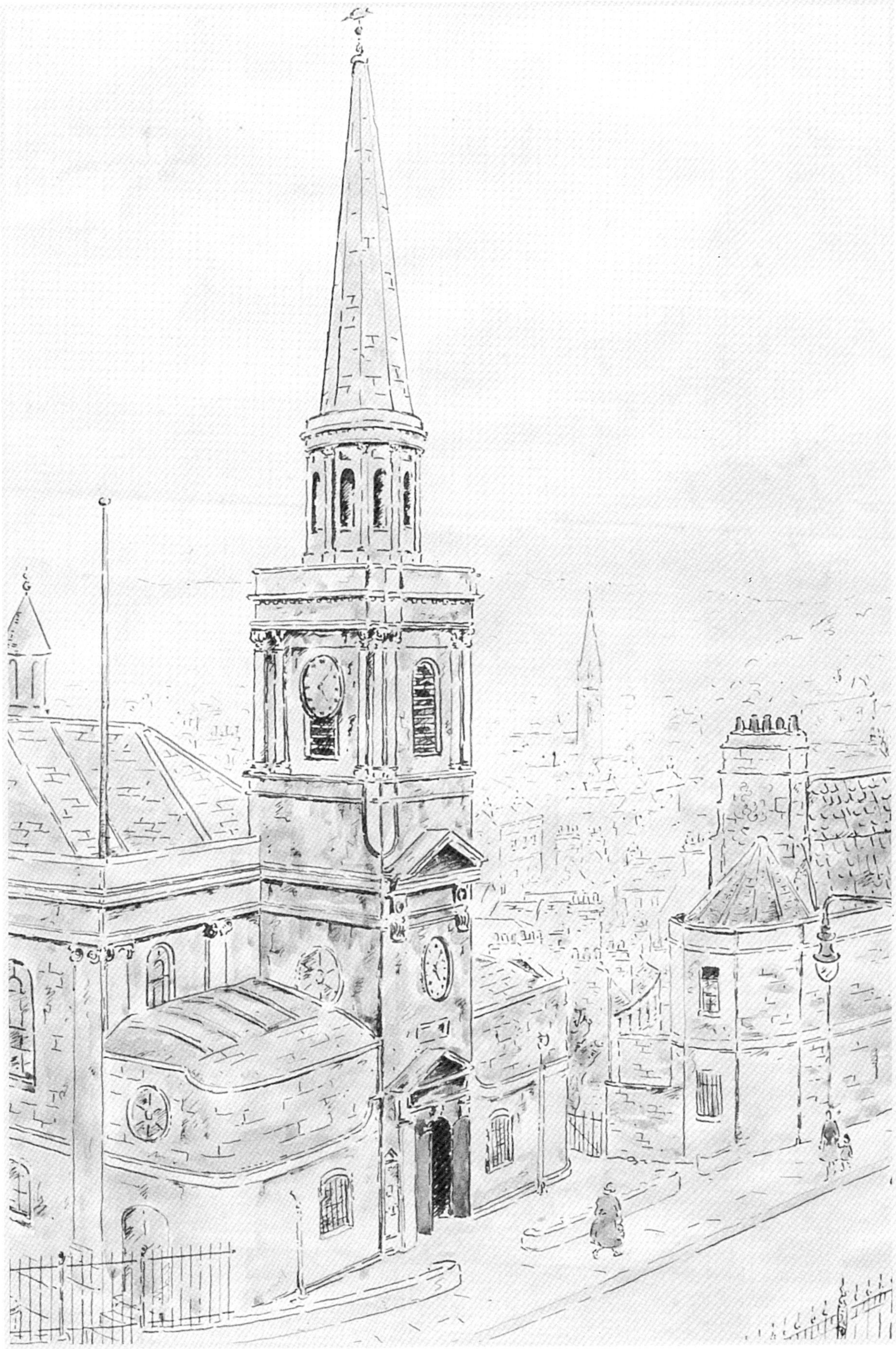

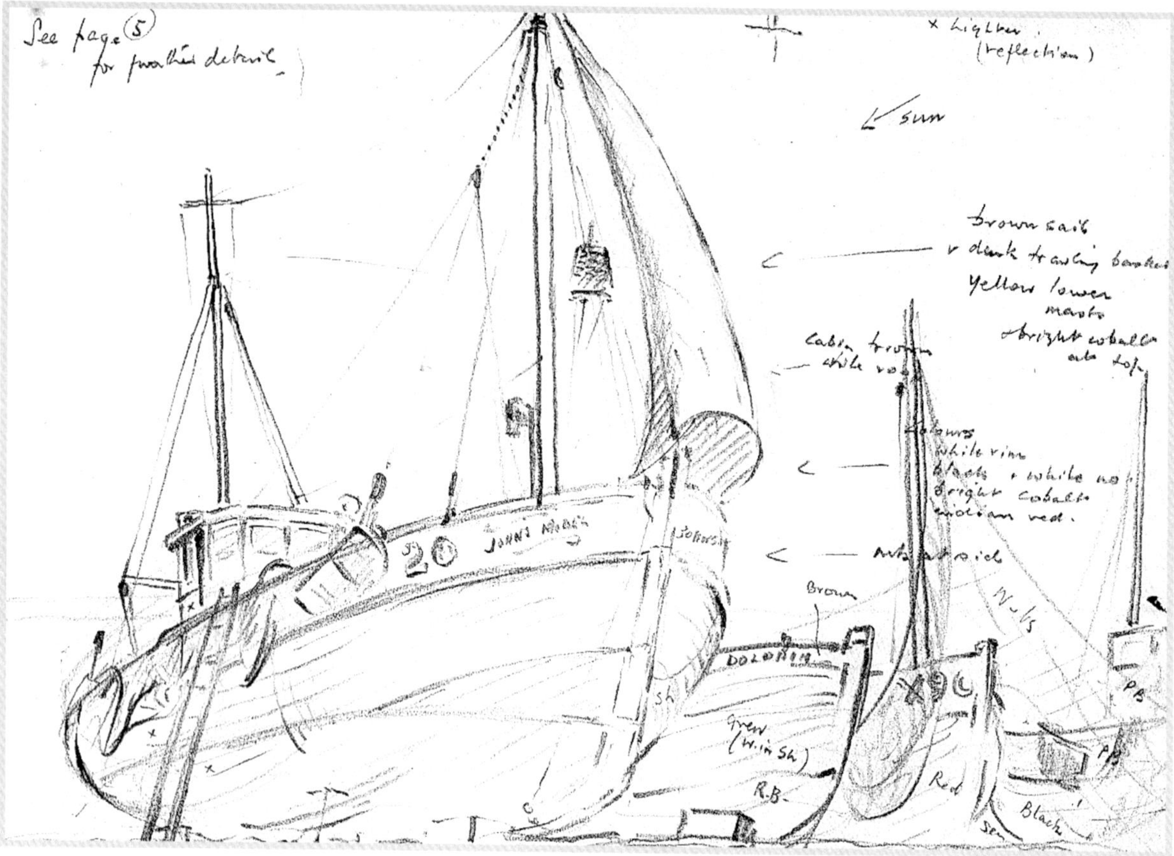

See page (5) for further detail
× Lighter (reflection)
sun
Brown sails
+ dark trawling baskets
Yellow lower masts
+ bright cobalt at top
Brown
Red

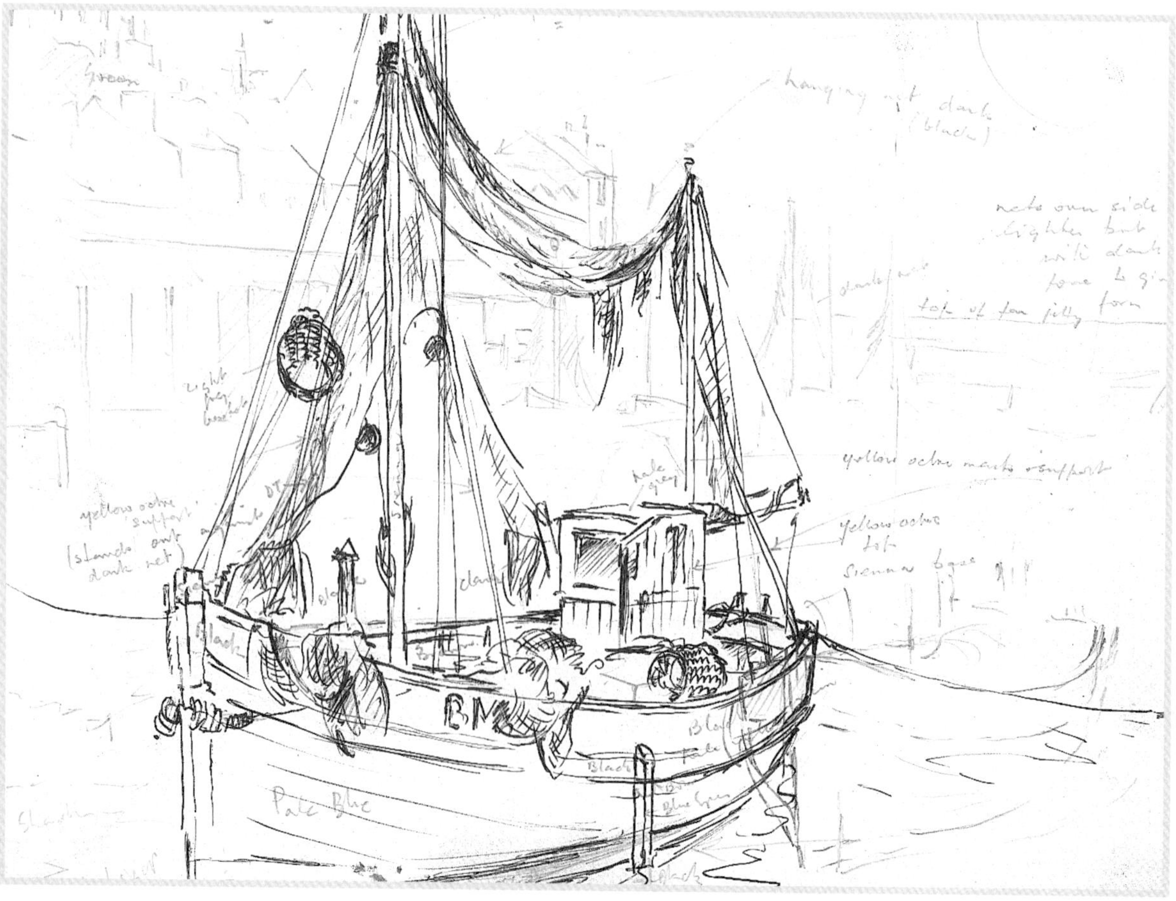

BM
Pale Blue

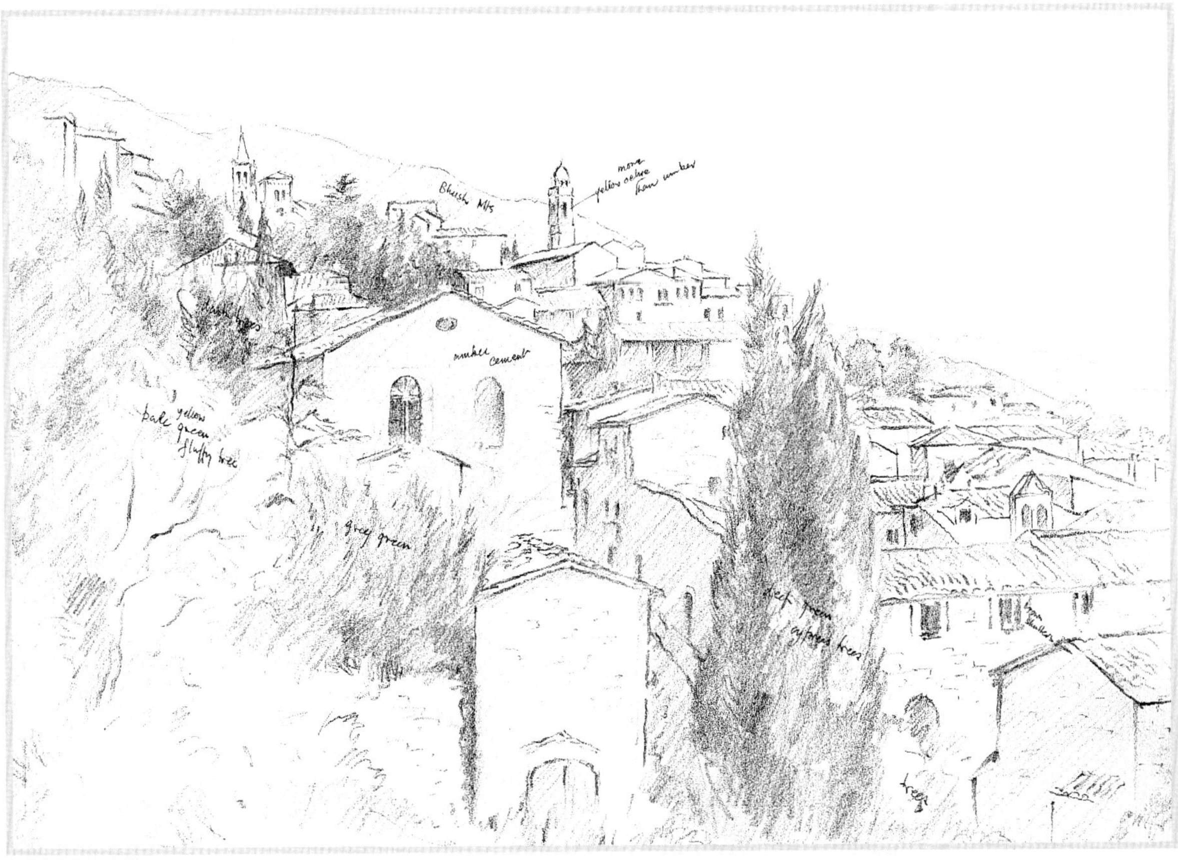
Bluish Mts
more yellow ochre than umber
umber cement
yellow
pale green
fluffy tree
grey green

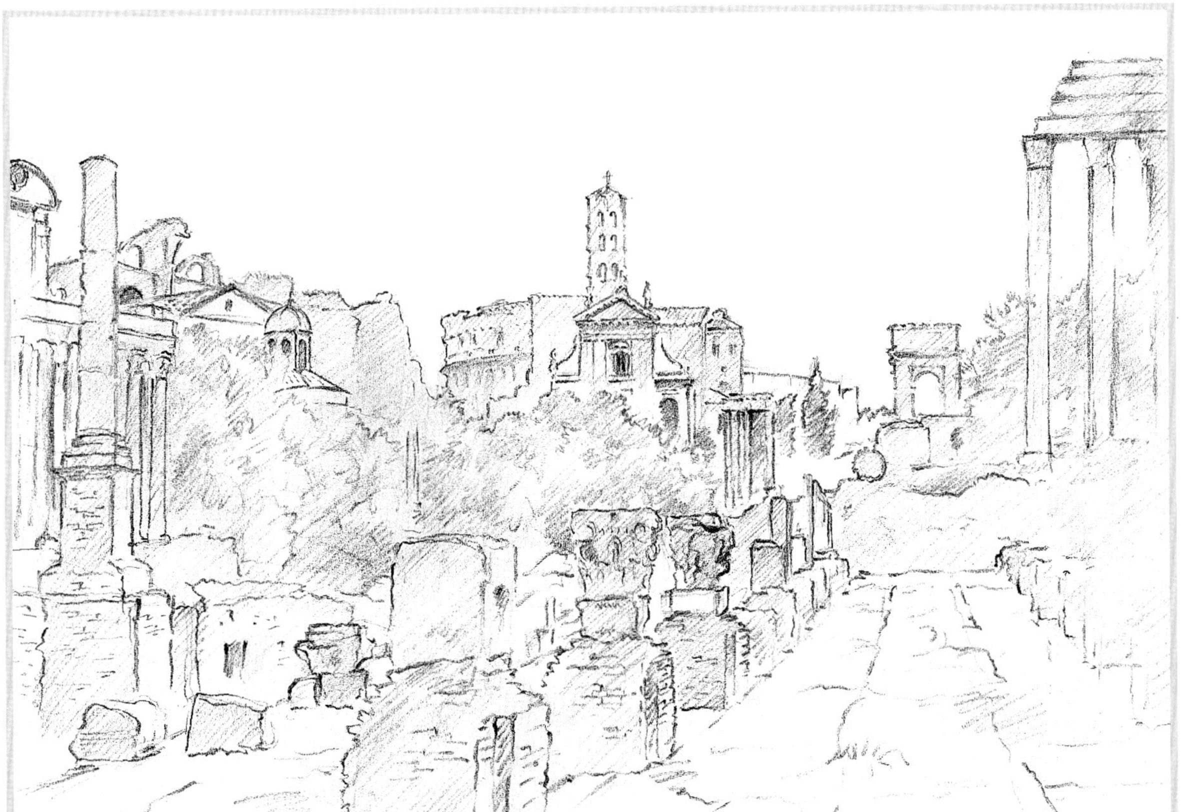
The Forum

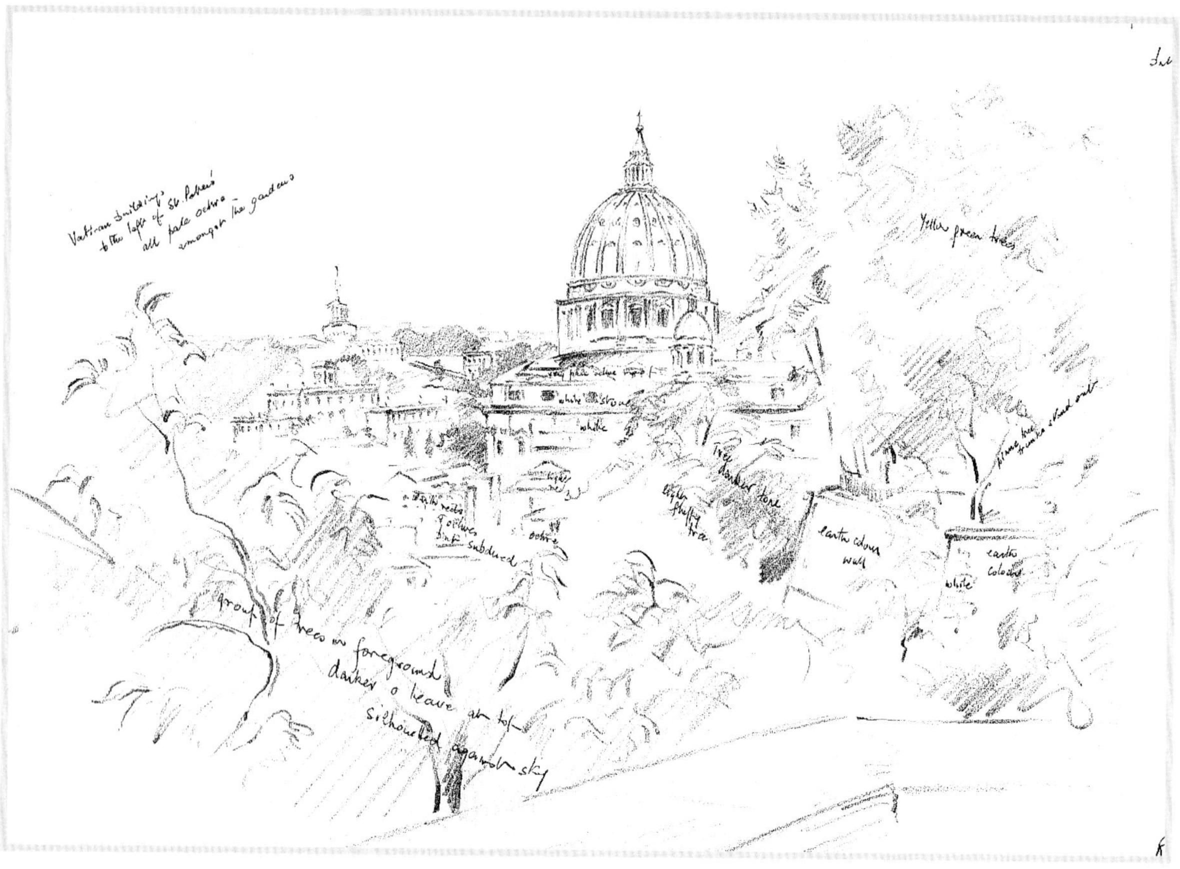
Vatican buildings to the left of St Peter's all pale ochre amongst the gardens
Yellow green trees
earth colour wall
white
group of trees in foreground darker o leave at top silhouetted against sky

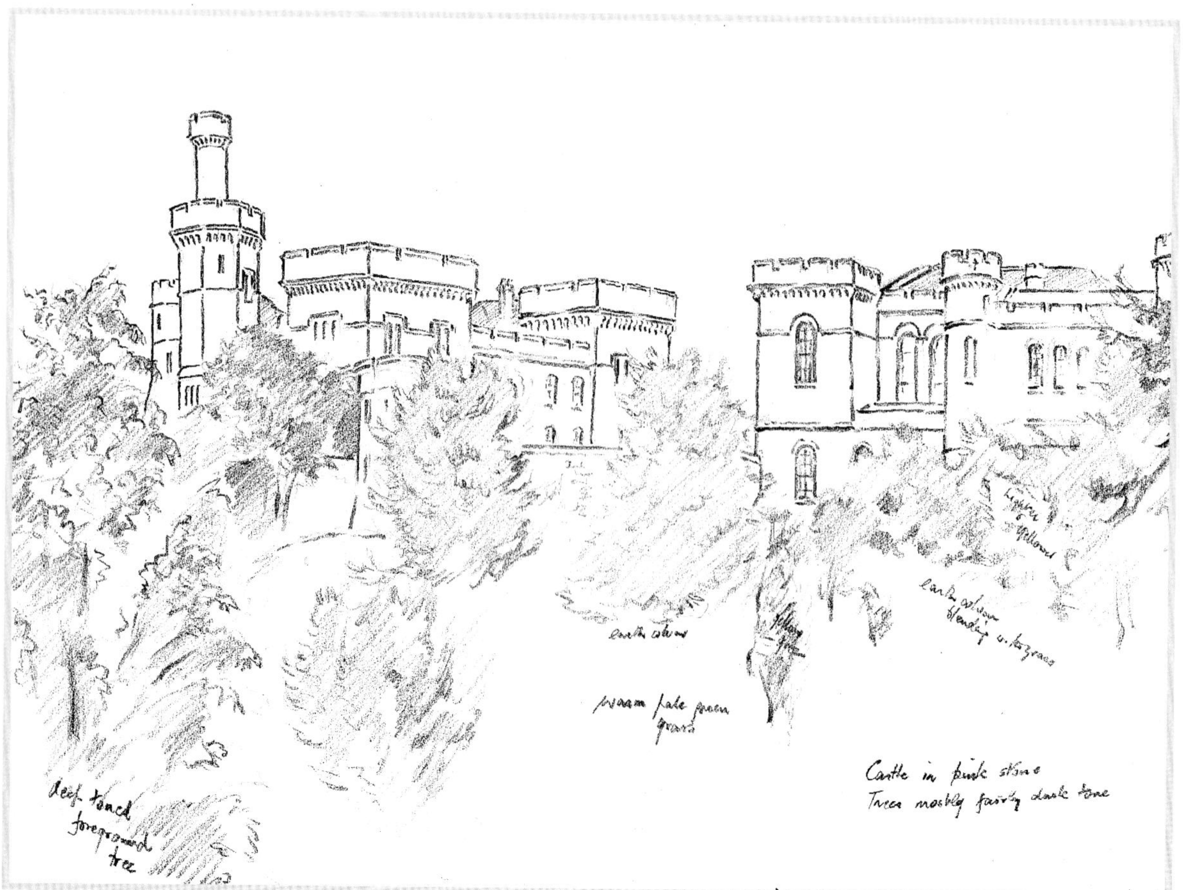
earth colour
warm pale green grass
Castle in pink stone
Trees mostly fairly dark tone
Deep toned foreground tree

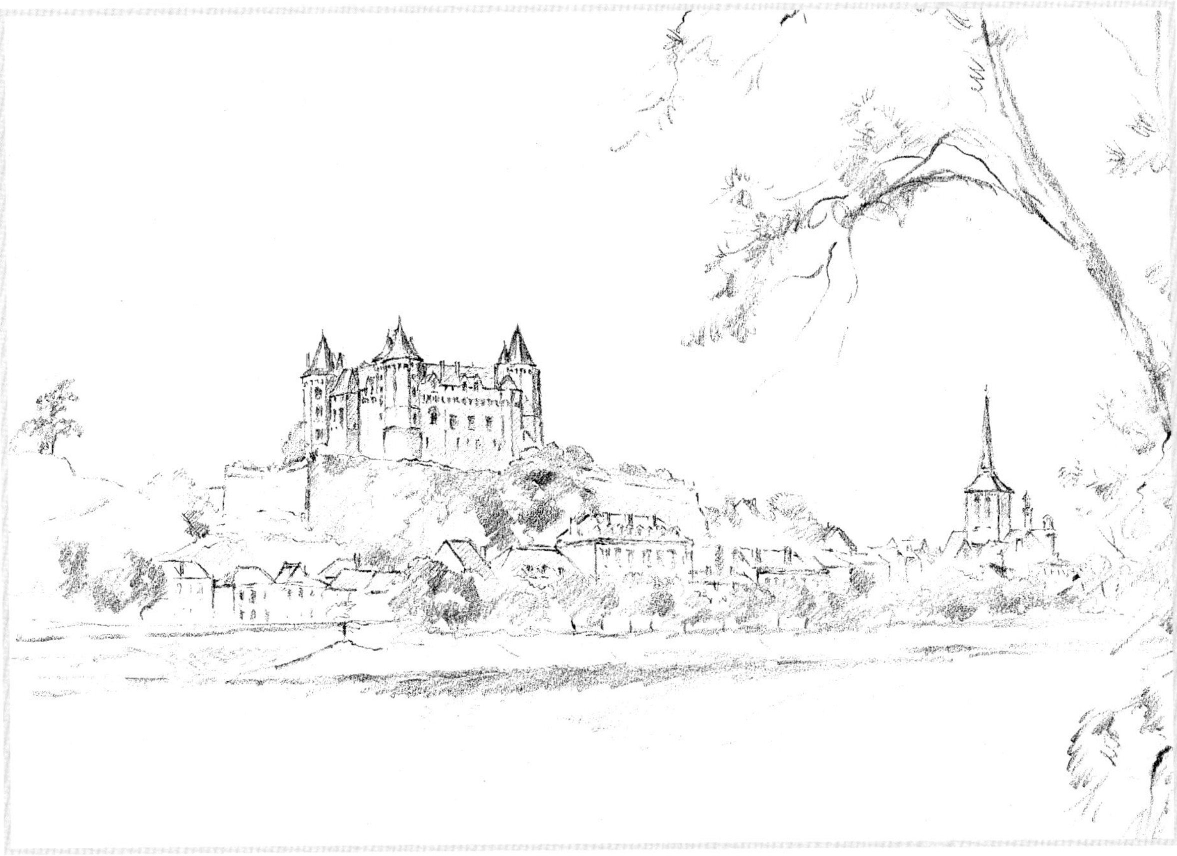

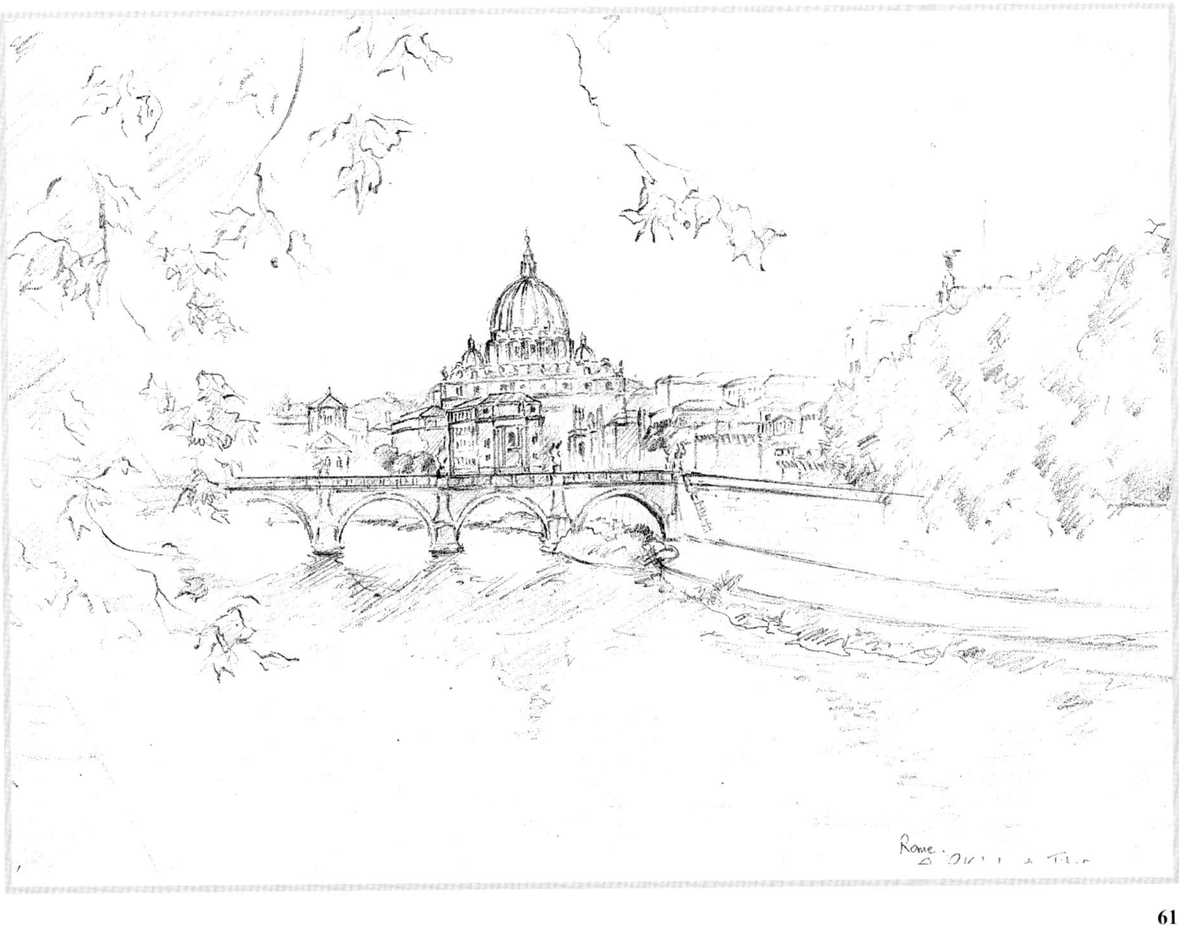
Rome:

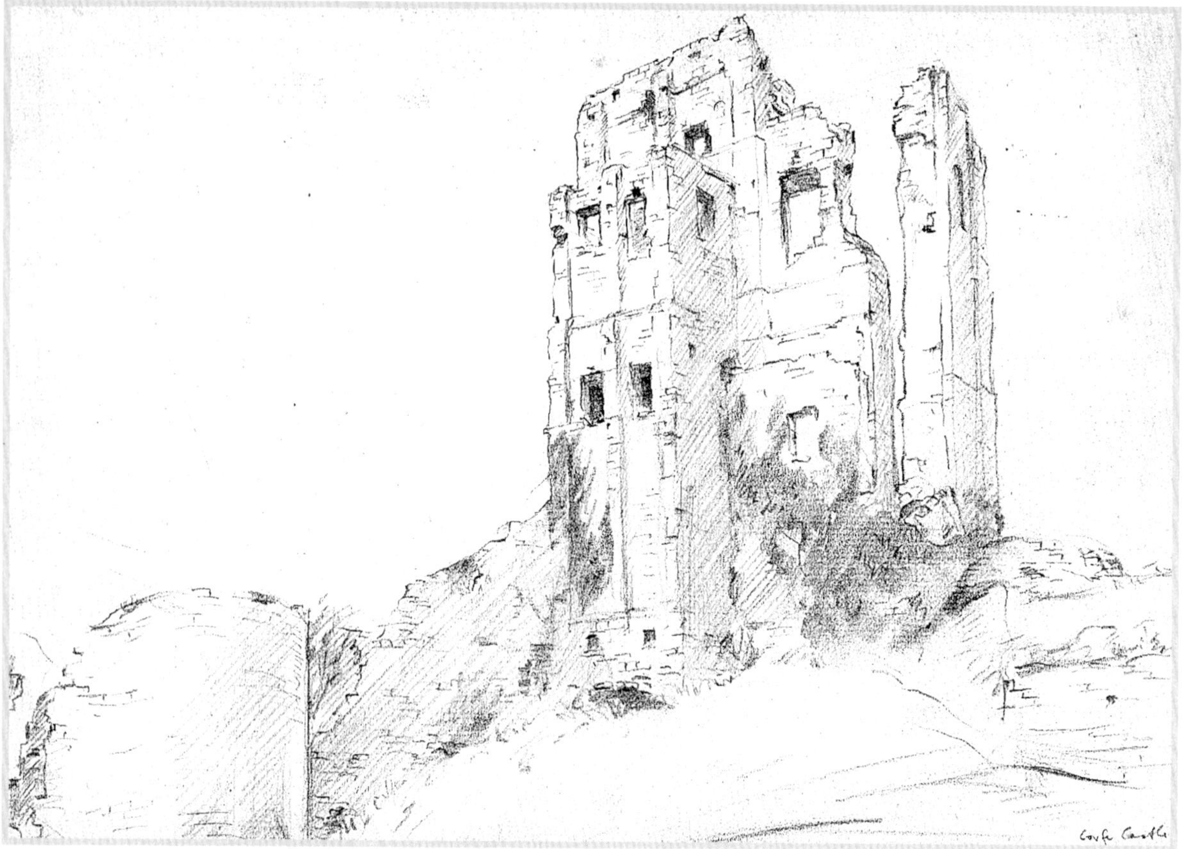
Corfe Castle

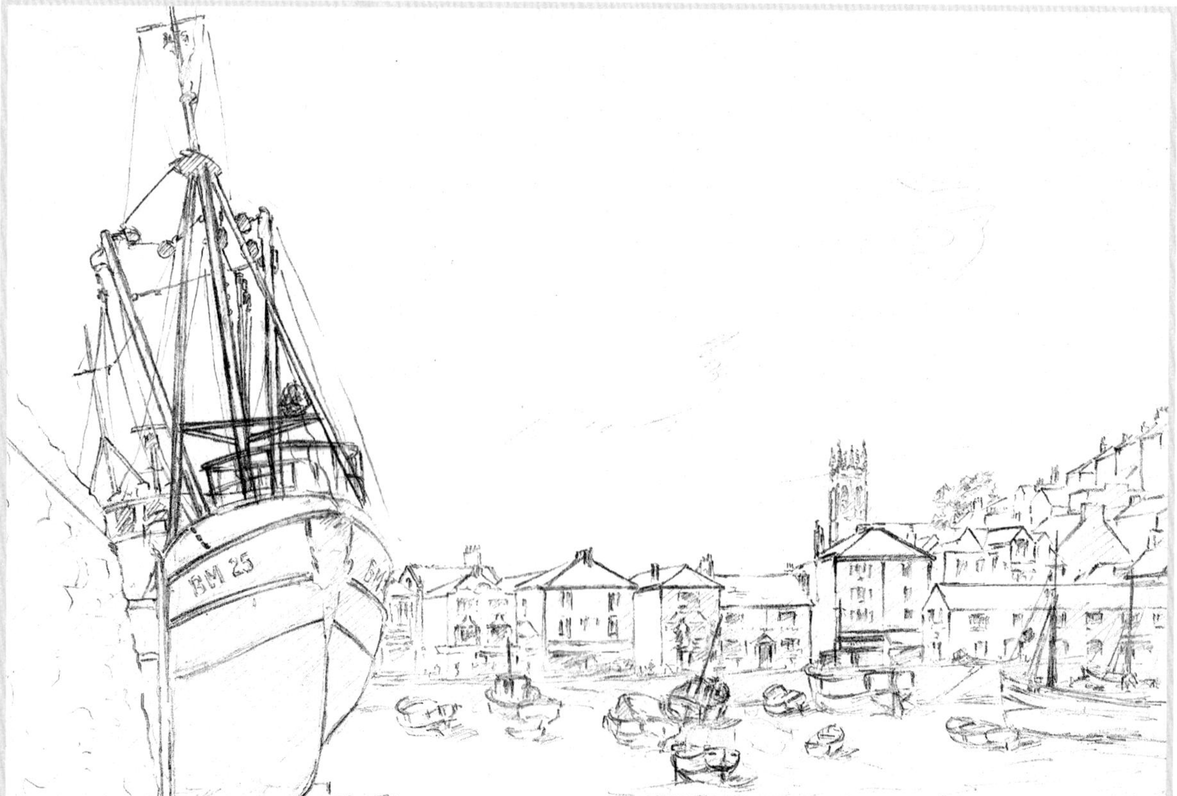
BM 25

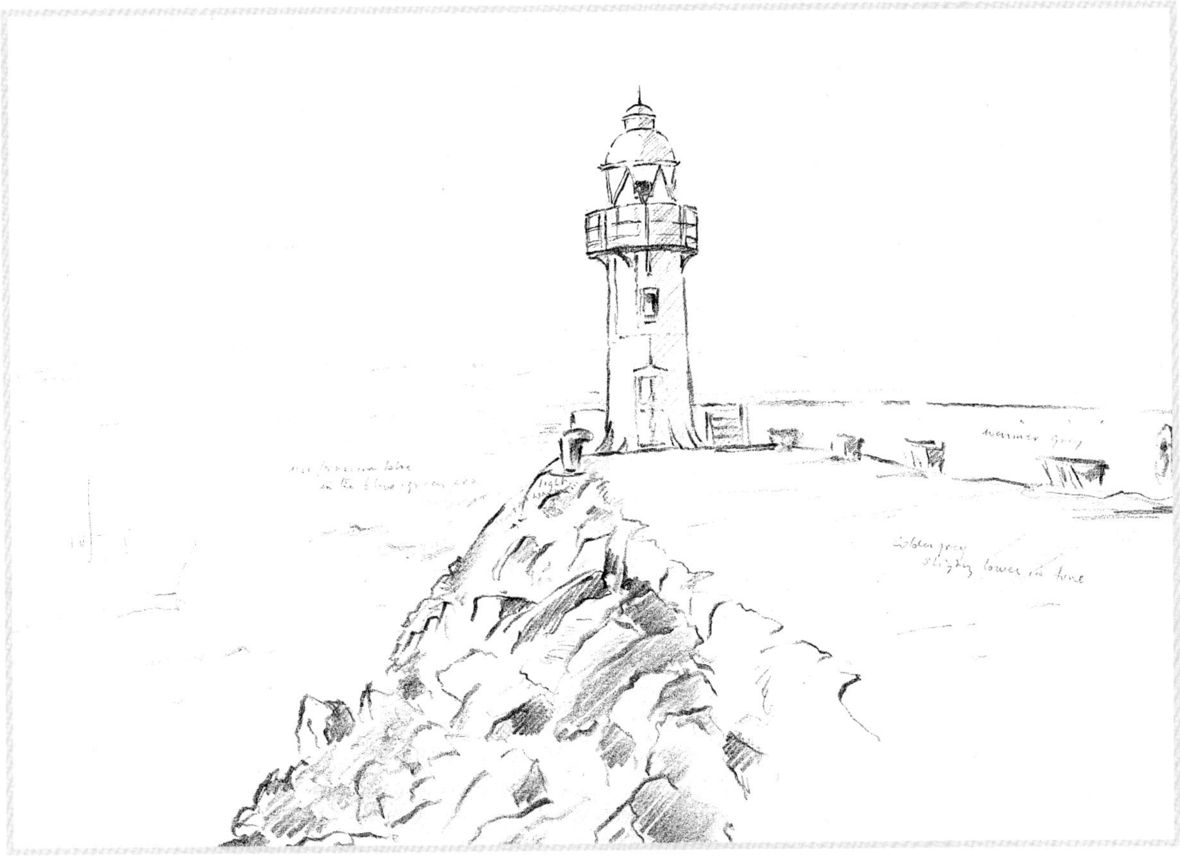

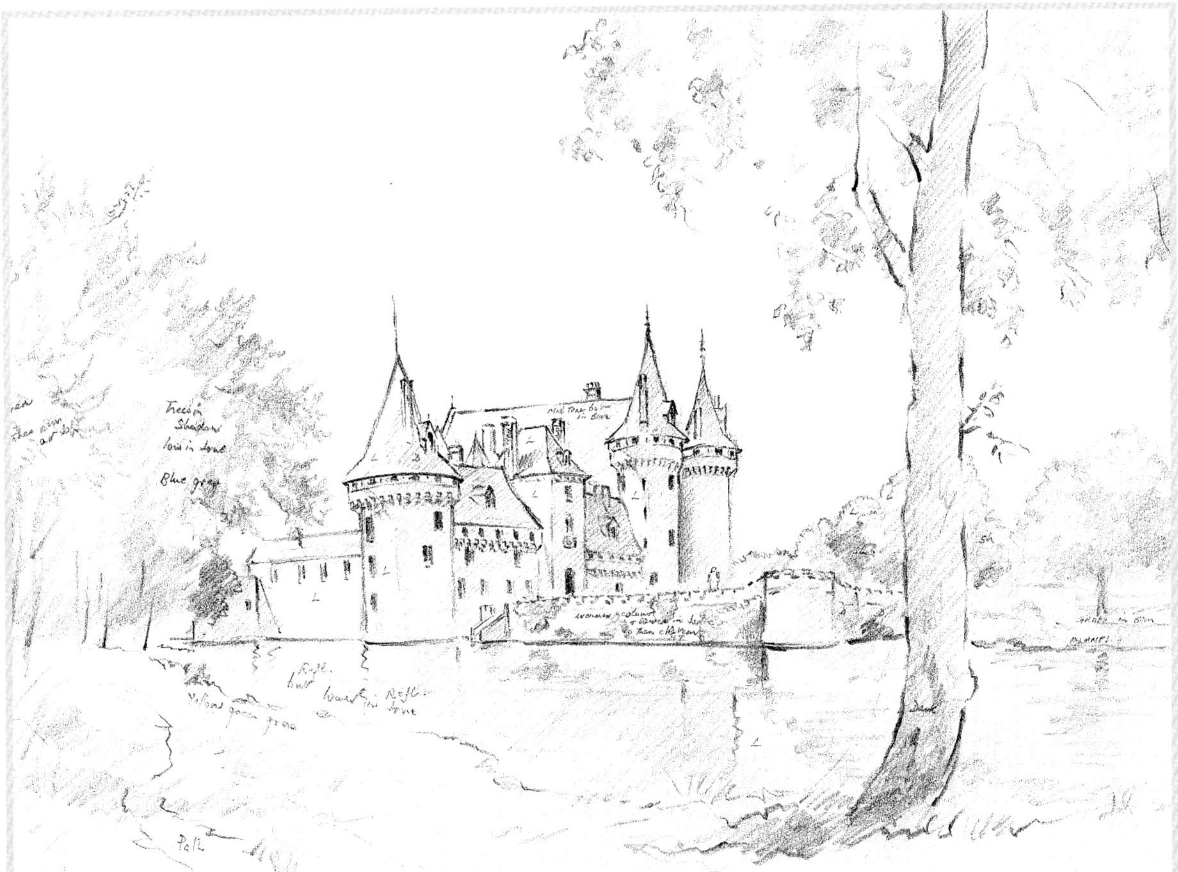

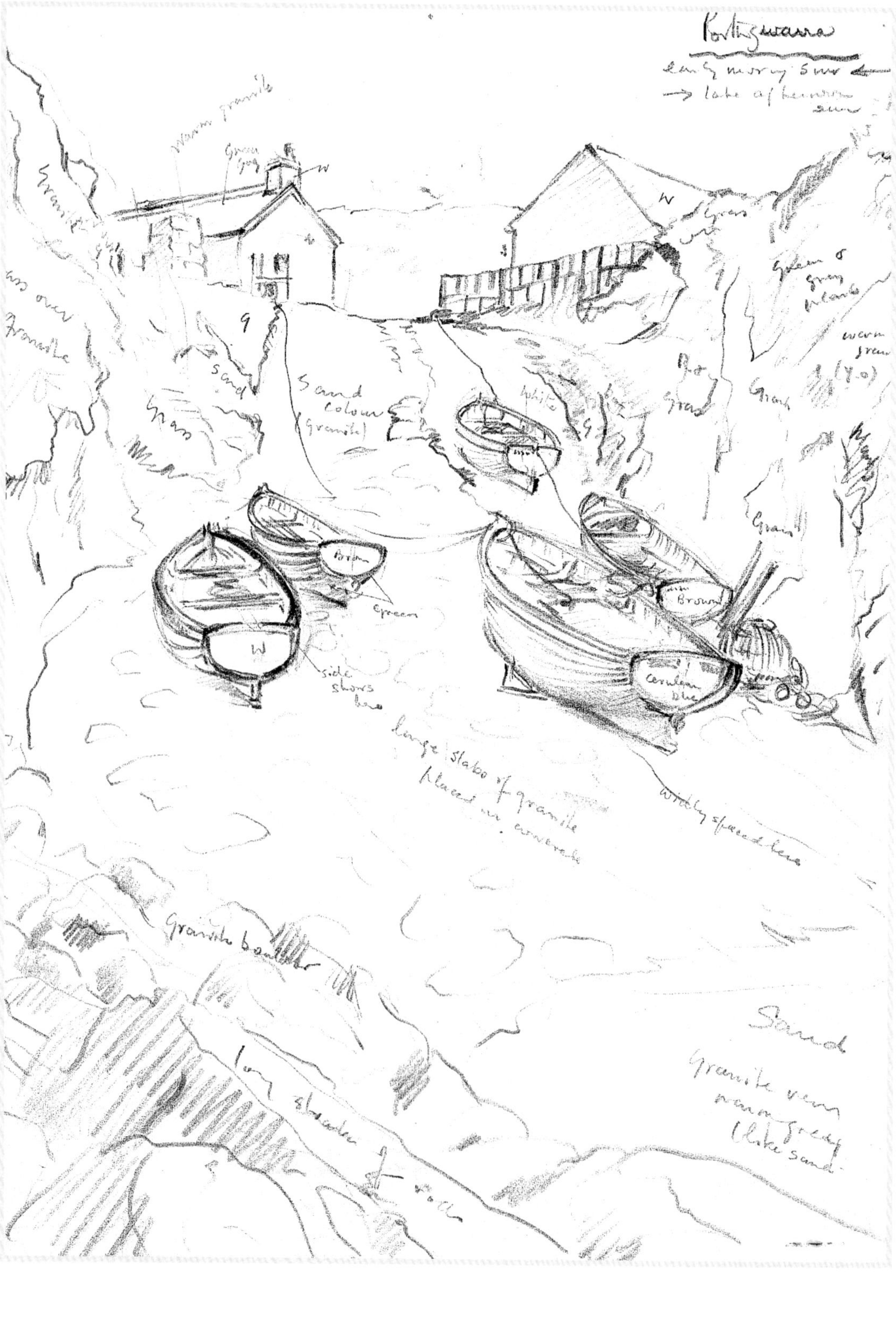
Porthgwarra
Sand
Granite veins
warm grey
(like sand)

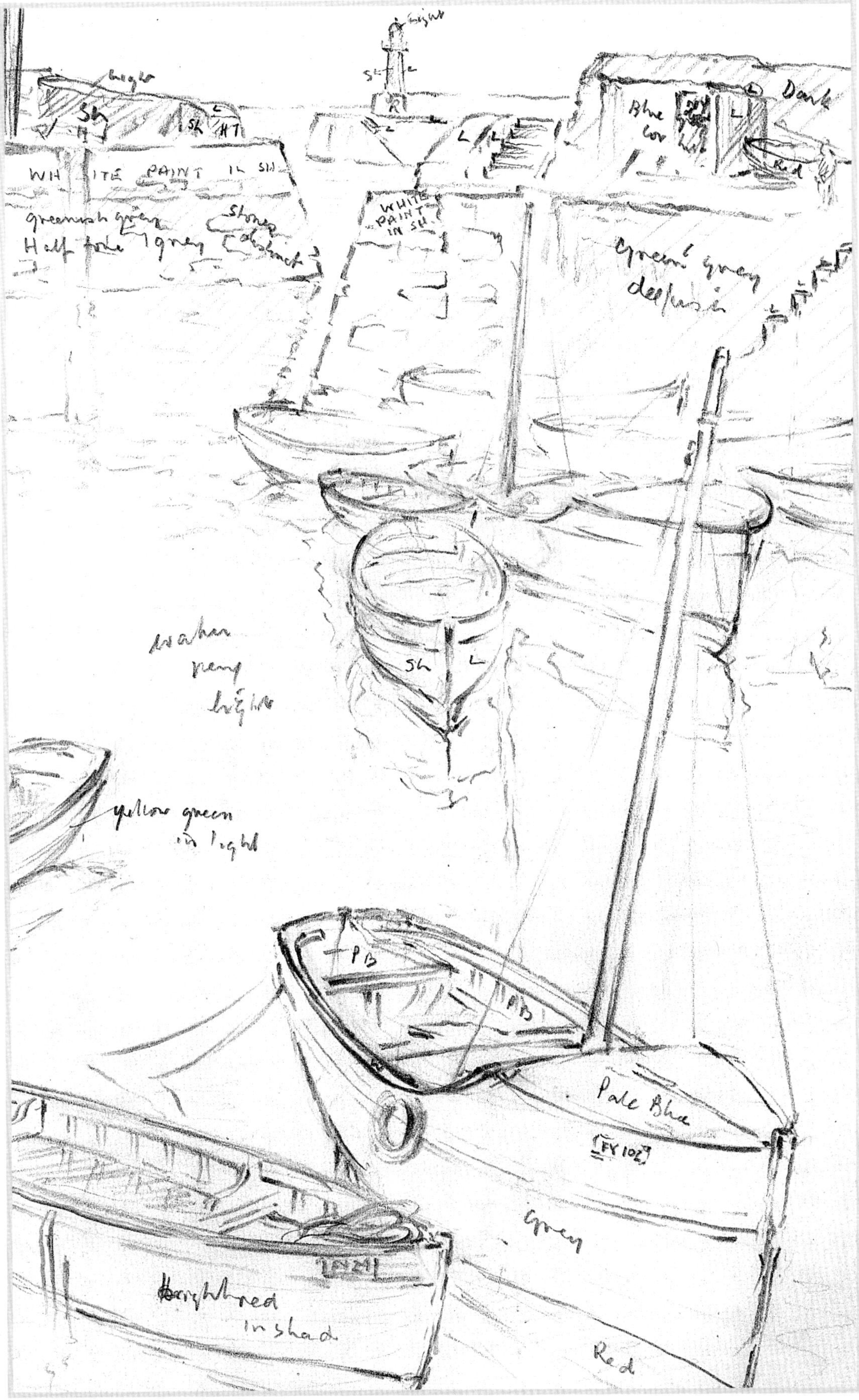
WHITE PAINT IN SH
Pale Blue
FY 102
Grey
Red
water very light
yellow green in light
Dark

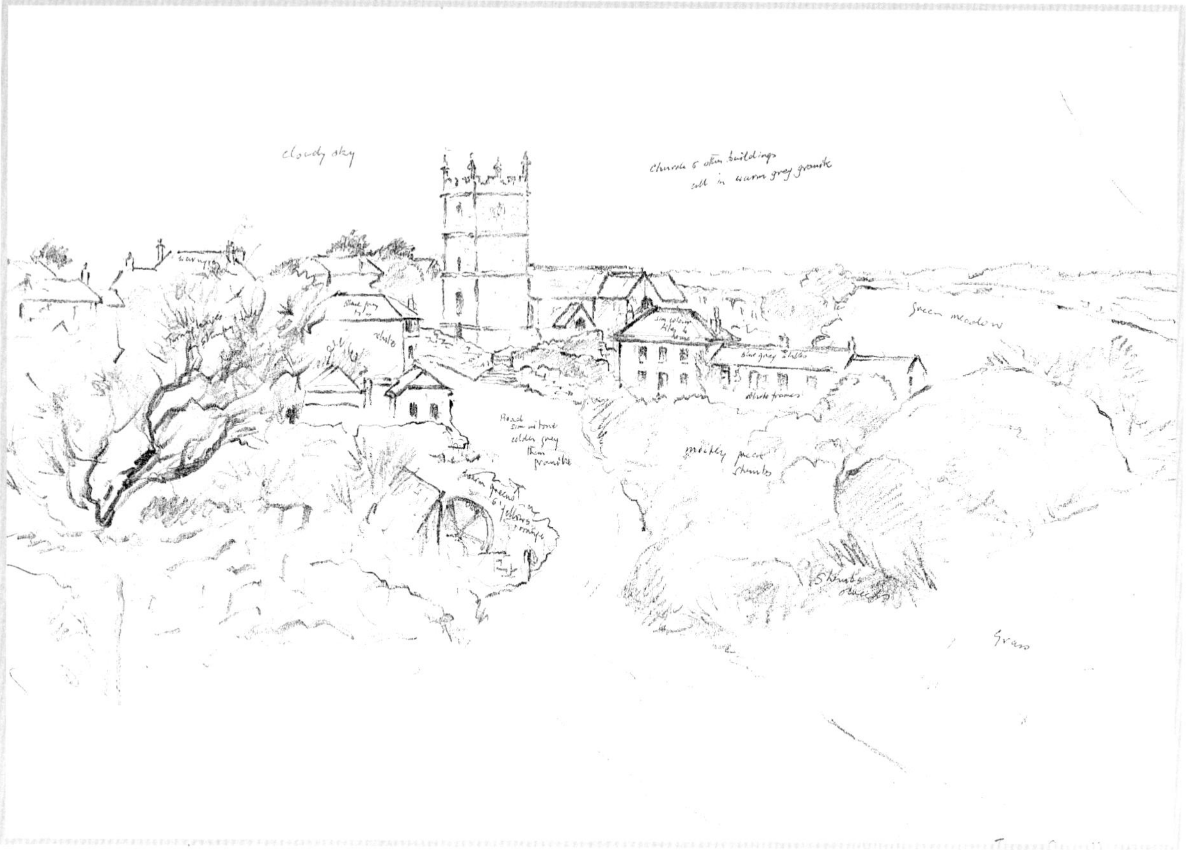
cloudy sky
Church & other buildings all in warm grey granite
Green meadow
white
blue grey slates
white frames
Road sim. in tone colder grey than granite
mottley green shrubs
Shrubs
Grass

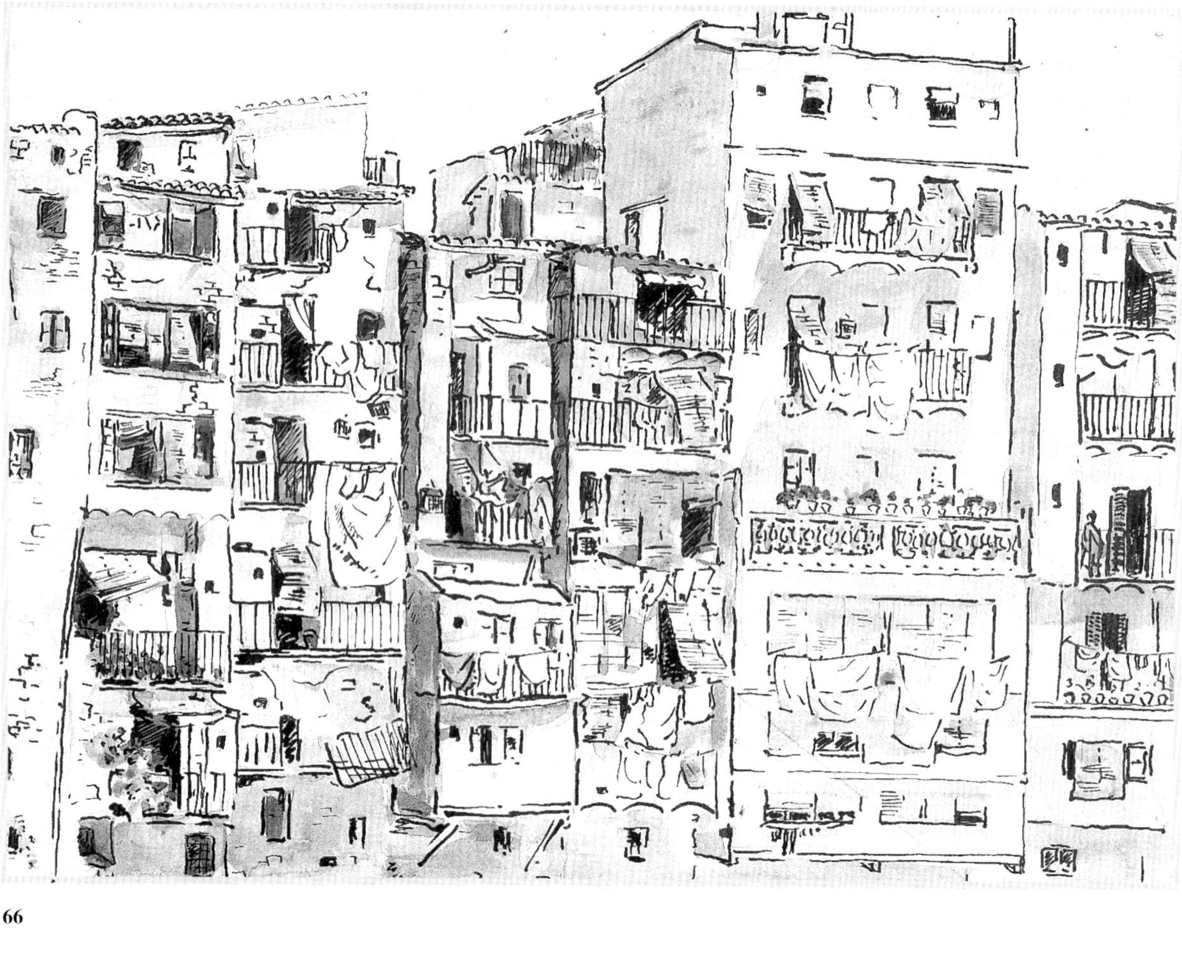

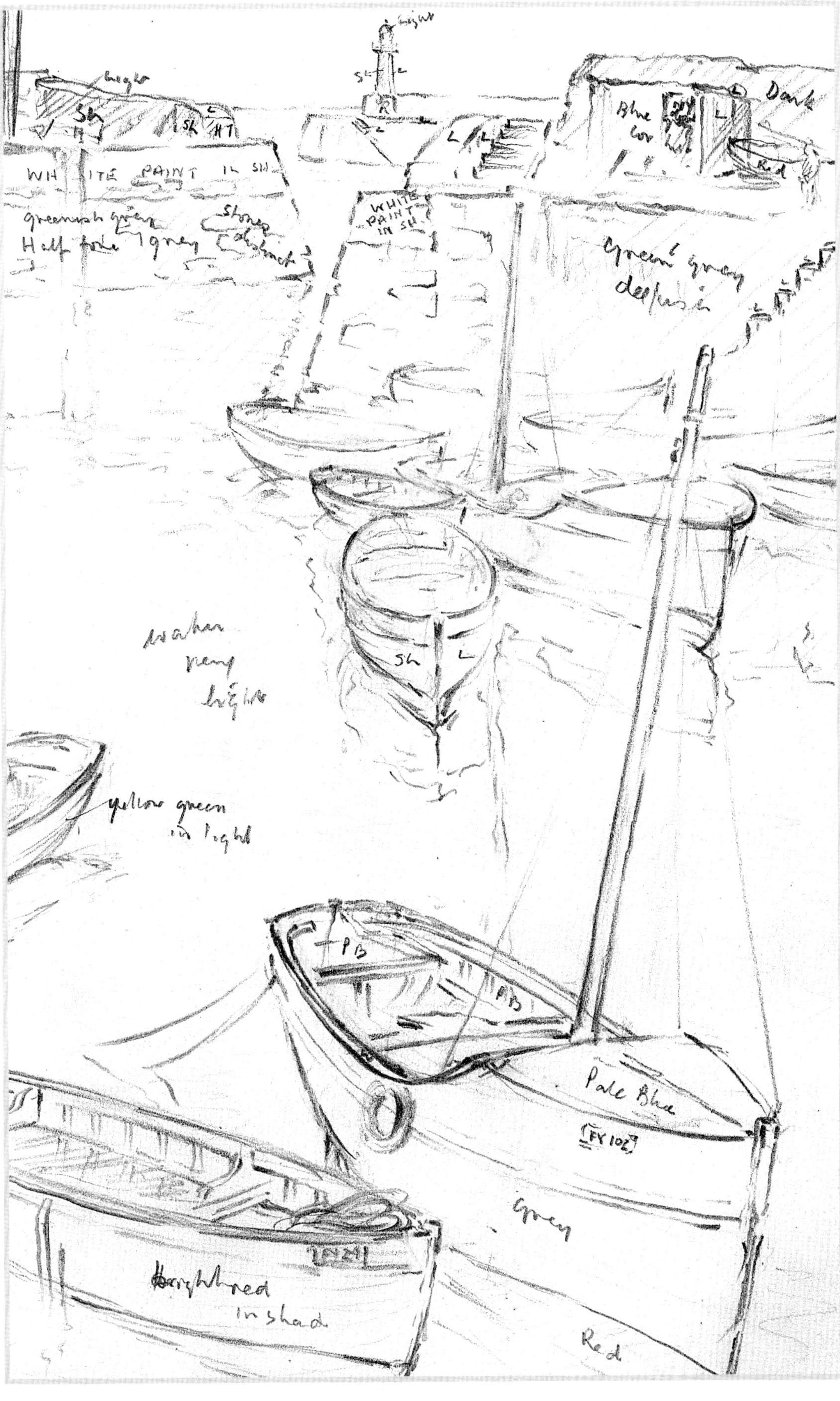
WHITE PAINT IN SH
WHITE PAINT IN SH.
Dark
Red
water very light
yellow green in light
PB
PB
Pale Blue
FY 102
Grey
red in shade
Red

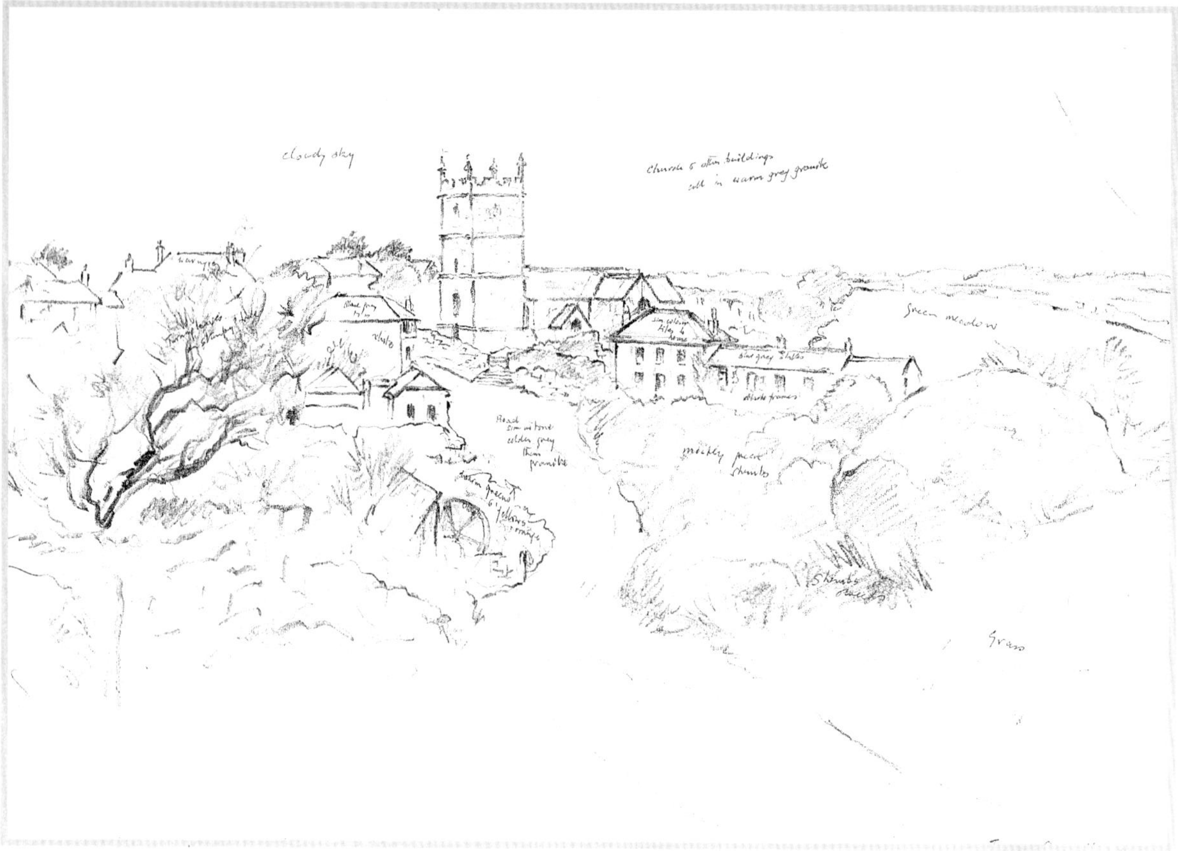
cloudy sky
Church & other buildings
all in warm grey granite
white
Green meadow
Grass

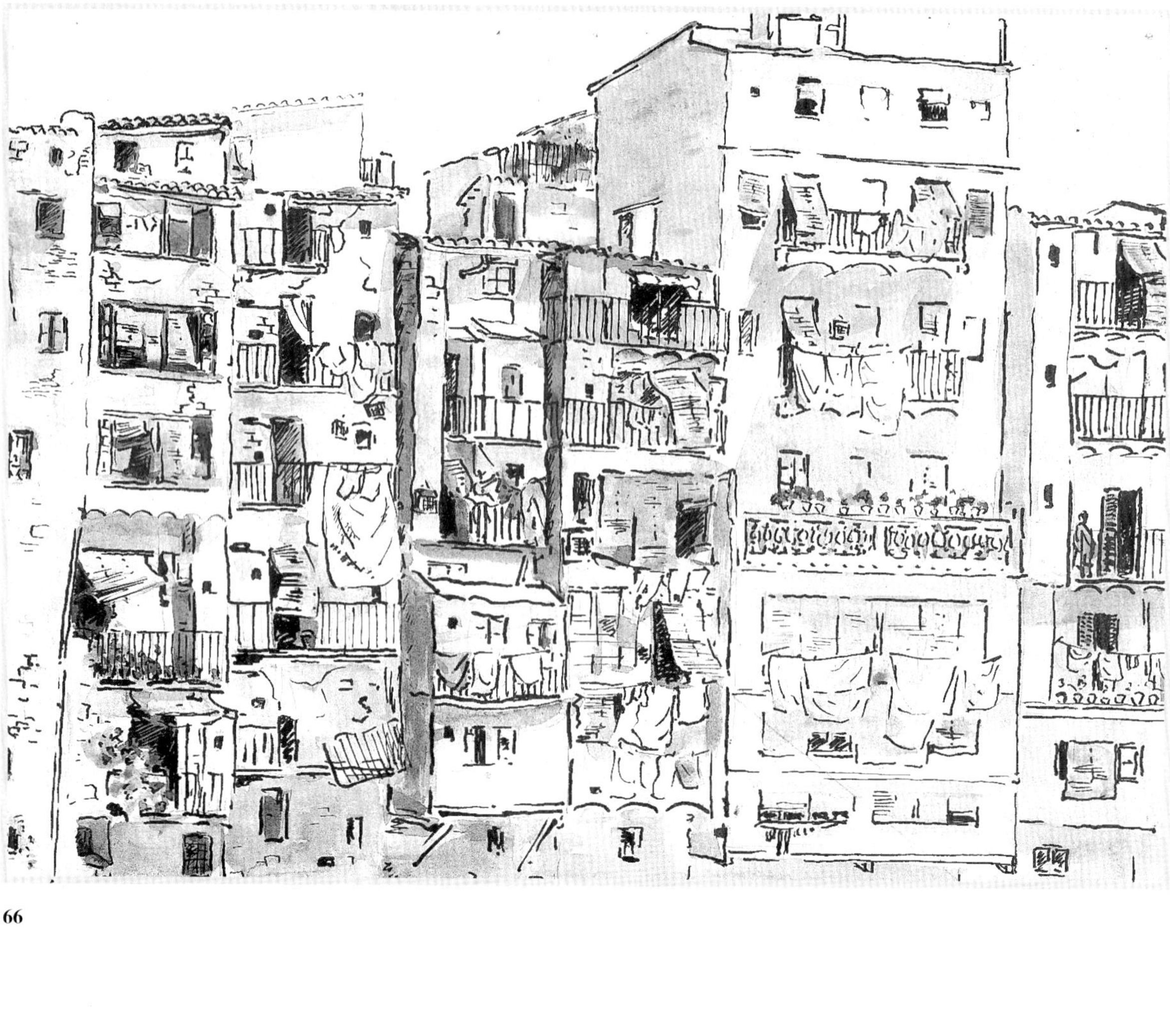

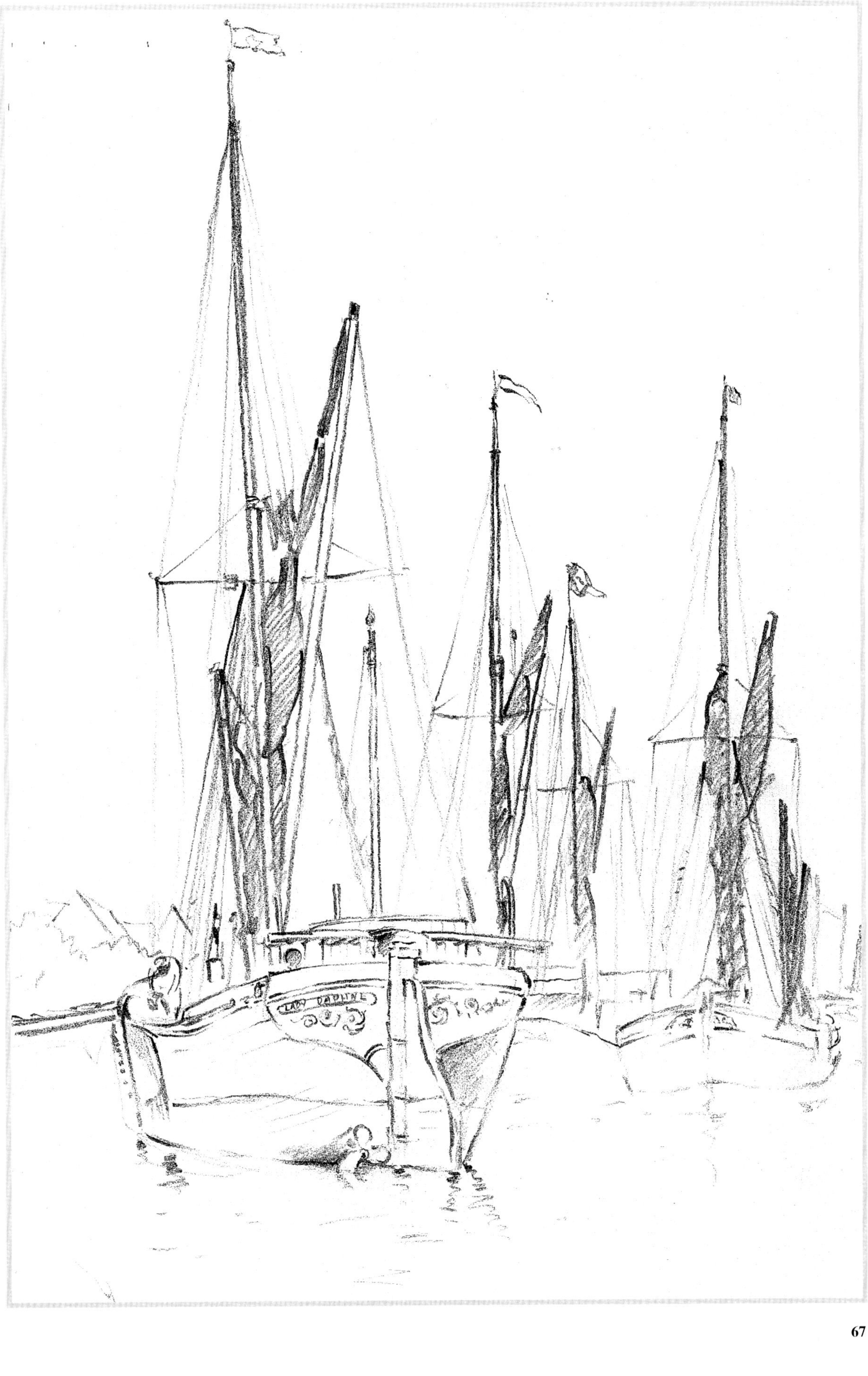
LADY DAPHNE

The Ernest Knight African Collection
Lusaka Northern Rhodesia 1954

In 1954 Kit was working as Physiotherapist-in-charge at Lusaka Hospital. The African patients came from many different backgrounds - domestic workers, farm labourers, clerks and some teachers. The schools in the villages were usually Mission schools so that the teaching had a strong Christian background. The long-term patients at the hospital were men and youths who suffered from poliomyelitis or tuberculosis and might spend months or years in hospital.

Ernest asked the management if he could introduce painting into the wards and the idea was greeted with enthusiasm: the Government would supply paints, paper and brushes. Africans are renowned for their skilled and imaginative stonecarving and woodcarving, but apart from cave painting and the decoration of village huts there was no tradition of painting among the local people. This was partly due to lack of materials but also because termites destroyed paper. Some who lived in the Bush had never seen a painting.

Many of the patients painted in their beds and Ernest helped them. He would not impose Western ideas on them but encouraged them to use imagination and memory to tell their stories pictorially, which they did.

No subject matter was suggested so the paintings were diverse in content; those with a Biblical subject were translated into unique unsophisticated illustrations. Ernest was able to draw out natural talent and some of the patients became so absorbed in their artwork that they painted all day.

The benefit of these classes was very great. One patient who was not expected to recover from tuberculosis was shown by X-rays to be clear of the disease. He was given a job at the hospital and continued to paint in his spare time. He earned extra money by selling his paintings. Other patients also benefited because many paintings were framed and hung on the hospital walls, cheering up the rather gloomy wards.

A collection of sixty of the paintings was exhibited by the Commonwealth Institute in London, Vienna, Canada and the provinces of the United Kingdom.

Ernest gave guidance, not teaching, and the result is a collection of extremely individual art.. The landscapes are full of happenings: tribal customs are illustrated, giving an insight into rural life in Northern Rhodesia in the 1950's. Dramatic incidents are recorded as in Martin Secondes 'Swarm of Red Locusts' and H.M. Chiyanas 'Man Attacked by Lion'.

Although the Africans lived near the big mines of the Copperbelt, one patient illustrated the early methods of smelting copper and other metals in the bush in Northern Rhodesia. He gave a written explanation of the method of smelting on the reverse of the painting.

Some of the figures in the paintings have goitre - a common complaint at that time amongst the indigenous population .

Painting was a new adventure for these artists, who showed a remarkable ability for story telling with a natural simplicity and an innate sense of colour and design. Ernest led them wisely, allowing them to express themselves by his encouragement.

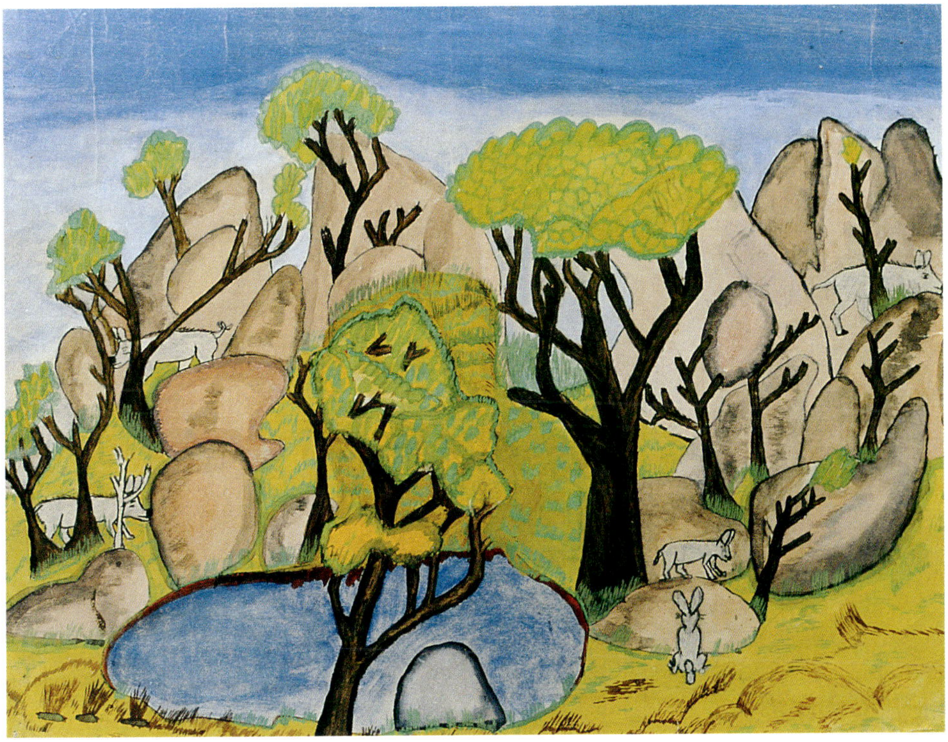

Kululu. Isaac Banda. Powder paint on paper. 63 cm x 51 cm. Plate 60.

Kululu is the 'little white hare' and is part of African folklore. Always sly and successful, he kept the hyenas at bay. The story was taken to America two hundred years ago by slaves and reappeared as Brer Rabbit.

Isaac Banda was an orderly at Ndola Hospital before he became ill with poliomyelitis. He was one of the few African patients who asked Ernest about perspective and he developed his own interpretation, which shows in Kululu.

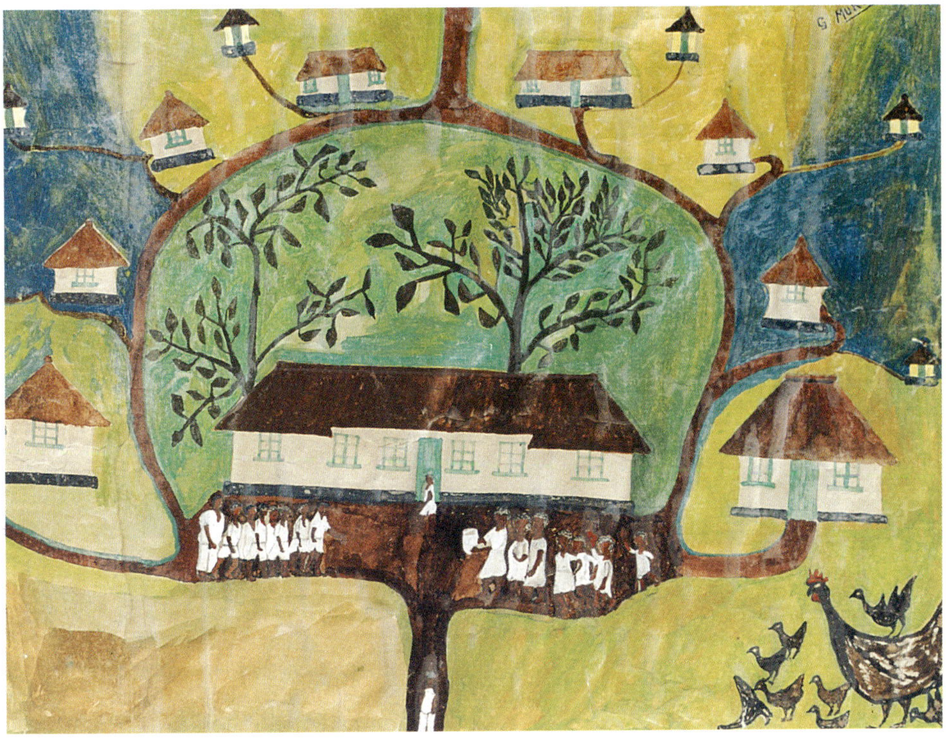

Tonga Village. Powder paint on paper. Plate 61.

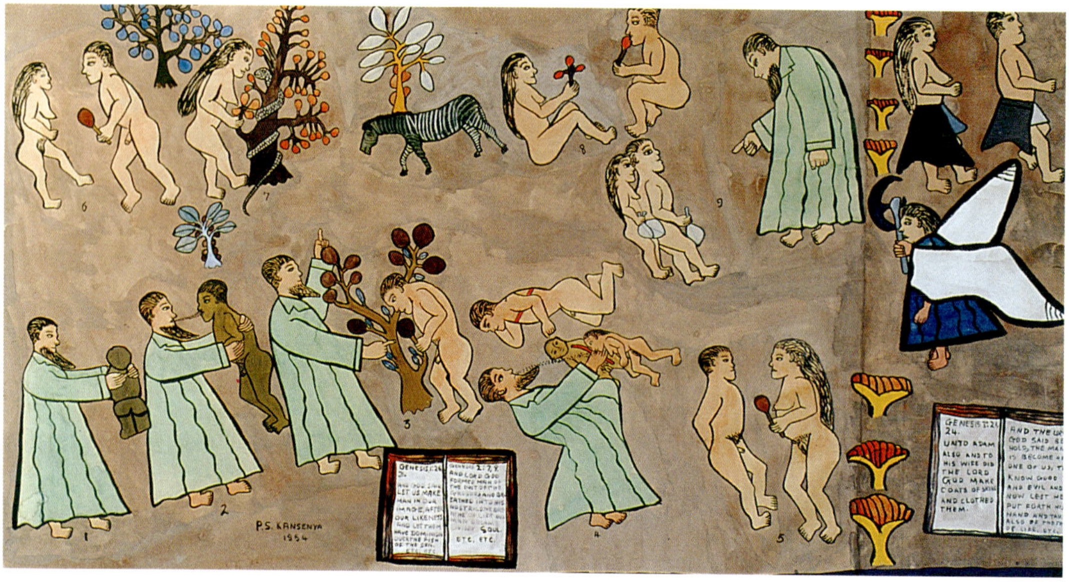

Creation Peter Kansenya (1954). Powder paint on paper. 76 cm x 54 cm. Plate 62.

Peter Kansenya paints the Christian story of Creation in an unconventional way, overlapping his Christian Mission education and the tribal belief in witchdoctors. Both religions rely on an unseen force which is symbolised in this painting by spirit 'dots'.

The story begins at the lower left-hand corner of the painting. God, in a green robe, makes a clay figure from the earth and breathes his Spirit into it, thus creating man. The Spirit is again seen in No. 3 when God takes Adam's rib to create Eve. The trees and leaves are wild fig and the tree of knowledge is abundant with fruit. The creation of animals is represented by a solitary zebra.

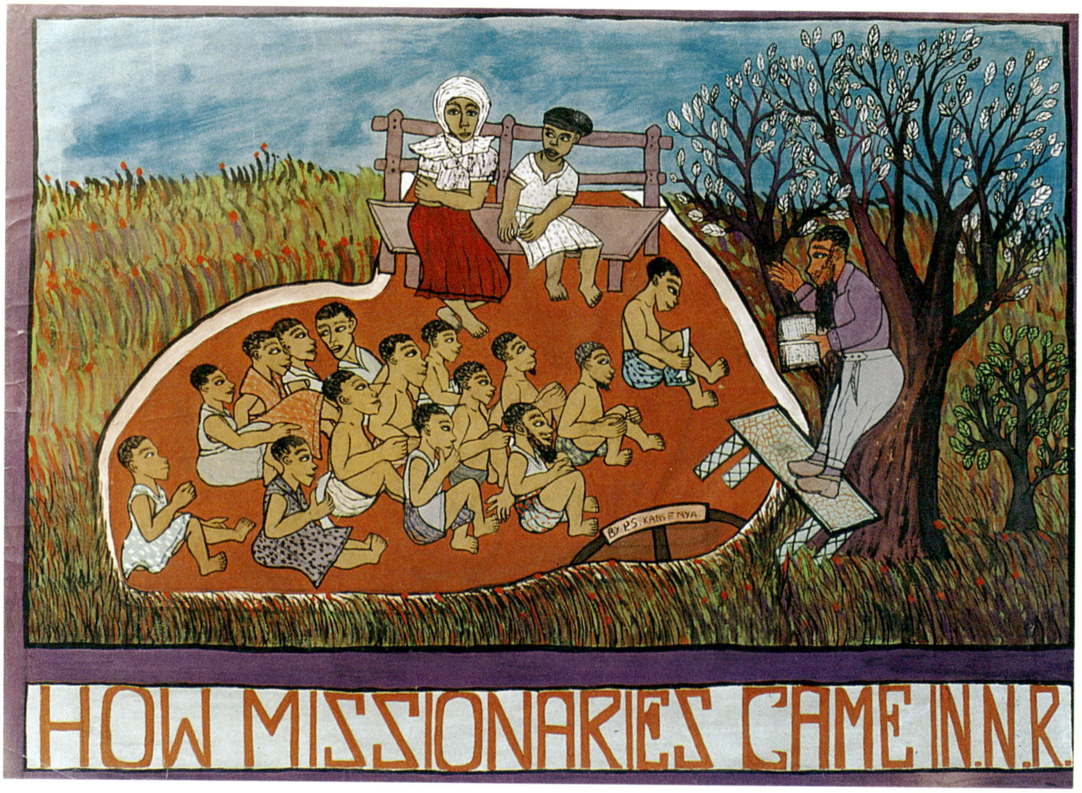

How the Missionaries came to Northern Rhodesia Peter Kansenya.
Powder paint on paper. 77 cm x 56 cm. Plate 63.

This is unsophisticated decorative story telling. Over generations the tribal stories had been recounted verbally, now this important influence is being recorded pictorially, simply and vividly.

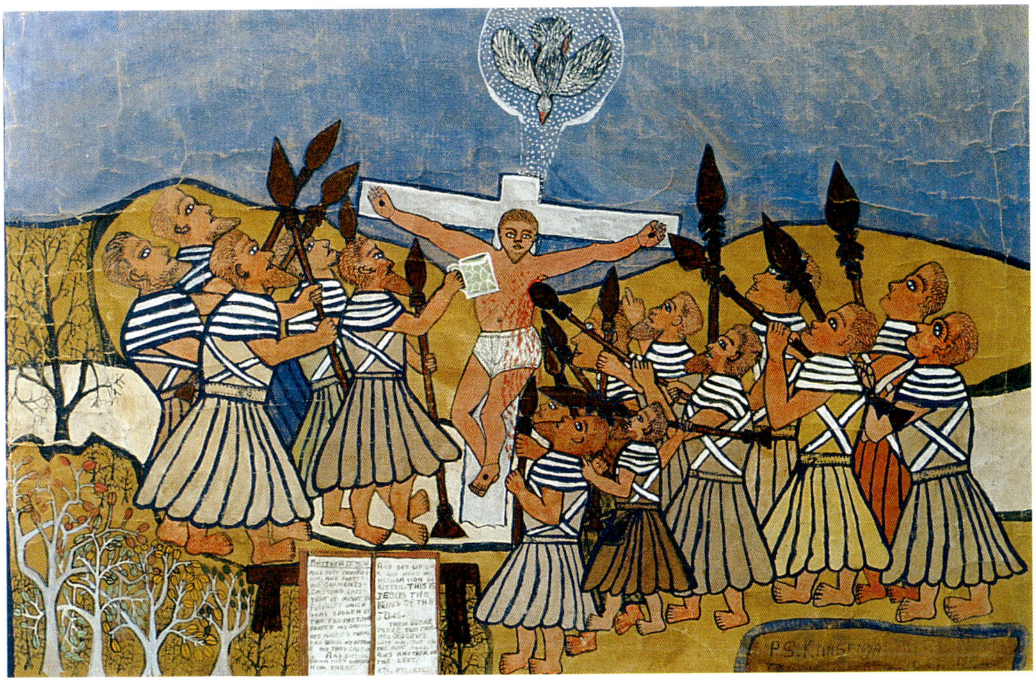

The Crucifixion Peter Kansenya. Poster paint on paper. 77 cm x 56 cm. Plate 64.

Peter Kansenya was a district messenger at Lusaka. His paintings fell into two groups: stories from the Bible and stories of tribal life and customs. In the Crucifixion he paints the soldiers in western clothing but God is represented symbolically by a dove, which is surrounded by the 'dots' of the Spirit, as in his witchcraft paintings. He was asked why, in his paintings of The Temptation (not illustrated) he had made our Lord smaller than Satan. He explained this was because our Lord was feeling humble but Satan was full of pride.

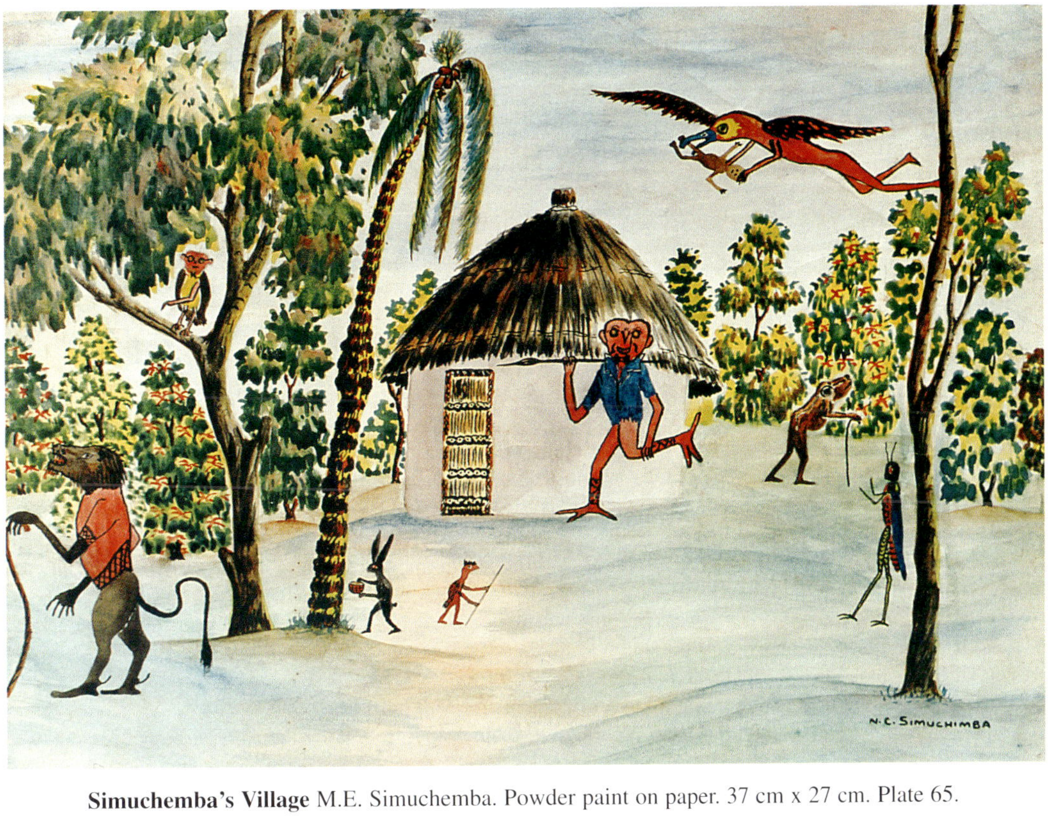

Simuchemba's Village M.E. Simuchemba. Powder paint on paper. 37 cm x 27 cm. Plate 65.

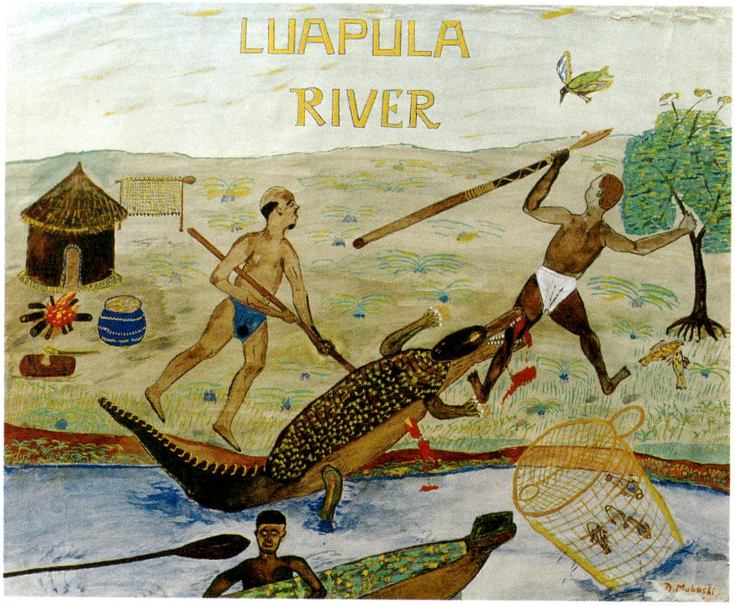

Luapala River, N. Rhodesia. D. Mukoshi. 61 cm x 52 cm. Plate 66.

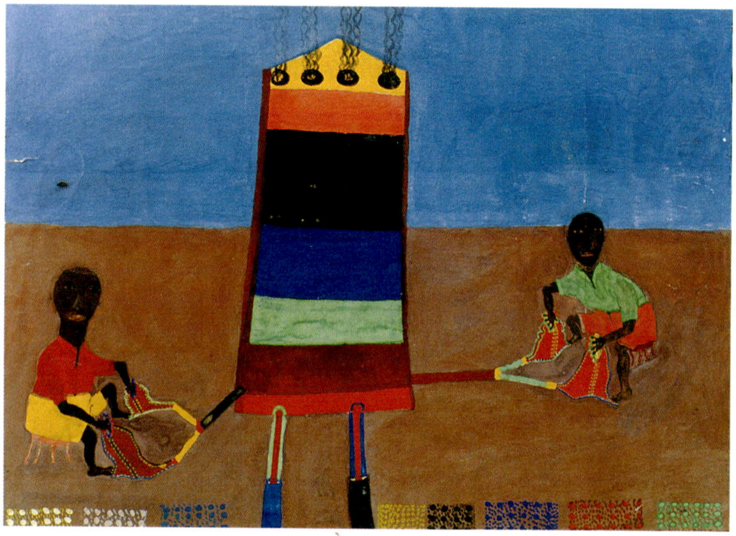

African Smelter. Poster paint on paper. 49 cm x 36 cm. Plate 67.

This description of metal smelting was written on the reverse side of the painting. (sic)

1. Something standing between the picture is a smelter.
2. Let us start from the bottom of smelter.
   (a) You see first space decorated in red colour - it is red because of kept on burning so long time.
   (b) Second space in dark brown. They used on putting small stones of different colour as shown under.
   (c) Third and fourth spaces kept on putting other kinds of stones.
   (d) Fifth part used for charcoal.
   (e) Sixth part used for other-colour stone (because they did not know which colour of stones will give iron or metal. That is why they were mixing).
   (f) Seventh part used for soda. They were burning waste things left from millet ashes put on something and put on pull on water. Water from ashes is pulled on to let these burn soon.
   (g) You will see smoke from inside and wall.

A man is sitting on stool holding air tub pumping to let things in and wall burn.
They keep pumping all day until something starts coming out red in colour, following the path into a pot put ready.
When it is cool they take out mud and iron remains or metal.
Under you will see stones, charcoal, ashes etc. used.

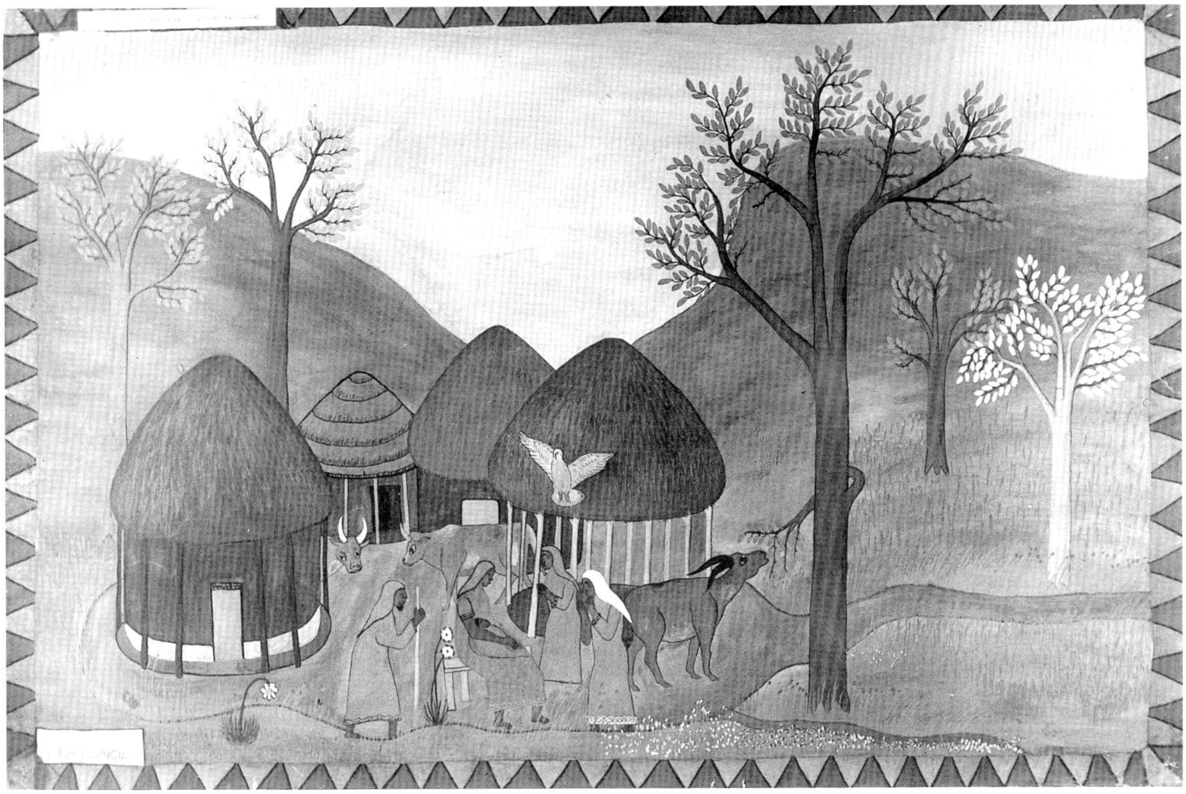

The Nativity. Samuel Katilunga. Poster paint on paper.

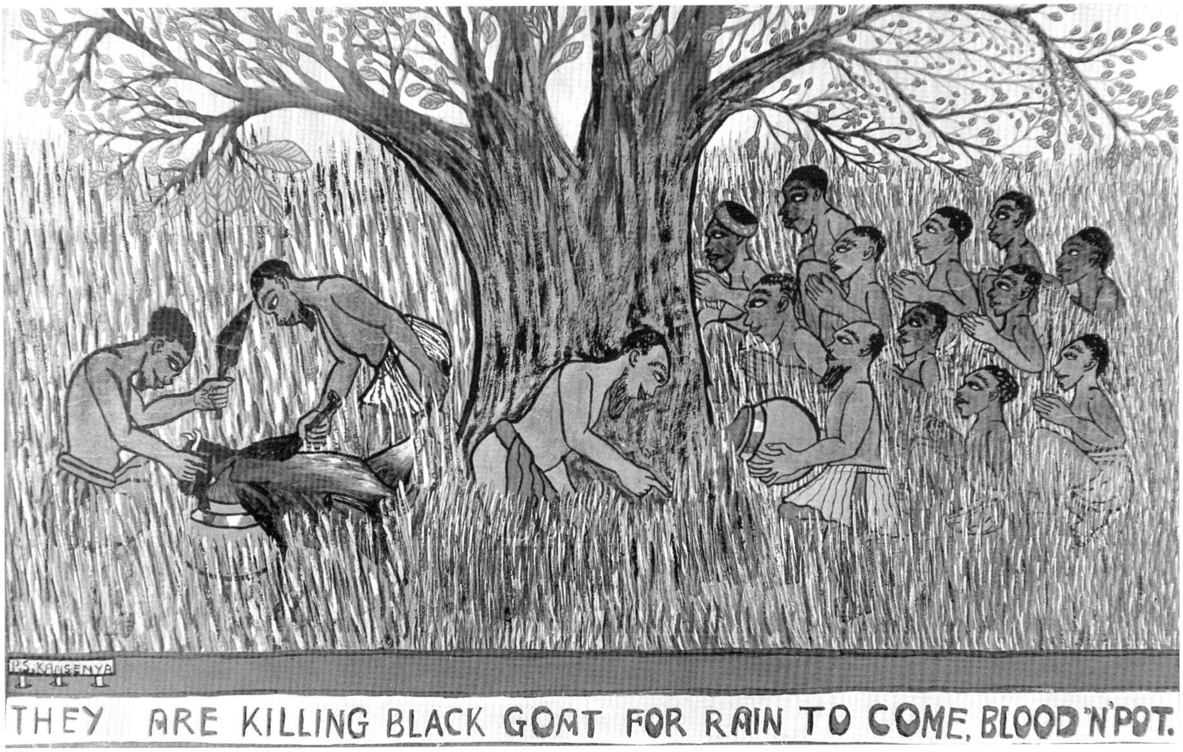

Rainmaking. Peter Kansenya.

This is a painting of a Tonga custom in times of drought. A goat is killed and its blood is drained into pots and then poured around the roots of a sacred wild fig tree. While this is done the villagers chant and clap.

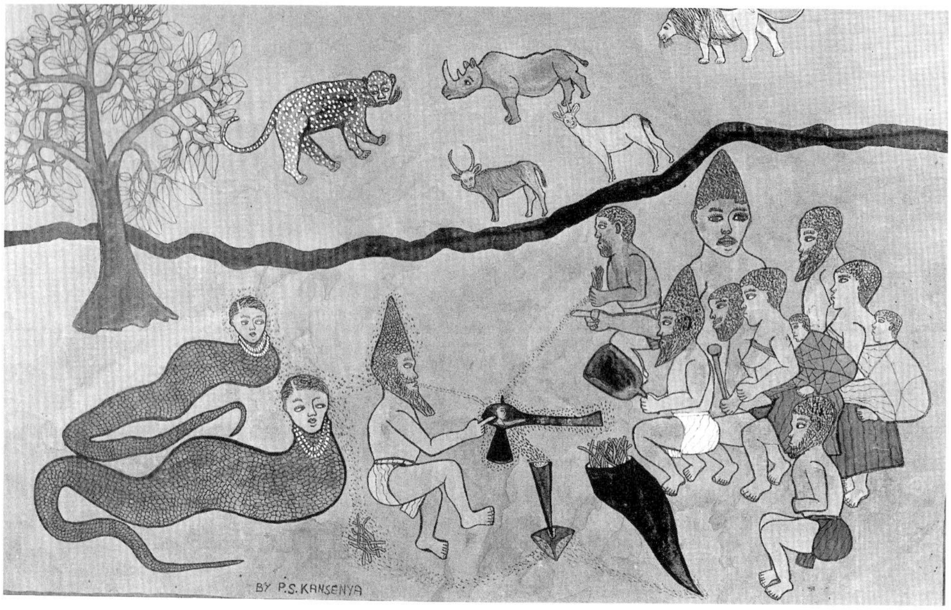

Witchdoctor At Work. Peter Kansenya.

Africans are reluctant to speak of their tribal customs but Peter Kansenya was able to describe pictorially the way in which a witch-doctor seeks out a 'culprit'. The witch-doctor is surrounded by his artefacts and behind him are two 'Ilomba' or human headed snakes. The Ilomba is a familiar of the witch-doctor and is created by him, sharing his identity. To create an Ilomba a sorcerer will come in the night and bring a concoction of medicines and put them into a pot with the tooth of a snake. After a few days a maggot will appear and will develop into a snake with a human head. Some Ilomba feed on a victim's shadow to drain his strength.

None of the witch-doctor's objects in the painting can be seen by others as they are surrounded by the spirit dots. The magic dots emanate from the witch-doctor and his Ilomba through the horn of medicine and then to the 'culprit', who knows he is doomed. The axe would belong to the client who wants the wrongdoer identified. The cone of hair of the witch-doctor identifies him as being of the Ila tribe.

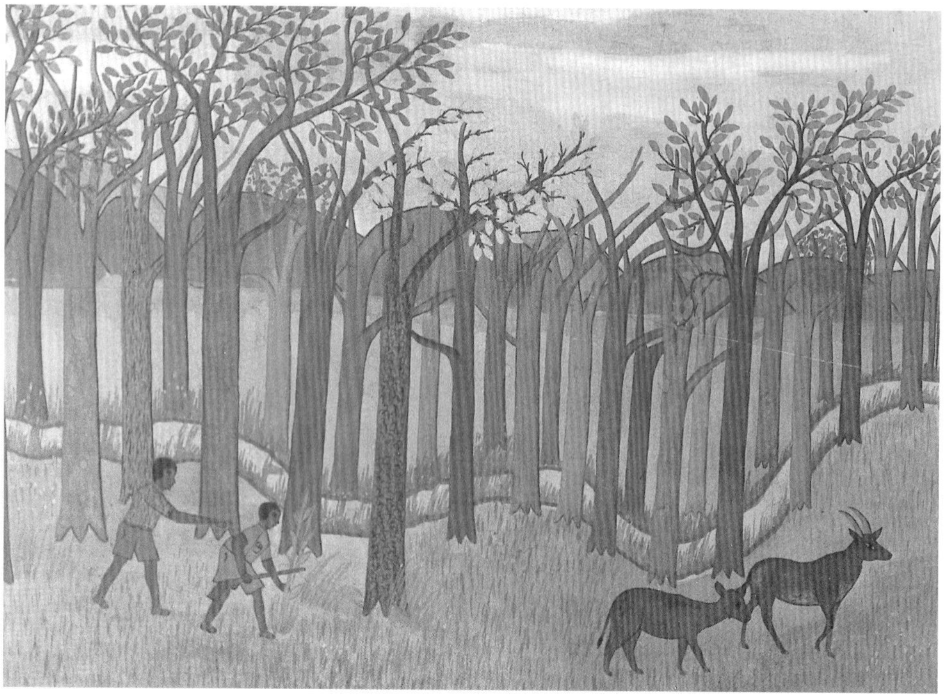

The Hunters. Samuel Katilunga. Poster paint on paper.

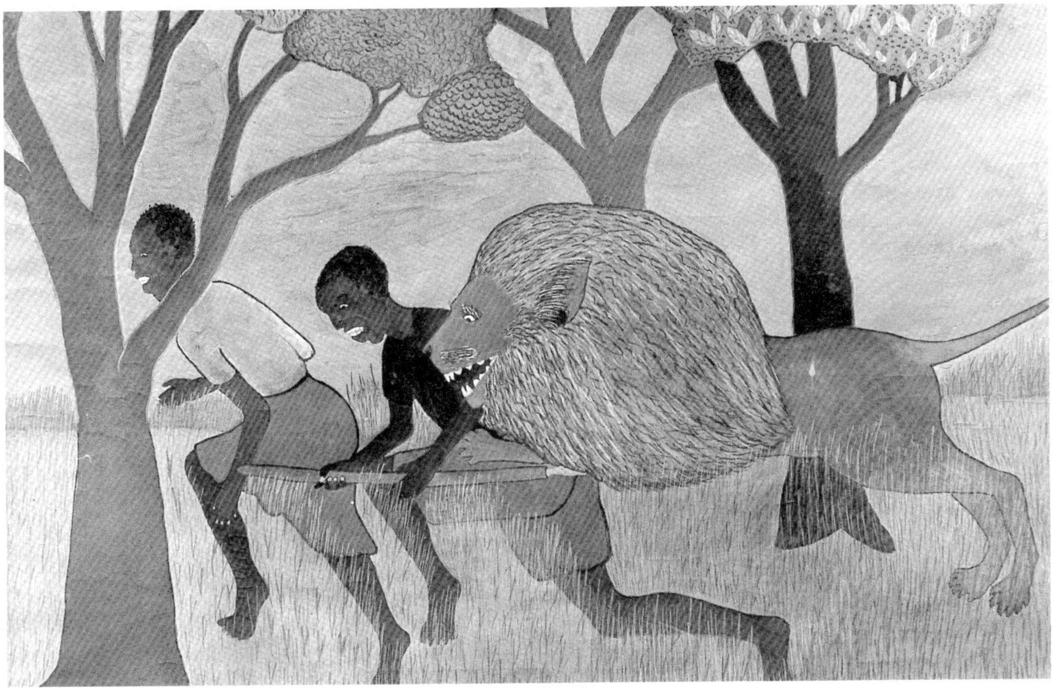

Man Chased by Lion. H.M. Chiyana. Poster paint on paper.

Chiyana came from a village on the border between the Belgian Congo and Northern Rhodesia. He has shown the power of the lion and the fear of the men and although this painting is more realistic than others he has retained the intuitive decorative element.

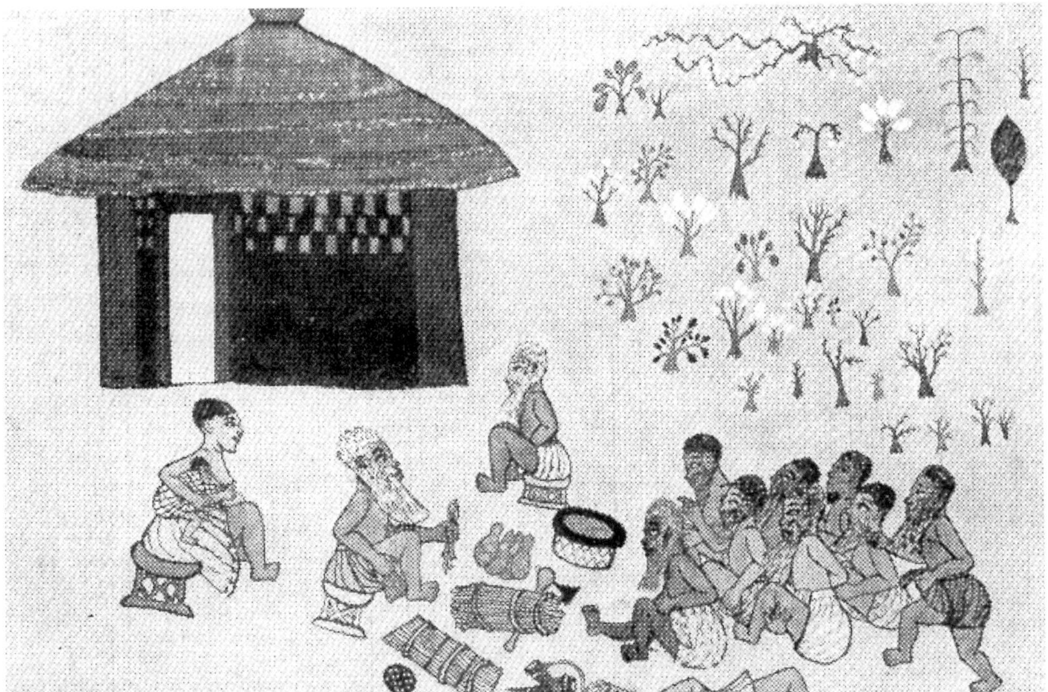

Witchdoctor. Peter Kansenya. Powder paint on paper.

"In a village many people were dying and it was thought that they were killed by one of their tribe. They go to an old witchdoctor who had two horns and he made each person hold them in turn. When the guilty one took hold of them he fell down and died.

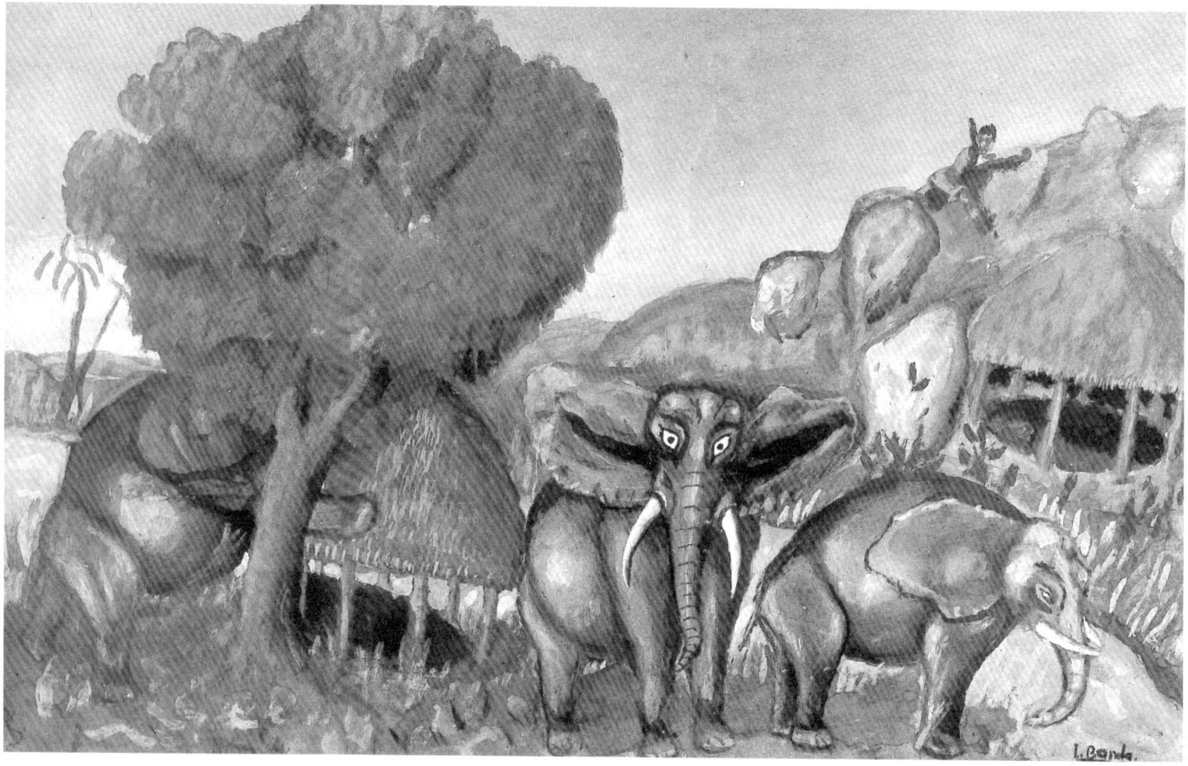

Elephant Raiding a Village Grainstore. Isaac Banda. Poster paint on paper.

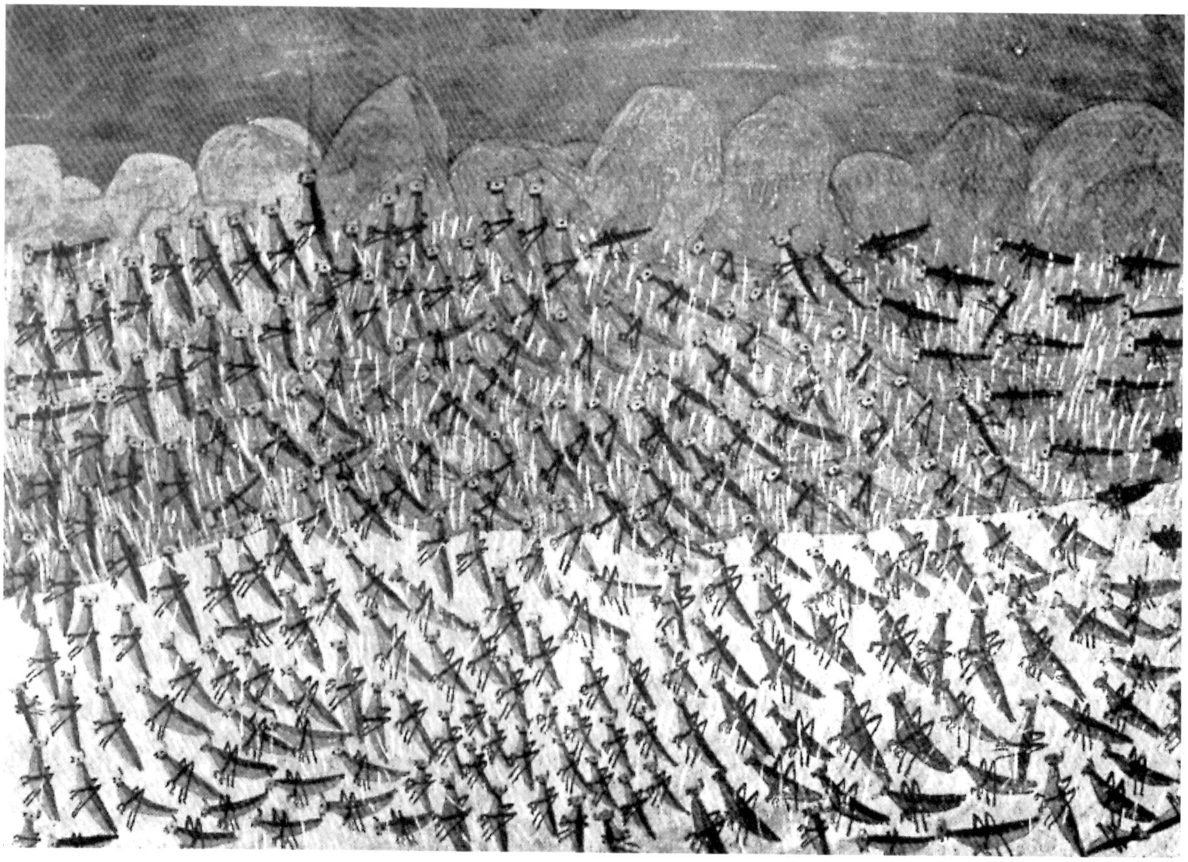

Swarm of Red Locusts. Martin Seconda.

Martin Seconda lived on the edge of Lake Tanganyika near to the International Red Locust Control Area. His painting shows, with the delicacy of lace, the dramatic devastation the locust swarms can cause.

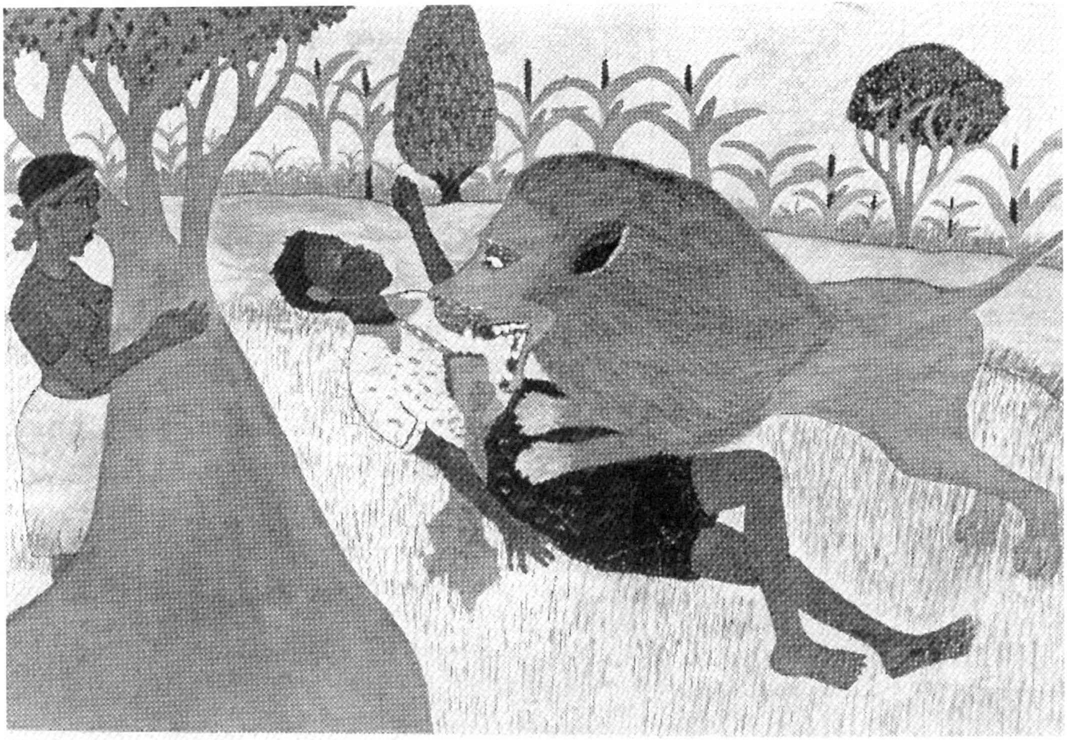

Man Attacked by Lion. H.M. Chiyana.

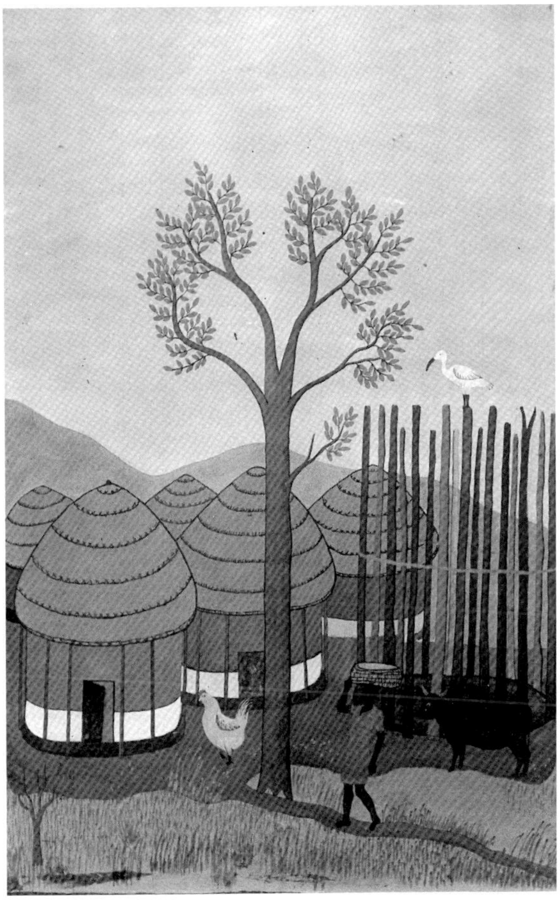

The Village. Samuel Katilungu. Poster paint on paper.

The cattle kraal is a typical construction and the bird on top is probably a stork.

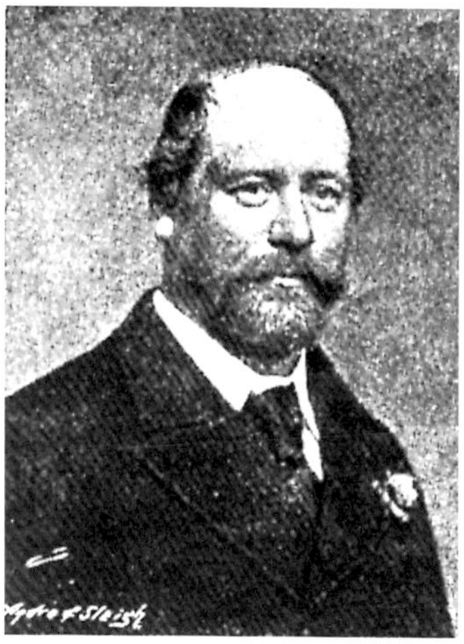

Ernest Griset
Victorian Artist and Illustrator 1843-1907

Ernest Griset was born in Boulogne, France but his family came to live in London when he was about nine years old. They lived near Regents Park and from an early age he studied and sketched the animals in the Zoo. The family also kept many small animals in the home. He was fluent in French and English, which stood him in good stead when he studied art under Lois Gallant, a Belgian painter. He became familiar at this time with the French and English caricaturists, who appealed to his innate sense of humour.

Back in London he sketched and painted prolifically and he sold his pen and ink sketches and watercolour paintings from a small bookshop in Leicester Square. His work was noticed by publishers and soon he was producing comical drawings for Punch, Boys Own Paper, Little Folks and many others.

In 1859 Darwin had published 'The Origin of Species'. The book had caused much controversy; Griset was influenced by this and his illustrations became anthropomorphic. He enjoyed drawing animals but not people and by his clever observations he made his unusual collection of humorous caricatures.

Griset was a prolific illustrator but alongside this were serious paintings of animals and birds, especially stork and eagles. He had several commissions to illustrate books, including Aesop's Fables.

In the early 1870's Griset married Laura Foley. They had several children and in order to maintain this large family and because of increasing competition from other illustrators, he was under great pressure. He never refused a commission, even if he was not interested in it, and he increased his output and illustrated copious children's magazines and annuals.

Griset was described as a caricaturist of the highest richest order and his work was imaginative and fun. An Exhibition of his work was held at the Victoria and Albert Museum, where several of his paintings and illustrations are held. He died in Highgate on 27 March 1907. His daughter Florence Annabella married Herbert Knight and they had two children, Ernest and Isabella. Ernest inherited his grandfather's gift of humour and his skill as an artist.

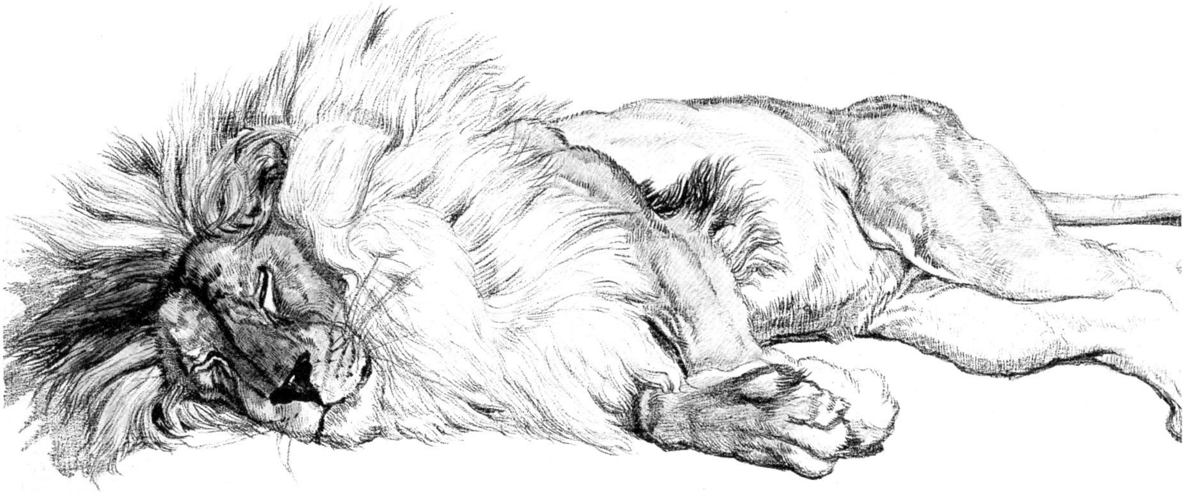

Nubian Lion Ernest Griset.

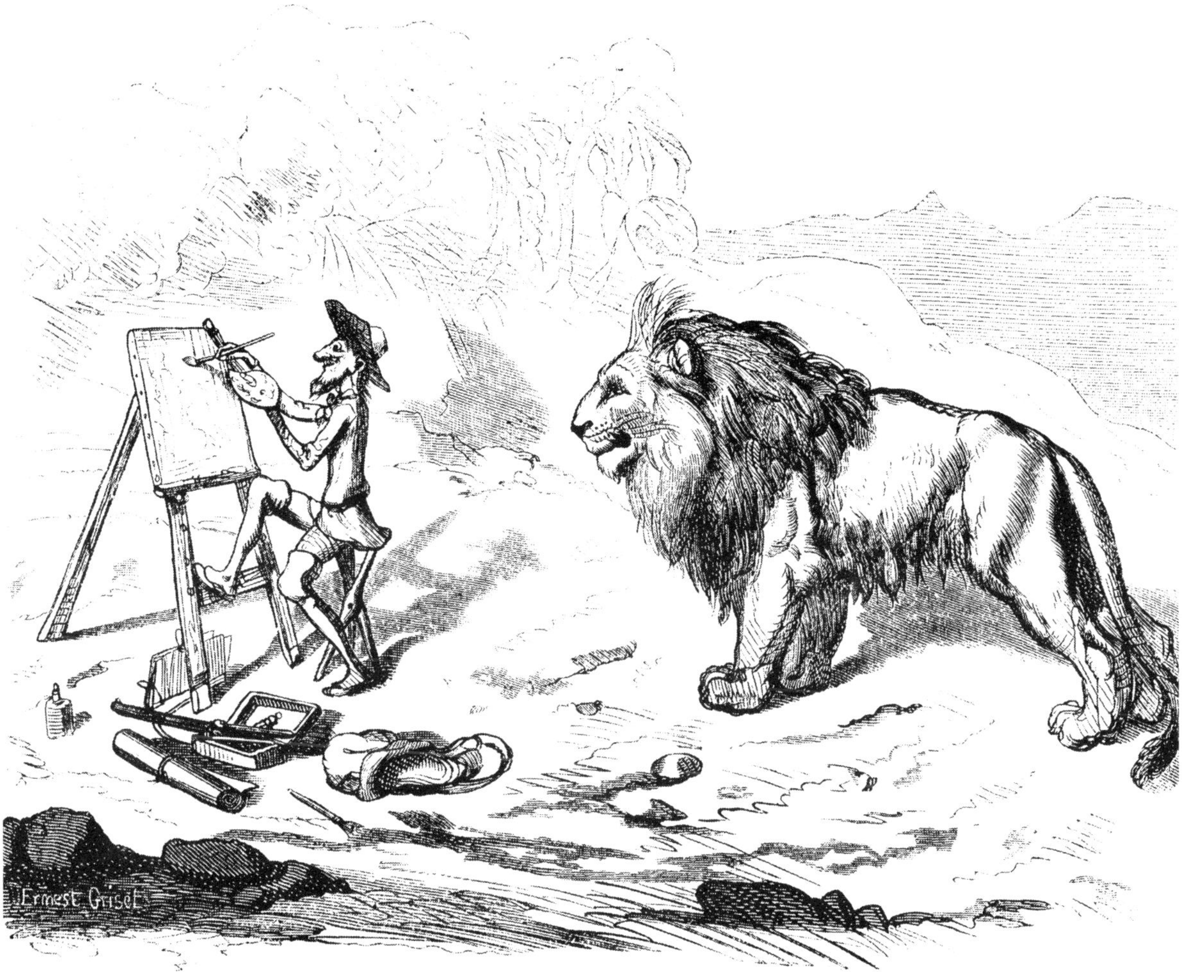

The Artist and Onlooker Ernest Griset

The Theatre of Nature

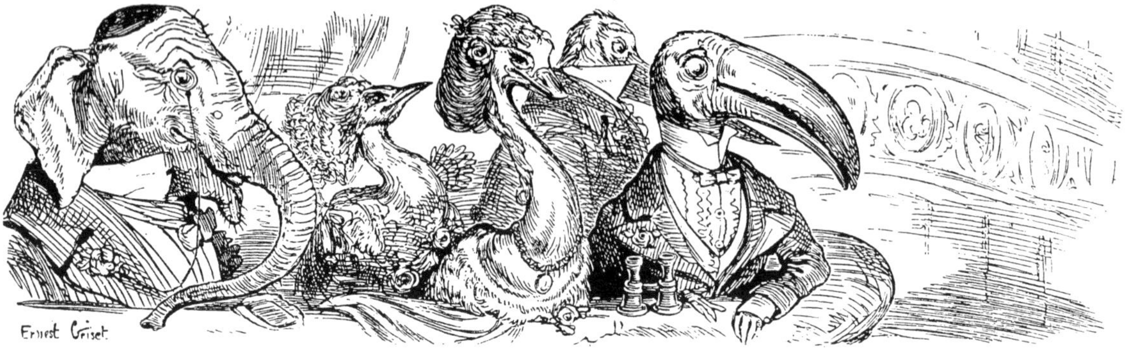

BOXES

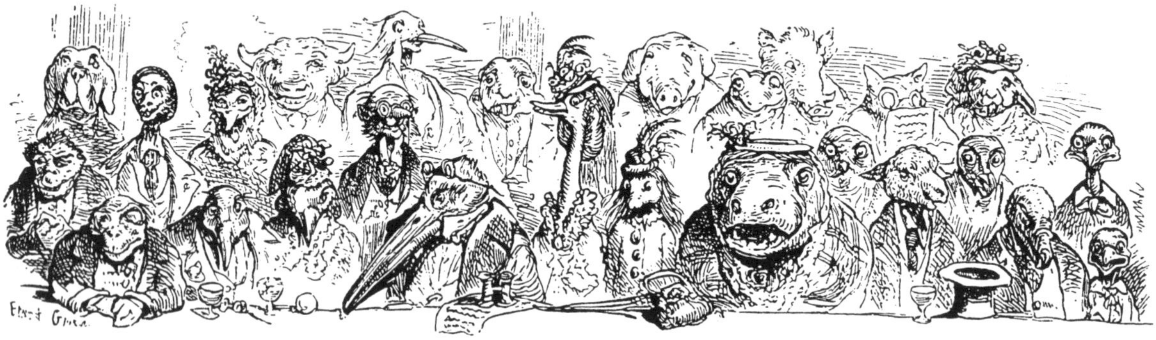

PIT

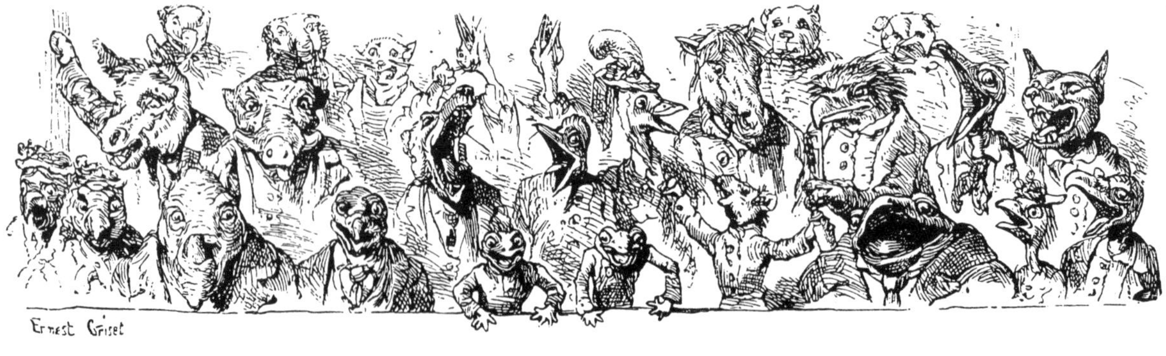

GALLERY

The Theatre of Nature Ernest Griset

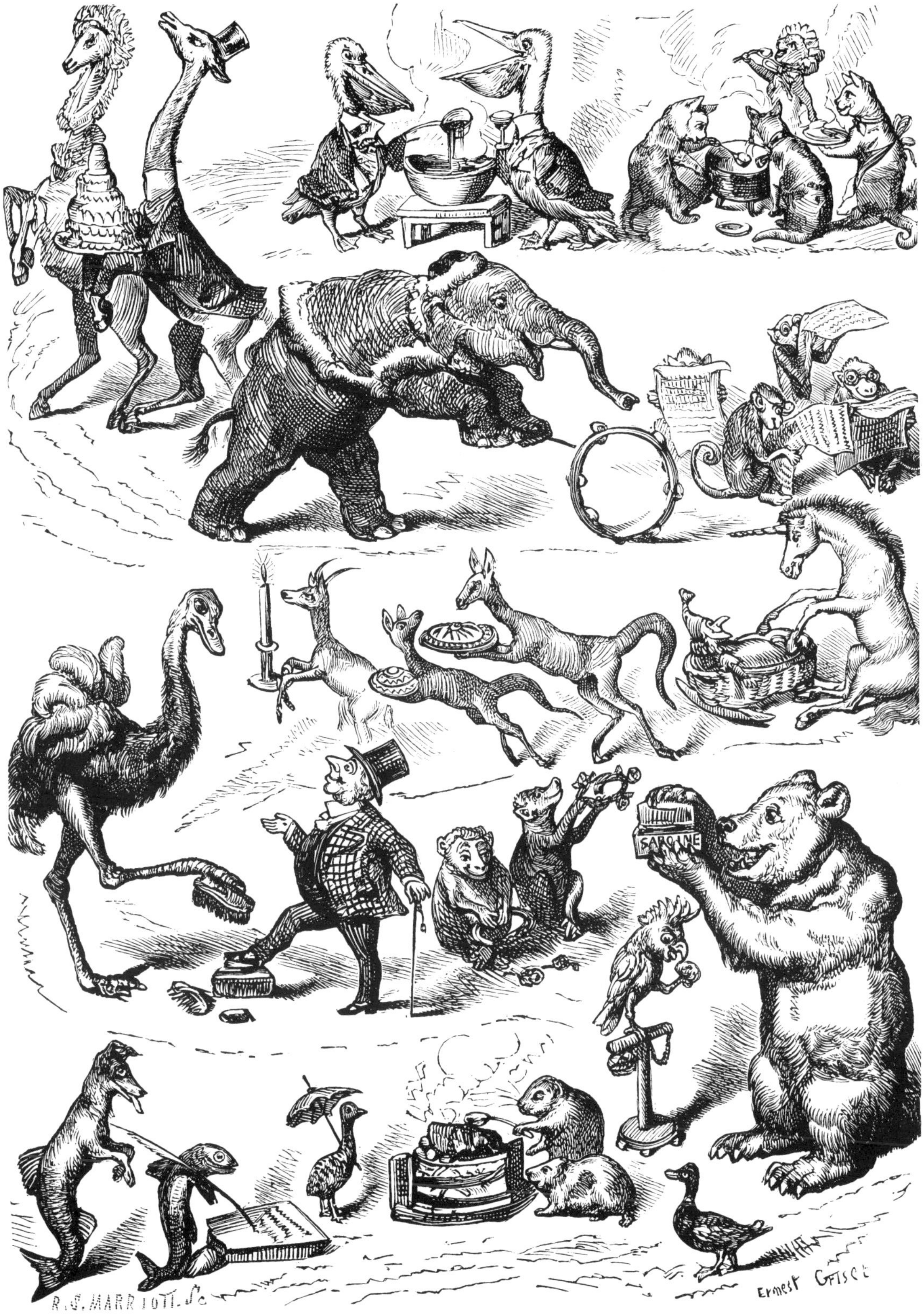

A Page of Improbables. Little Folks 1871. Ernest Griset

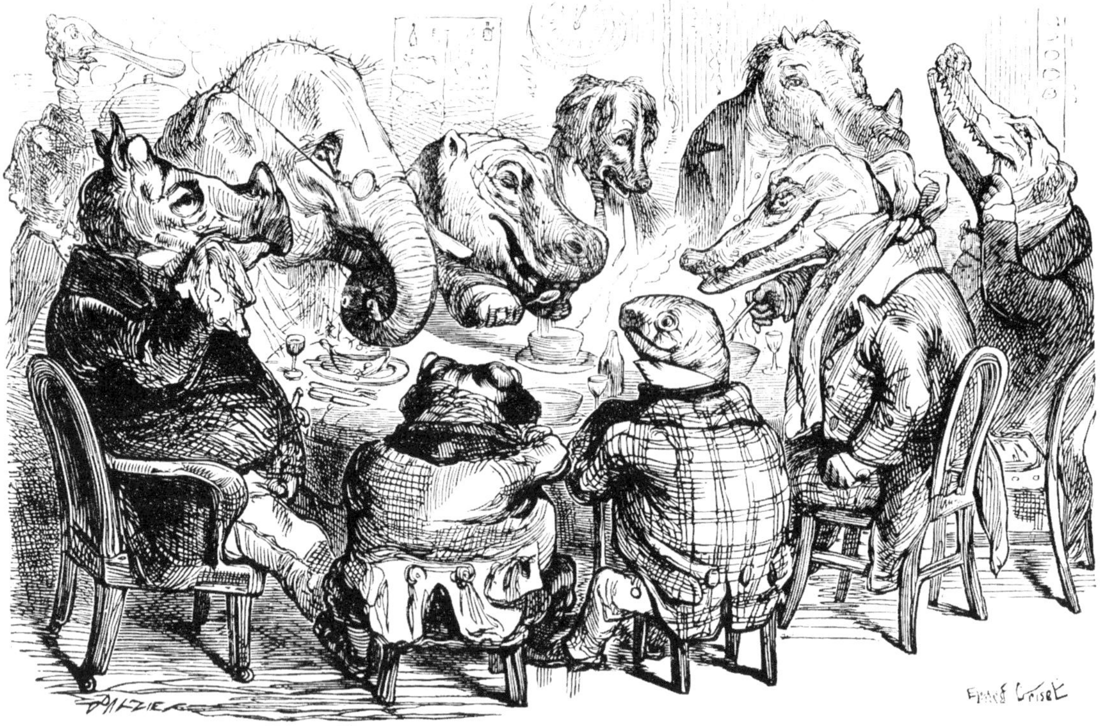

'A Lord Mayor's Dinner? O dear, no. You would not insinuate that anybody makes a beast of himself there!'
Ernest Griset

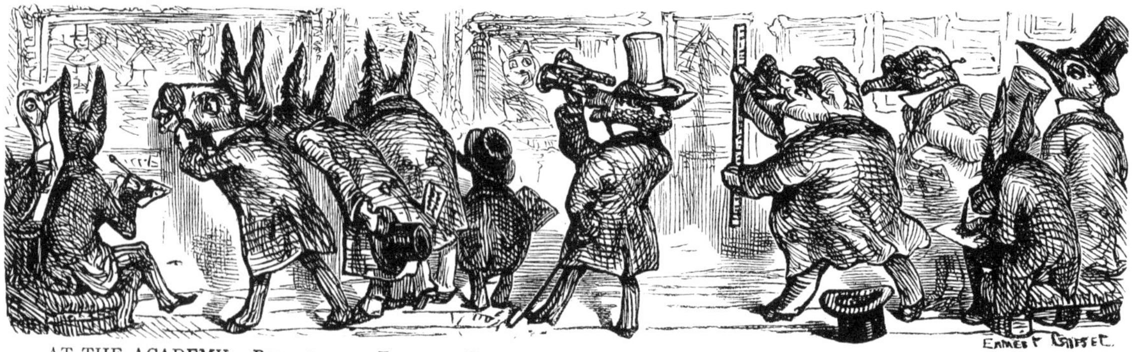

AT THE ACADEMY.—PORTRAITS OF EMINENT CRITICS.—"Only a moment to stop. Ten columns of criticism to do to-day!"

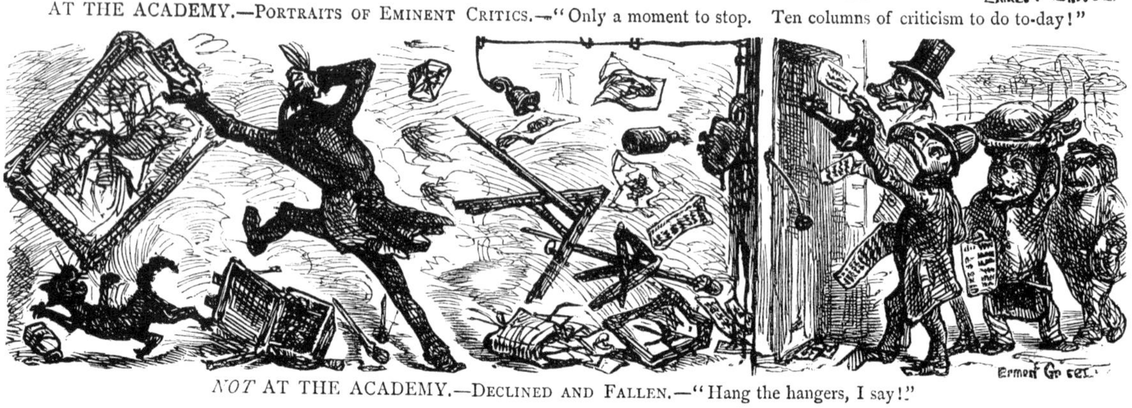

NOT AT THE ACADEMY.—DECLINED AND FALLEN.—"Hang the hangers, I say!"

Fun Almanac. Ernest Griset

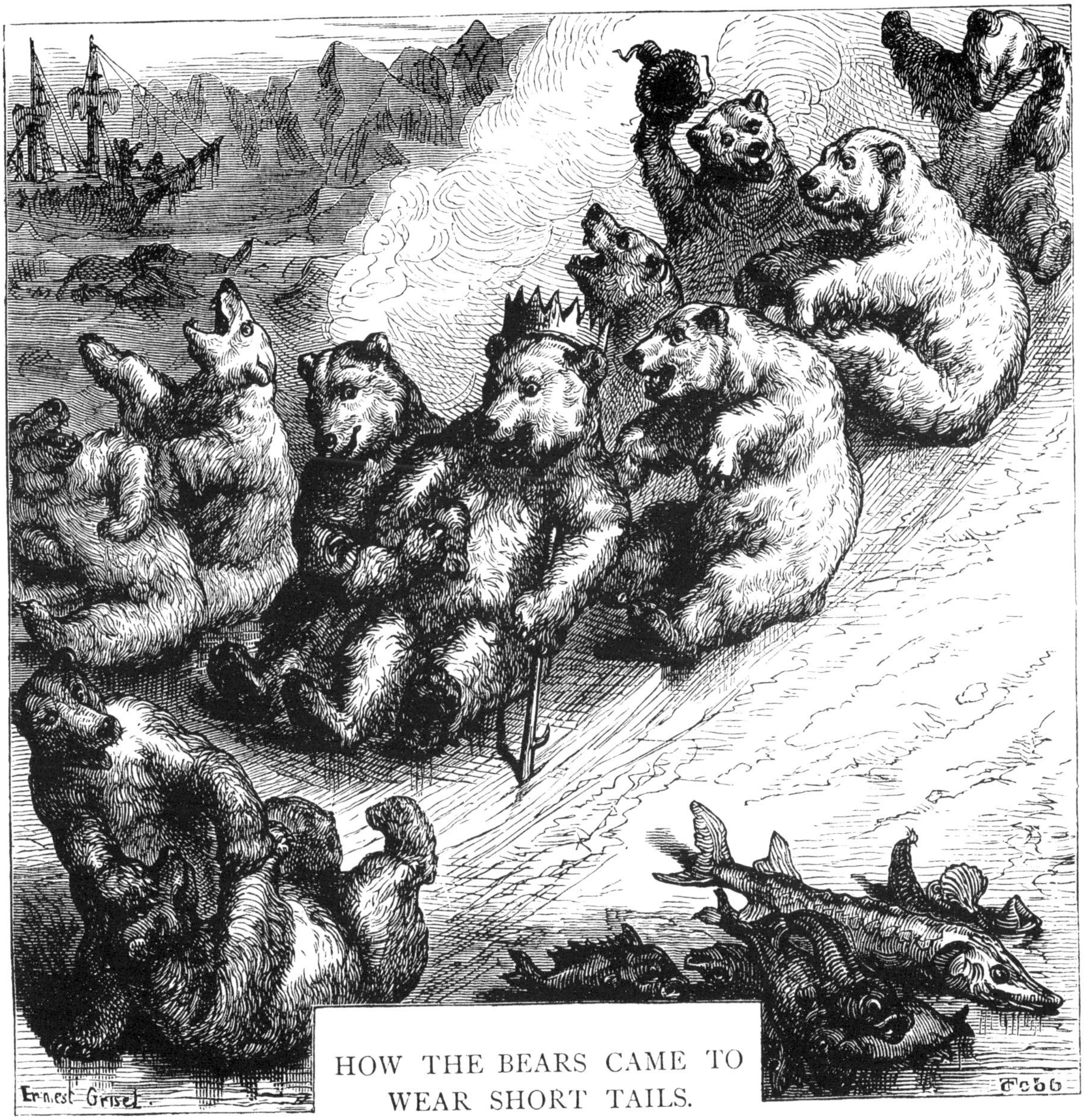

Little Folks 1872. Ernest Griset

THE ANIMALS' BALL.

REPORTED BY THE MARCH HARE.

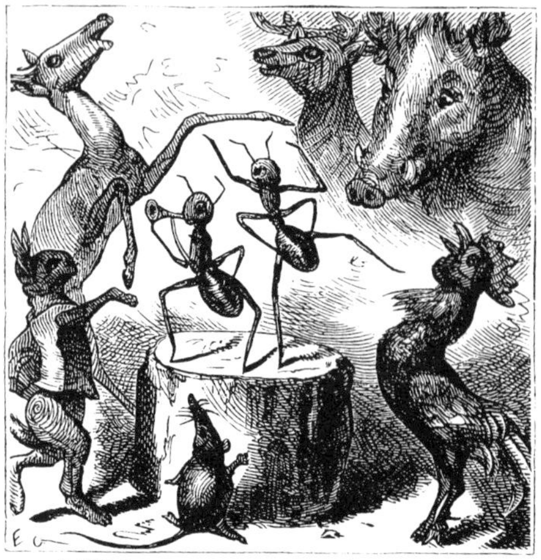

"'WE'LL DANCE ALL NIGHT,'
CRIED THE ANTS WITH DELIGHT."

"WE'LL dance all night,"
Cried the ants, with delight.
"Pray tell me why?"
Inquired a fly.
"Because it's nice,"
Explained the mice.
"Oh, very well!"
Laughed the gazelle.
"Yes; but where?"
Demanded a hare.
"Somewhere near,"
Suggested the deer.
"Why not here?"
Crowed chanticleer.
"Yes, this will do,"
Said the kangaroo.

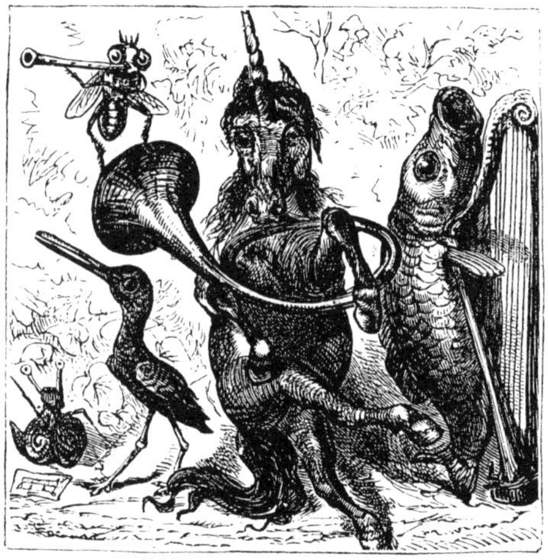

"'I'LL PLAY THE HORN,'
SAID THE UNICORN."

"I've lost my wig,"
Sobbed the pig.
"Give me a chain!"
Cried the crane.
"My shirt's too narrow,"
Complained a sparrow.
"What will you do?"
Sighed the kangaroo.
"None fine as I,"
Remarked the fly.

"Who will play
For us to-day?"
"I'll play the horn,"
Said the unicorn.
"Who will pipe?"
Asked the snipe.
"Why, I!"
'Said a fly
"And I'll play the harp,"
Added the carp.

"Let's be smart!"
Remarked the hart.
"Fetch our gloves,"
Cried the doves.
"And my glass,"
Brayed the ass.
"Where's my brooch?"
Howled the roach.
"Curl my back hair,"
Ordered the mare.
"Don't step on my tail!"
Pleaded the whale.
"Please take care!"
Begged the hare.
"Oh, my cravat!"
Screamed a gnat.

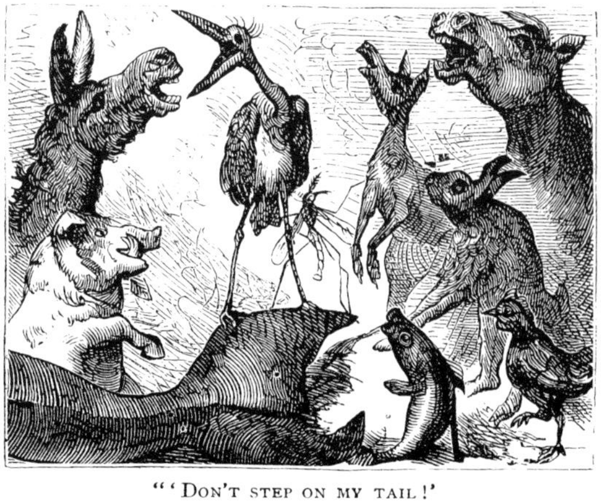

"'DON'T STEP ON MY TAIL!'
PLEADED THE WHALE."

"We are all ready now,"
Spoke out the cow.
"Then form a row,"
Said the buffalo.
"And now we'll dance,"
Again said the ants.
Then danced he cuckoo
With the kangaroo,
The cat with the rat,
The cow with the sow,
The dog with the hog,
The snail with the whale,

The Animals Ball, Little Folks Magazine. Ernest Griset

The wren with the hen,
The bear with the hare,
The lark with the shark,
The ram with the lamb,
The fox and the mare
Made the last pair.

" Now we will feast,"
Remarked a beast.
" Take an ice ! "
Begged the mice.
" Do drink this wine,"
Invited the swine.
" Not just now,"
Objected the sow.
" Let 's have some beer,"
Said the deer.

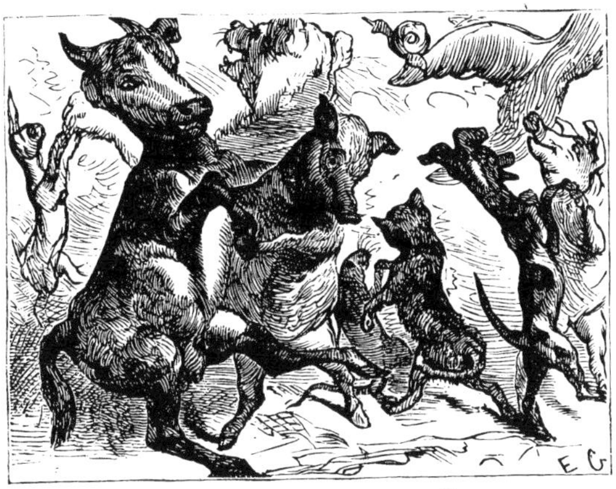

"THE COW WITH THE SOW."

" But I prefer cider,"
Whispered a spider.
" You must not think
So much about drink,"
Said the cow
With a bow ;
" It 's a bad habit,"
Shouted the rabbit.

At last the fly,
With a tear in his eye,
Gave his arm to the lark
And went off in the dark.

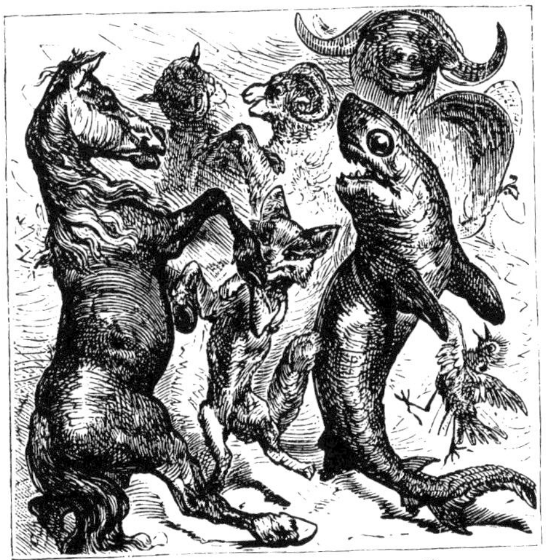

"THE LARK WITH THE SHARK."

Away in a trice
Scampered the mice.
Then the skate
Said, " 'Tis late."

" I must go now,"
Remarked the sow.
" It is too soon,"
Growled a baboon.
" Not a bit, not a bit,"
Chirped a little tom-tit.

And all the rest
Agreed it was best,
To say good-bye,
And homeward hie.

So the cow
Made her bow,
The rat donned his hat,
The whale fetched her veil ;
" Now, all farewell,"
Sighed the gazelle !
Farewell echoed all,
At the animals' ball.

Thus then it did end,
My dear little friend ;
And you may depend,
That if you are kind,
And gentle in mind,
And loving in word,
To both beast and bird,
When they next give a ball,

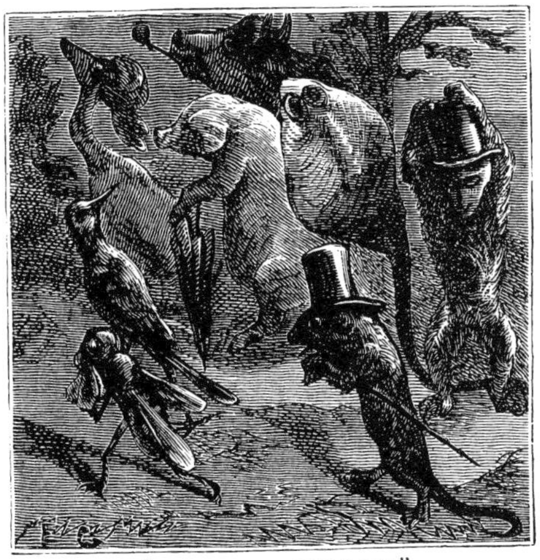

"WENT OFF IN THE DARK."

They 'll think of you all !
And send you (I say it without hesitation)
A carefully-worded polite invitation.

The Animals Ball, Little Folks Magazine.

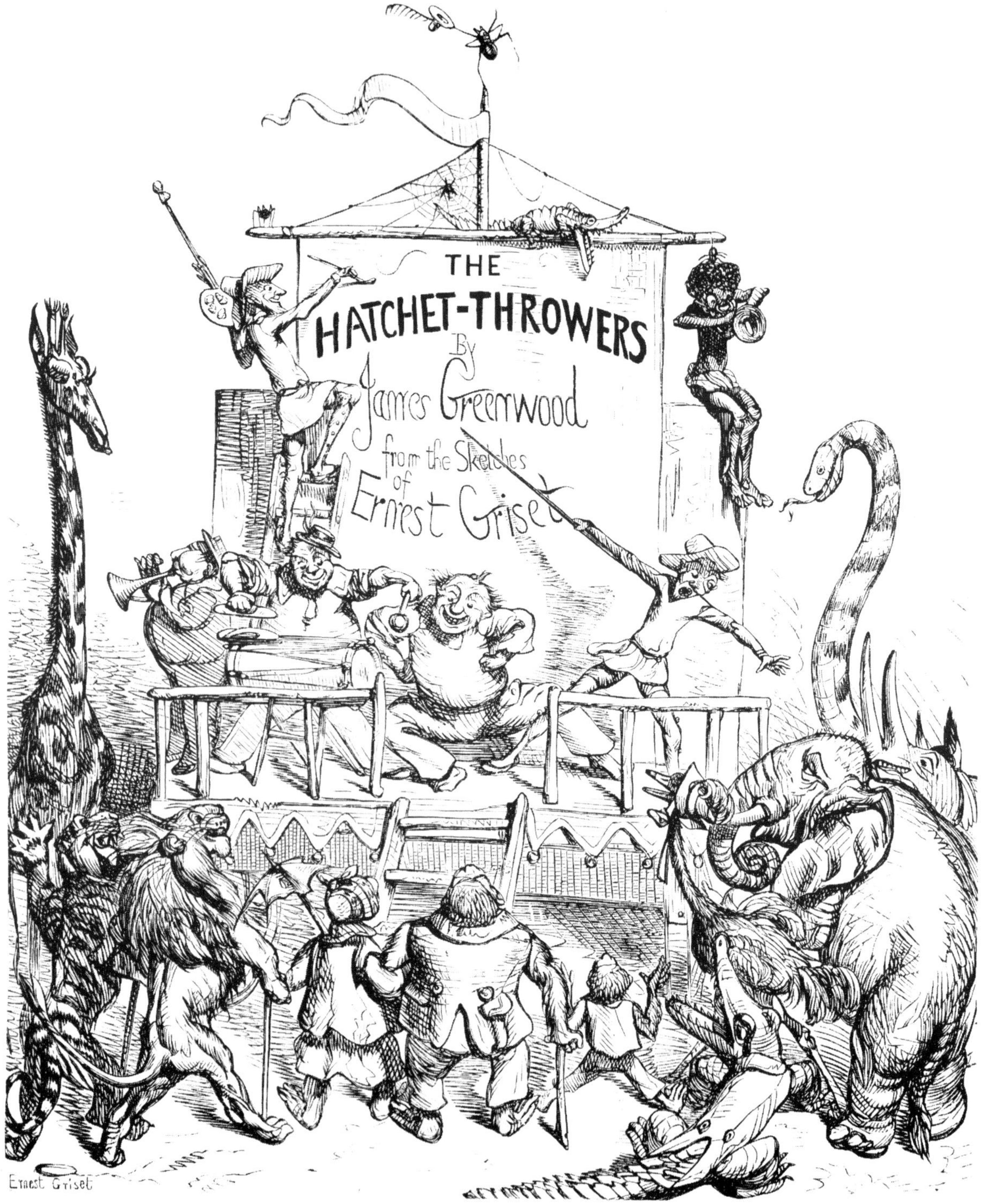

Hatchet Throwers. Ernest Griset

Griset greatly enjoyed drawing title papes and here portrays himself adding the finishing touches. He is surrounded by other characters from the book, including the author who is pointing to his own name.

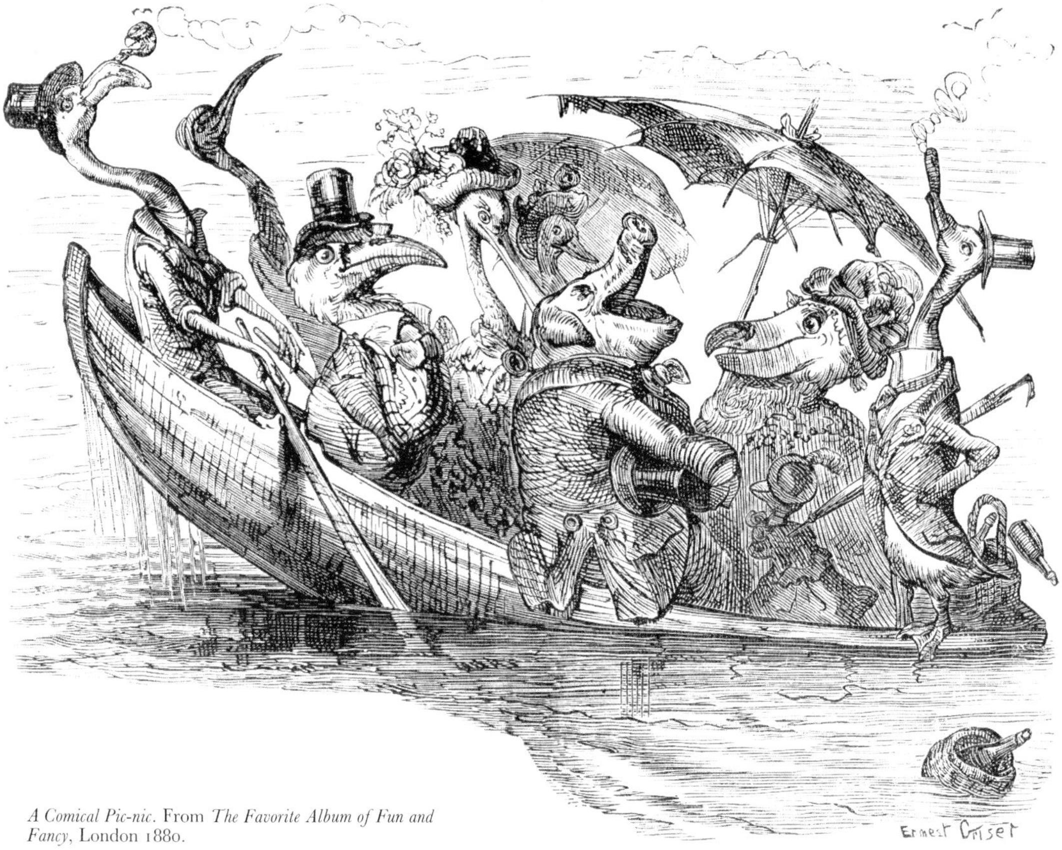

A Comical Pic-nic. From *The Favorite Album of Fun and Fancy*, London 1880.

A Comical Picnic. Ernest Griset

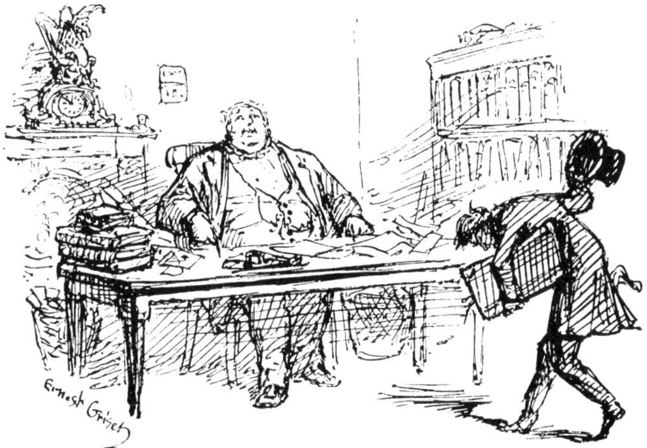

Griset portrays himself nervously greeting the editor, a portfolio of new designs under his arm. From *The History of Punch* by H. M. Spielman, London 1895.

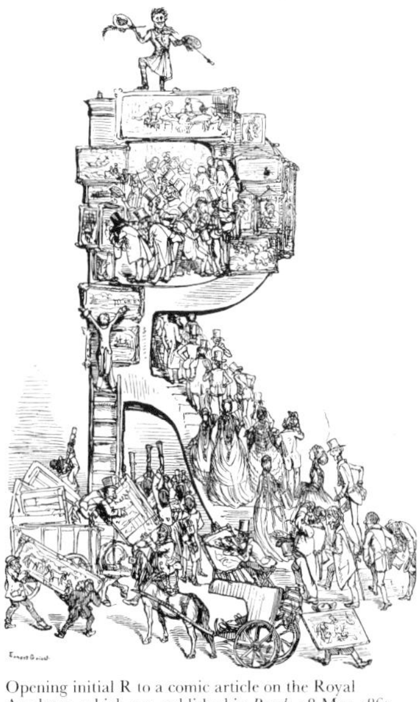

Opening initial R to a comic article on the Royal Academy, which was published in *Punch*, 18 May 1867.

Punch

From 1867 to 1869, Griset was employed as a staff caricaturist on the most famous of all English comic journals, Punch. The experience was not a happy one, for his own highly individual style and specialized interests made it difficult for him to supply the variety and number of caricatures required by the editor.

Remembering Ernest Knight

"We entered the peaceful world of Ernest and Kit Knight in the summer of 1984, having followed a convoluted path originating in California, passing through the Victoria and Albert Museum, and ending on Dartmoor. The V & A had held an exhibition, curated by Lionel Lambourne, of the work of Ernest's grandfather, Ernest Griset. A family friend on the West Coast had brought home a copy of the catalogue which came to us. Drawn strongly to the work, we wished to know more about the artist. Moreover, as Griset is an uncommon name and also Mary's maiden name, there was the added curiosity about possible kinship. Through the goodness of Lionel Lambourne we got off a query to the Knights. Happy for us that a letter arrived from Ernest with a warm invitation to visit Torcroft. So it was that we commenced sharing a deep friendship with two of this world's dearest people from whom we gained so much in truth, beauty and goodness.

Our discovery that Ernest was himself an accomplished painter deepened the richness of our time together. Torcroft in those days was ever an irresistible feast to the eye, with canvasses of Venice, Rome, Assisi, Naples, Brittany, Normandy, Chartres, French market scenes, Loire valley château, the Lake District, Dartmoor perspectives and so much more. Today, as we look around our home, adorned with beauty from the hand of our much-missed friend, our hearts are warmed by Ernest's joyful spirit, abundantly evidenced in his paintings.

How do we remember Ernest Knight? We remember his kind and generous temperament. We remember his gentle though repeated admonitions to pause to savor the glories of earthly existence. We remember his love of books and his passion for peace. We remember long dinners with good wine and talk. We remember cool evenings before the fire. We remember his standing on the train platform either greeting or bidding adieu, his snow-white beard and wisp of hair blowing in the wind. Above all, we remember his spirit through his joyful sense of colour, and we treasure his continuing presence in our lives."

Jim and Mary Holland

Sheperdstown, USA.

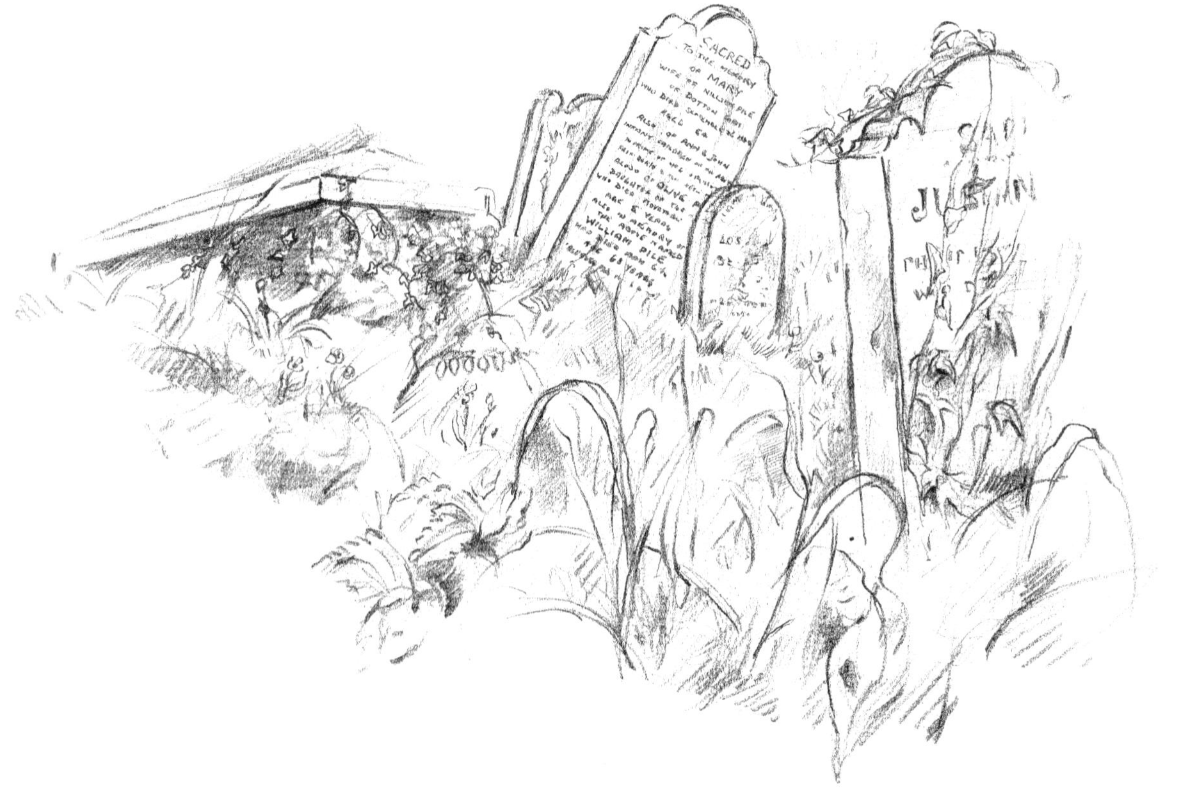